CHARISMATIC CAPITALISM

CHARISMATIC CAPITALISM

Direct Selling Organizations
in America

Nicole Woolsey Biggart

The University of Chicago Press
Chicago and London

NICOLE WOOLSEY BIGGART is associate professor of
management and sociology at the University of California at
Davis and coauthor of *Governor Reagan, Governor Brown:
A Sociology of Executive Power.*

The University of Chicago Press, Chicago 60637
The University of Chicago Press, Ltd., London
© 1989 by The University of Chicago
All rights reserved. Published 1989
Printed in the United States of America

98 97 96 95 94 93 92 91 90 89 54321

LIBRARY OF CONGRESS CATALOGING IN PUBLICATION DATA

Biggart, Nicole Woolsey.
    Charismatic capitalism : direct selling organizations in
America / Nicole Woolsey Biggart.
        p.   cm.
    Bibliography: p.
    Includes index.
    ISBN 0-226-04785-7 ISBN 0-226-04786-5 (pbk.)
    1. Direct selling—United States.   2. Sales personnel—
United States.   3. Commercial agents—United States.
I. Title.
HF5438.25.B52   1988
658.8′4—dc19   88-19833
                                                              CIP

∞ The paper used in this publication meets the minimum
requirements of the American National Standard for
Information Sciences—Permanence of Paper for Printed
Library Materials, ANSI Z39.48-1984.

To the memory of Barbara Mann Biggart

Contents

Preface

Like all authors, I approached my book with an intellectual agenda that has shaped what and how I have written. First, I wanted to write an organizational analysis that connected formal organizations with other social phenomena. Much of what I have written about in this book—family relations, ideology, gender, business culture, economic history—falls outside the usual categories of organizational analysis. I hoped to show that these can be critical factors in understanding how organizations come to be and why they take the forms they do. Although organization theorists in recent years have recognized that the institutional environment of an organization is important to its form and survival, not many studies have shown in any detail *how* the environment works to shape structure and social action. I thought that a close look at a single industry, and the social worlds it creates and responds to, would be a useful analytic bridge between the study of organizations per se and the study of the social environment.

It is curious that the three central works of sociology, Marx's *Capital*, Weber's *Economy and Society*, and Durkheim's *Division of Labor in Society*, are all about the relationship between economic structure and social structure. Despite our intellectual forefathers' agreement on the importance of studies of the economy, economic matters have usually been subsumed under political sociology—when they have been considered at all by sociologists. This is just beginning to change, though, and I view the change with excitement. As a sociologist with an appointment in a management school, where an economic paradigm reigns, I am especially aware of the contribution that sociology, anthropology, and social history can make to our understanding of economics. Studies of consumption, the meaning of money, the social structure of markets, the relation of economic action to religion, to culture, and to ideology, the cultural variability of risk aversion and opportunism—all these important topics and more lie outside the usual bounds of what my economist colleagues choose to study. Even those topics of central concern to economists demand reexamination by social scientists not committed to the utopian and Western assumptions of neoclassical economics. My second aim item has been to make a contribution to what I hope will be the new economic sociology.

Finally, my approach has been shaped by my belief that the ideas and methods of Max Weber are useful to the study of organizations. This is perhaps an odd statement, since Weber's writings on bureaucracy are de rigeur in any introductory course on the sociology of organizations. Rarely, though, have scholars marched into the field with a Weberian analytic framework in the same way that Marxist scholars have used the ideas of Karl Marx to direct their research. This book expresses my conviction that an institutional analysis of organizations, one that considers seriously the cultural, material, and historical bases of organization, greatly benefits from a consciously Weberian approach.

This idea, that Weber's work was *useful* and not just "important," had its source in my graduate years at Berkeley. I can remember Reinhard Bendix walking into a graduate seminar with that day's paper and asking how Weber would explain the headlines. Bendix made me appreciate, not only in class but in his own work, that Weberian sociology offered a valuable tradition for an explanatory social science. The work of another of my teachers, Philip Selznick, piqued my interest in organizations and led me to understand their essentially political and moral nature.

I have pursued my agenda with the help of a lot of advice, much of which I used. Howard Aldrich, Annette Lareau, and Gary Hamilton read every word of the manuscript, and I am indebted to them for giving me necessary amounts of both criticism and encouragement. Woody Powell was a careful line-by-line reviewer, and his comments helped me clarify my thinking and my prose.

Because this book goes beyond conventional organizational analysis, I often found myself at the limits of my knowledge. Judy Stacey read the chapter on family and gender and gave me confidence in my ideas. Manuel Castells allowed me to sit in on his course on the economic institutions of capitalism during a sabbatical leave, and I have tried to follow his advice to "look for connections."

I tried out bits and pieces of my analysis on audiences at the University of North Carolina, the University of Chicago, and the Berkeley and Santa Barbara campuses of the University of California. I appreciated invitations to test my ideas extended by Howard Aldrich, Paul Hirsch, Wendy Griswold, Glenn Carroll, and Roger Friedland. The Bay Area Women's Research Seminar, a group of accomplished feminist scholars (and warm colleagues), encouraged me to think about the relation of gender to organization.

The research and writing took four years and would have taken longer without some very skilled assistance. Norm Coontz, Beverly Lozano, Barbara Purdy, and Cindy Stearns helped me in the library, in the field, and in coding the data. Sasha Bessom and Josephine Chu cheerfully did miscellaneous typing chores. I owe a special debt of gratitude to Guy Whitlow, who transcribed all the interviews. Turning a conversation into a readable document takes a good ear and a lot of patience. Guy had both.

This research would have been far more difficult without the assistance of the Direct Selling Education Foundation and the Direct Selling Association. Marlene Futterman, executive director of the DSEF, cleared the way for my contacts with industry executives. Neil Offen, president of the DSA, helped me understand the political environment of the industry. Jay Hescock, vice-president of the DSA, pulled all kinds of things out of his prodigious memory and helped me enormously by reading a draft of the entire manuscript. I thank them all for the generous gift of their time and for supporting my efforts to understand their industry. I received a great deal of assistance from participants in the industry, both distributors and executives, but the graciousness and openness of the staff at Mary Kay Cosmetics was special.

Research is expensive, even when done on a shoestring.

I am grateful for a series of Faculty Research Grants given to me by the University of California at Davis. The sponsorship of Dean Gary Walton at the Graduate School of Management was crucial to my receiving a Faculty Development Award just when I needed the time to write.

My son Scott was born in the midst of all this, making me appreciate both the strain of juggling work and child care and the blessing of a supportive and sharing spouse. Thank you, Jeff.

CHAPTER ONE
Introduction

On Wednesday night 11 December 1985, 4,000 people came to Sacramento, California, to hear what they knew would be a rousing call to action. Most came with their spouses, and not a few brought their children to hear the speaker. The gathering of nicely dressed men, women, and children resembled nothing so much as a congregation of the faithful assembled to hear a touring evangelist.

Indeed, the speaker was a charismatic man who had come to lead them on a "crusade" to overturn an "evil" and predatory force in American society. A gifted orator, he painted pictures of how American families were imperiled by this evil force, a powerful enemy he was committed to annihilating by the year 2000. He was in Sacramento to encourage his followers in what he knew was a difficult battle and to seek new members for the crusade. He promised the audience that he would show them not only how to aid other families, but how to profit from their good work.

The speaker's reception at the end of the talk was wildly enthusiastic. People jumped to their feet applauding loudly, obviously moved by his words. An observer could only conclude that the mission was a success and that many new converts had been made.

The speaker's name is Art Williams, and the evil he is committed to overturning is the whole-life insurance industry.

Whole life insurance seems an improbable enemy and an unlikely focus for an emotional crusade. But in less than ten years Art Williams has built a 155,000 member, multimillion-dollar enterprise with his moral appeal to middle American families. The members of his organization sold more term

1

life insurance in 1986 than Prudential, the previous industry leader.[1]

That the A. L. Williams Company is a success must be attributed to many factors, including the vibrant personality of its founder and also a desirable product. But a critical factor in the company's success has been its ability to engage the energies of thousands of people and shape them into a highly productive organization.

Productive workers are the perennial aim of capitalist enterprise, of course. At least since Frederick Winslow Taylor's espousal of scientific management techniques at the turn of the century, American business has attempted a variety of strategies for getting people to work harder and better. At different historical moments the strategies have ranged from carrots—money, benefits, a "warm" corporate culture—to sticks such as machine-paced technology, piecework pay, and close supervision. But whether the management fashion has been to run a tight ship or a loose one, the ship of American industry has almost invariably been bureaucratically built.

The A. L. Williams Company and other members of the direct selling industry, such as Amway Corporation, Tupperware, and Mary Kay Cosmetics, have stopped trying to fine-tune bureaucracy in the search for productivity. Instead, they have adopted a form of organization that dates from this nation's colonial past and have shaped it to fit the circumstances and aspirations of contemporary Americans.

They have been amazingly successful. In 1984 direct selling organizations, or DSOs, sold *$8.6 billion* in goods and services. More surprising, perhaps, 5.8 million Americans, *5% of the labor force*, were members of DSOs in 1984. More than one in four households in this country has had a member involved in direct selling. Significantly, 80% of all direct salespeople are women.[2]

Direct selling organizations have achieved this financial stature and widespread social appeal through an unusual combination of organizational practices and management strategies. To an outsider, life in a DSO is surprising, sometimes even bizarre. It is as though the activity of a traditional firm were viewed in a funhouse mirror; nearly every familiar feature of corporate life is either distorted or missing. Direct selling organizations not only are different, they violate many of the most accepted tenets of management practice today.

For example, corporate America spends millions of dollars trying to recruit and select the best possible workers. Psychological testing, in-depth interviews, and checks of credentials and references are standard practice in many businesses. The entire executive search industry is predicated on its ability to find exactly the right person for the job through a skillful blend of knowledge, art, and connections. Businesses are willing to spend time and money to locate good workers because poor ones are both useless and costly. Firms such as IBM and Xerox, with large sales forces, have made a science of picking and training salespeople.

One might think that DSOs, as sales organizations, look for outgoing, self-motivated, and experienced personnel, people comfortable with presenting products and asking for the sale. In fact, most DSOs have no recruitment criteria at all. Many DSO salespeople, usually called distributors, have never sold anything when they join. Anyone willing to try is welcomed through the open doors of many DSOs.

Most American businesses accept and even encourage a competitive spirit among workers. Capitalism works because people pursue self-interest, and organizations benefit from employees' maneuvering to get ahead. Workers trying to be a bit smarter or a bit harder working, in hopes of promotion or a bonus, are good for business. Books such as Michael Korda's *Power! How to Get It, How to Use It*[3] teach corporate players techniques for getting ahead in the competition for jobs at the top. Michael Maccoby's study *The Gamesman*[4] attests how widespread intraorganizational competition has become. Even such recent books as Rosabeth Moss Kanter's *The Change Masters*,[5] which argue for the superiority of teamwork over employee competition, support the view of organizational life as a competitive world.

Not only do DSOs not encourage competition between distributors, they often actively discourage it. Distributors are taught to help each other be successful, sometimes even at the cost of their own success. Many DSOs include the Golden Rule—"Do unto others as you would have them do unto you"—in their published corporate philosophies. Mary Kay Cosmetics, one of the largest DSOs, even offers a prize for the most selfless distributor. The "Miss Go-Give" award is a highly coveted symbol of the organization's disdain for competitive behavior at the expense of others.

In 1956 William H. Whyte's best-selling book *The Organization Man*[6] described a generation of organizational workers who had been molded by the needs of the corporation. As Whyte described them, they were conservative, impassive little gray men. Their lives in the organization were routine and largely unemotional. "The executive is very gregarious when he sees some utility to the gregariousness. But if he doesn't see that utility, good fellowship bores him to death."[7]

The flat picture of organizational relations Whyte painted is often, but not universally, true today (as perhaps it was not always true then). In particular, companies that are self-conscious about their "corporate culture" work hard to provide a friendly atmosphere. High-technology firms such as Apple Computer and Genentech routinely have, for example, much-publicized employee mixers to promote good times along with hard work.

Even the most upbeat corporate culture of traditional American business, however, pales beside the daily round among direct sales distributors. Relations in most DSOs are not just friendly, but highly personal. Distributors become involved in each other's private lives and often describe themselves as "family." Their meetings are frequently characterized by displays of joy, tears, and pride. One gathering of Tupperware distributors I attended, with its paper hats and noisemakers, more closely resembled a New Year's Eve party than the monthly business meeting it was. Mary Kay Cosmetics holds annual "Seminars" at the company's corporate headquarters in Dallas. In 1986, 28,000 cheering, singing, applauding women attended at their own expense. Other direct selling companies, such as Amway and Shaklee, also sponsor lavish celebrations that encourage effusive and expressive behavior.

There are emotional moments in even the sternest, most conservative company, of course. What is distinctive about DSOs is that they actively encourage emotional attachment and expression and that such expression is a *routine and expected* aspect of organizational life. Occasionally the president or chief executive of a traditional company is the focus for employee commitment and even emotional expression: certainly, for example, auto executive Lee Iacocca is a much-admired top manager who evokes pride and loyalty from his subordinates. While "charismatic" leaders are not expected in American business, they are not unknown.[8] Every generation of executives has its Iacoccas, managers of ability and personality who inspire others and seem larger than life.

The direct selling industry, too, has had its share of winning personalities. What is unusual, though, is that it has had so many of them. Distributors in Mary Kay Cosmetics and Amway Corporation are not just admirers of Mary Kay Ash or Amway founders Jay Van Andel and Rich DeVos. They are devotees who orient their lives around the words of these executives. They listen to every pronouncement carefully. They read books by and about them.[9] Mary C. Crowley, founder of Home Interiors and Gifts, a DSO that sells decorative items for homes, published her philosophy of life in several works. One, a small collection of aphorisms, was in its twenty-ninth printing in 1985, with more than 600,000 copies in circulation.[10] When A. L. Williams distributors went to hear Art Williams in Sacramento, they went not only to listen to his words but to see *him*, a man who represented a way of life as much as a business opportunity. Not all DSOs celebrate the lives and beliefs of their leaders, but many of them do.

Direct selling organizations rarely recruit for experience or ability. They sometimes discourage even friendly competition among distributors, promoting a "go-give" spirit, not a "go-get" attitude. They do not believe that emotionalism, or even partying, gets in the way of business. They continually celebrate business success and corporate ideology. The emotionalism that often attaches to a charismatic leader sometimes gives DSOs a cultlike character.

Compared with traditional firms, DSOs appear loose and out of control. They represent an apparent management nightmare that only a thick rule book and a platoon of managers could keep together. In fact, DSOs have almost no rules and, compared with most firms, few managers. Home Interiors and Gifts, for example, with 30,000 distributors, has only thirty-five managers.

THE LOGIC OF ORGANIZATION

How can an organization with few rules, little management, and an open door survive, much less prosper? Why are so many Americans attracted to organizations that are emotional—by most standards, excessively so? Is the emotional character of DSOs what attracts so many women? If DSOs are not bureaucratic firms, what are they?

At first glance, DSOs appear to be eccentric firms, companies that have taken traditional American business practices to the extreme. After all, one can find examples in many industries of companies with lax recruiting policies, friendly relations, and popular chief executives. And not all organizations are run with a rule book; seat-of-the-pants management is practiced in a lot of smaller and some larger firms.

What is different about DSOs is not that they have such characteristics, but that they have all or most of them at the same time. These are *typical* and maybe *essential* characteristics of modern direct selling organizations. They are expressions of a central organizational logic. If one understands the institutional logic, the characteristics of DSOs are a sensible and even predictible result, not eccentric at all.

Most businesses today are *firms*, or bureaucratically organized enterprises. Although *bureaucracy* has a pejorative connotation in everyday speech, to a sociologist "bureaucracy" or "firm" is simply a form of organization with particular characteristics.[11] Bureaucracies have such familiar features as chains of command, rules and regulations, and relatively impersonal relations. Bureaucratic officials tend to relate to each other in terms of the positions they hold, not as individuals. Such firms are usually nine-to-five organizations: when you're at work the boss is in control, but when you're at home your time is your own. Bureaucracies espouse a meritocratic hiring and promotion policy. At least officially, it's what you know, not who you know, that leads to success.[12]

Bureaucratic firms, the organizational mainstay of an industrial economy, like DSOs have a central logic that makes all their features add up to an integrated whole, a form of organization that makes sense and seems right to the people who work within it. Nepotism or favoritism in promotion, when it happens in a bureaucracy, seems wrong because it goes against the logic of impersonality and merit. In a family enterprise, though, nepotism is acceptable and even expected because the logic of organization is different.

Direct selling has a logic too, but it is radically different from the logic of bureaucratic organizations. In fact, direct selling developed and persists as a challenge to the bureaucratic organization of enterprise. Direct selling organizations offer a conscious alternative to firms as a way to organize economic activity for a profit, as a technique for managing labor, and as a means of earning income. DSOs are surely capitalist enterprises, but they are not corporate capitalism of the sort that dominates the American economy.

Direct selling organizations differ in important ways from most firms. For example, firms are typically staffed by workers who do not own the enterprise. Bureaucratic workers are usually employees who earn a wage in return for their labor.[13] Social theorists Max Weber and Karl Marx described the separation of ownership from work as the critical social relationship of capitalism: workers lose control of the means of production,[14] and the profits of their labor go to the people who own and manage the enterprise.[15] Weber saw workers' disfranchisement and subordination to rational management processes as a critical technical requirement for the development of industrial capitalism, and he considered bureaucracy the main vehicle of this subordination. For Marx, control of workers by management is a peculiar feature of a capitalist economy, not a necessary feature of industrial development.[16]

Despite their differences, both scholars turned our attention to the alienating potential of modern work arrangements where workers labor not for themselves, but for the people who hire them. Scholars following the lead of Weber and Marx have described the numerous strategies managers have used to exact productivity and to focus workers' energies toward organizational ends under conditions of employment. In the early stages of Western industrial capitalism a common managerial strategy was totalistic control, that is, encompassing the worker's whole life, including family members, within the production process. Company dormitories and company towns, for example, placed even off-the-job activities under the employer's surveillance.[17] As organizations grew larger, that strategy yielded to one of erecting a barrier between the workplace and the home to maintain industrial discipline. Workers were expected to exclude their outside lives while at work and to concentrate totally on the job. Although this barrier is being questioned now through modest experiments with, for example, work-site day care, for most workers family, religion, friends, and other nonwork "disturbances" are best left at home. The barrier remains in place.

Direct selling organizations differ fundamentally from firms both in their social relations and in their managerial strategies. DSOs concentrate ownership, management, and labor *within* every distributor. Every distributor is legally the owner of a business run under the direction of an often revered corporate leadership to which the distributor is morally, but not legally, subordinate. In addition, DSOs repudiate organizational arrangements that exclude people's nonwork lives. Direct selling organizations promote policies that incorporate distributors' families and friends, and even their churches, into their selling activities. The industry did not develop this alternative form of enterprise as a principled attack on overrationalized capitalist work arrangements. Rather, DSOs pursue these arrangements in order to better control workers.

MANAGING SOCIAL NETWORKS FOR PROFIT

Whereas bureaucratic firms seek to exclude nonwork social relations in order to control workers, the direct selling industry pursues profit in the opposite way, *by making social networks serve business ends.*

Industry executives both create and manipulate social relations. Under the guidance of corporate leaders, independent distributors are transformed into an entrepreneurial community dedicated to each other's financial and personal success. Managers create the conditions under which social and financial bonds flower and fine-tune arrangements to yield maximum profits without destroying the personalized character of the organization.

Even "outside" social relations are brought within the

bounds of the business. Private networks are transformed into pecuniary relations or are managed as obstacles. For a truly committed distributor, work and play, friends and competitors become indistinguishable.

The melding of personal and pecuniary relations is ideologically supported and maintained. Direct selling is not merely an instrumental means to an income. Making money is a moral endeavor, a "crusade" to achieve both public and private ends. Committed distributors see their work as a superior way of life that embraces political values, social relations, and religious beliefs. It gives them not a job, but a worldview, a community of like-minded others, and a self-concept. DSOs are businesses run very much like social movements.

These characteristics make the direct selling industry a particularly good vehicle for exploring the interpenetration of economic action and social relations in modern society. Many social scientists, particularly but not exclusively economists, have in recent decades adopted the position that economic activity becomes severed from other institutional arenas under advanced capitalism. As Mark Granovetter put it:

> This view sees the economy as an increasingly separate, differentiated sphere in modern society, with economic transactions defined no longer by the social or kinship obligations of those transacting but by rational calculations of individual gain. It is sometimes further argued that the traditional situation is reversed: instead of economic life being submerged in social relations, these relations become an epiphenomenon of the market.[18]

This "market makes society" perspective is suspect with even a cursory examination of direct selling's weaving together of business with family, religion with profit. In fact, there is a temptation to argue the opposite, that society makes a market: DSOs take people's social networks and transform them into financial networks.

It is possible, of course, that direct selling is an exception to a historical trend, an anomalous vestige of traditional society left over from its origins in Yankee peddling. This "vestige," however, grew explosively in the 1970s. Direct selling organizations, with their ability to attract millions of contemporary Americans, must therefore be explained not as an anachronism, but as a recent socioeconomic phenomenon produced under current conditions.

Why should a "less rational" form of organization, one that creates and manipulates social bonds, grow precisely when a market mentality seems to be spreading inexorably throughout the developed world? This study suggests that neither market factors nor social factors alone can answer this question. It is the intersection of economic and social conditions, of pecuniary and cultural orientations, that produced and sustains the direct selling industry. Economic action is pursued *through* social networks and beliefs, not in their absence.

For example, there is rational calculus on the part of industry participants, but the calculus is made not apart from, but *considering* the subjective aspirations and material conditions of distributors' lives, both factors being products of an advanced industrial society. Industry executives are astute observers of the hopes, fears, and realistic possibilities of their recruits. Business strategies are conceived not abstractly, but with an understanding of actors' life chances and cultural predispositions. Likewise, recruits evaluate the moral, affective, and status consequences of alternative forms of economic participation as well as the financial ones. They project themselves into different economic roles—as an independent Amway distributor, as an employed clerk-typist—and make their choices. It is social knowledge and valuation as much as objective economic conditions that have dictated the organizational form and development of modern direct sales.

My approach to understanding direct selling organizations and their distinctive socioeconomic character is largely inspired by the concerns of German sociologist Max Weber. For Weber, a full explanation of social life had to include three conceptual dimensions: material concerns, ideal or value interests, and the way these are combined in social structures. How does people's desire for gain or well-being undergird their social relations? How do "higher" values and systems of belief influence social action? When social relations are organized, why do some people feel empowered to direct others, and how and why are those directives obeyed? [19]

In this book I am concerned with why distributors choose to participate in direct selling, particularly with how they perceive their economic alternatives. I am also interested in the ways DSOs serve the "ideal" interests of distributors—that is, the way direct selling supports members' values, such as a belief in individualism and the importance of family. Finally, how do both material and ideal interests form the basis for organized economic action in DSOs?

A combination of material and ideal factors has been influential since the industry's beginnings. In the nineteenth century direct selling was promoted by organizers as a more effective distribution channel than bureaucratically organized retail establishments. Early distributors were solicited with the promise of riches, but also with the chance for travel and adventure. Dreams of city life attracted thousands of farm boys to door-to-door sales in a period of rapid urbanization.

More recently, direct selling organizations grew because they resolved what became problems for two usually competing social groups—capitalist businesspeople and a pool of modestly educated labor, particularly women. DSOs allowed business owners access to a large labor supply without what are now the substantial costs of maintaining an employment relation. Moreover, this is a labor supply that is ideologically conservative and unlikely to organize. In fact, the very structure of DSOs precludes labor organization.

For workers today, DSOs are a way to enter the labor force without the usual liabilities of bureaucratically organized work. Participants maintain control of their work hours and are at least apparently free from supervision. Distributors integrate spheres of life normally separate in modern society: children, spouses, neighbors, and even political and religious values are brought together in the enterprise. Most important, perhaps, direct selling promises, and occasionally grants, status and recognition to workers largely excluded from both in most workplaces. The economic health of the direct selling industry depends in large part on the exclusionary, discriminatory, and rationalized character of modern work settings. DSOs have prospered because they provide an alternative environment for work that many people, especially women, find attractive. As one industry executive put it, the greatest threat to direct selling is the improvement of working conditions for women in firms.

How do such organizational features as personalized relations, noncompetitive behavior, and ideological appeals create a viable basis for business? How can nonrational relations provide conditions for the pursuit of economic rationality? This paradox is only apparent: *affective and ideal bonds can be powerful motivators of economic action, not necessarily impediments*. DSOs, legally constrained from using the control strategies available to employers, control distributors through their desire for esteem, through their bonds of friendship, and through family authority relations. The industry creates social bonds and manages existing ones to support economic activity.

The social relations of direct selling are supported by a characteristic set of beliefs. All business organizations are based on beliefs, of course, often simply an economic ideology of efficiency and profits. DSOs, however, incorporate a substantive or value-based belief system. This usually takes the form of belief in the moral virtue of entrepreneurialism, sometimes combined with a product-related ideology espoused by a leader. Art Williams's life insurance crusade is not atypical of direct selling. For some, direct selling functions as an extension of worship or as a secular religious substitute.

Direct selling does not appeal to everyone, and there are important limits to what DSOs can accomplish as a form of organization; they have distinctive liabilities for both management and workers. But for a substantial number of people direct selling provides income, meaningful social relations, and the chance for self-esteem. For a management that successfully appeals to those aspirations, the industry provides profits.

LIMITS OF COMPARISON

In the course of my research I concluded that DSOs are not only not bureaucratic but even antibureaucratic, and at times it has been instructive to compare them with the bureaucratic firm. A comparison with bureaucracy entails important caveats, however. DSOs are not an alternative to the bureaucratic firm for many economic functions.[20] They are appropriate for distributing products and services, not for manufacturing or for many other economic tasks. Companies interested in distributing products, however, can choose between a bureaucratic sales force, direct-mail marketing, telemarketing, retail sales, and direct selling.

In fact, a conventional economic analysis might describe DSOs as firms with a market of independent buyers (distributors) who further distribute products to consumers. While the DSO headquarters of Mary Kay Cosmetics and A. L. Williams are indeed firms and that legally correct definition might suffice for some forms of economic analysis, it does not capture the social reality of relations among distributors. Distributors do not operate like a market: they are anything but socially or financially independent of each other, and they are often morally proscribed from competitive relations.

Nor does the legal reality describe the social reality of relations between distributors and the headquarters organizations. The corporate headquarters is not just a source of products that distributors contract to sell; it is the moral and ideological center of the enterprise. Like congregations of worshipers, distributors are "members" of a "church" of direct selling; they are as much a part of the organization as the "ministers" who provide guidance and inspiration. To atomize distributors analytically does violence to the web of social relations that binds them together and creates the conditions for economic success at the level of the firm.

At another important level the comparison between bureaucratic corporations and direct selling organizations is apt: *from the points of view of the actors involved, DSOs and firms are directly comparable.* Direct selling participants, both executives and distributors, continually compare the conditions of work under bureaucratic employment, the only alternative most distributors have, with conditions in DSOs. For them bureaucracy represents a social world with a distinctive array of benefits and liabilities, a distinctive way of life in the economy. Direct selling represents an alternative work world with its own carrots and sticks.

THIS STUDY

Where did this world of work come from? What social and economic forces prompted its emergence and shaped its current existence? In chapter 2, I describe the beginnings of direct selling in this country from its origins in independent Yankee peddlers through three successive forms of organized direct sales. I discuss how the industry responded to larger economic and social changes, in particular the rise of mass merchandising and the social welfare reforms of the New Deal. DSOs developed as an alternative to the employment relation for both managers and workers.

Chapter 3 examines the changing working conditions of post–World War II America. I describe how a transformed environment of work created economic and social dilemmas, particularly for women. During this period the large-scale movement of women into low-pay, low-prestige occupations, the rise of large corporations as an important place of work, and the increasing insecurity of even white-collar employment made direct selling an attractive occupational choice for millions of people. These conditions provided fertile ground for the growth of direct selling in the 1970s, a growth that ran counter to the slowing of the larger economy.

Chapters 4 through 6 examine the social relations of DSOs, in each instance showing how they represent an alternative to bureaucratic relations and impersonal control strategies. In chapter 4 I argue that whereas most firms attempt to separate work and family direct selling pursues different tactics: DSOs attempt to co-opt distributors' families, either by integrating them into the organization or by directly managing them as impediments. Moreover, direct selling organizations are run as "metaphorical families," and distributors are encouraged to see themselves as having familylike bonds. This gives DSOs a decidedly "feminine" character, with noncompetitive, nurturing relationships. I consider whether "feminine organization" is necessarily "feminist organization."

In chapter 5 I show how the direct selling industry uses social ideals to spur economic activity. Americans' belief in meritocracy and individualism forms an important basis for DSO recruiting: the dream of independent success is a powerful draw to people in the lower ranks of corporations and to those isolated at home. I discuss how DSO ideology, expressed as belief in the moral virtue of entrepreneurialism and a leader's vision, provides a basis for economic action. DSOs do not embrace economic rationality of the sort that undergirds the firm.

Chapter 6 explores the strategies of control used to maintain order in an organization that cannot oversee the day-to-day activities of dispersed participants—strategies that attempt to create and sustain a socioeconomic community. I argue that direct selling organizations are based on a "routinized charisma" and that organizational practices flow from that. I analyze the three principal social controls that substitute for bureaucratic management.

Finally, in the last chapter, I consider why an organizational form based on the commercialization of social relations should arise in an advanced industrial economy. The rise of direct selling and the development of "less rational" forms of organizational control in the firm may signal that we have reached the limits of rationality. Paradoxically, less rational controls may be economically more rational.

Data for this study come from a number of sources. The Direct Selling Association (DSA) and the Direct Selling Education Foundation (DSEF), both industry groups, provided me with statistical data about the industry as well as information about the legal and political environment in which the industry operates. In addition, the DSEF invited me to attend conferences and conventions sponsored by the industry for DSO managers and university faculty.

A substantial amount of literature on industry history and practices is available in popular books written for distributors and in the commercial press. I have used these materials to understand DSO origins and to gain an appreciation of the variety of business practices DSOs employ. At my request, some forty-two DSOs sent me information about their organizational structure, recruiting practices, and distributor profiles that has helped me understand the diversity of the direct selling form.

Much of the material for this study comes from fieldwork and an analysis of ninety-five interviews with distributors, DSO managers, and trade association executives. I selected distributors in different lines, at different levels, and with different degrees of apparent commitment. Where appropriate I interviewed both men and women distributors. I also interviewed a few disaffected and former distributors.

Because of the nature of social activity in DSOs, I visited

sales meetings in homes, in motels, and at regional and national conventions. I also attended, at the invitation of the
DSA and DSEF, industry-sponsored meetings. All quotations in
this book are from transcriptions of interviews or meetings or
from cited works.[21] Additional discussion of my method is
given in the Appendix.

THE STRUCTURE OF NETWORK DSOs

All direct selling is, quite simply, the face-to-face (salesperson
to consumer) sale of products or services away from a fixed
business location, usually in a consumer's home. Direct selling
is an industry that is bound together by a common organizing
strategy, not by a common product or service.[22] The salespeople or distributors are independent contractors, not employees. They earn an income by selling at a profit goods that
they buy wholesale from one or more manufacturers or distributors. Sometimes they are paid a commission by the
wholesaler.

This study focuses on a subset of the industry, what I call
network DSOs, such as Tupperware and Amway. Network
DSOs, in addition to the features above, have two distinguishing characteristics. The first is the presence of sponsorship
lines that create financial ties between distributors—ties that
become the basis for intense social relations.

In a hypothetical example, a distributor named Martha is
recruited by Anne, who becomes Martha's "sponsor" and im-
mediate "upline." Martha recruits Paul, Mary, and Alice, who
are "downline" from her (see fig. 1). As her personal recruits,
they are also known as her "frontline." Any of the people recruited by Martha's frontline and any others downline from
her are part of Martha's "organization," although, like Martha,
each is a legally independent entrepreneur. People recruited
by the same sponsors are on the same "level" and members of
the same "generation," although they may end up having very
different degrees of financial success. Sponsorship lines look
like family trees and in fact are often called "genealogies."

Compensation is based on several factors, not all of
which operate in all network DSOs. First a distributor makes
money on the goods personally sold, usually about a 30%

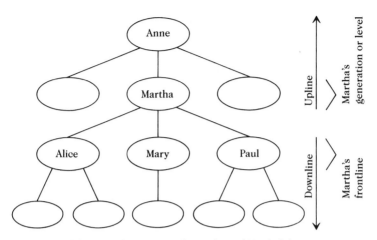

FIGURE 1: Organizational genealogy of Martha's line

markup between the wholesale and retail prices. Second, in multi-level marketing companies (where distributors buy products for wholesaling to downline recruits) distributors can earn volume purchase bonuses—the more one buys wholesale from the company, the less one has to pay. For a small order a distributor might get a 3% discount off the usual wholesale price; for a very large one it might be as much as 25%. Therefore it is in a distributor's interest to recruit people who buy lots of products (or lots of people who buy some products), presumably for reselling, but also perhaps for their own personal use. Sponsors charge the downline a bit more than they pay for the products, thereby profiting as wholesalers.

Third, distributors can earn royalties from the sales of their frontlines, as well as from the sales of people the frontline recruits. This royalty usually ranges from 3% to 5% in network DSOs. The number of levels down on which a DSO will pay royalties differs; in some there is no maximum, in others the company will pay fewer levels down but a higher percentage. The different arrangements influence whether a distributor will concentrate on working with distant downline distributors or the frontline, thus affecting the character of network or "family" interactions.

Fourth, distributors can earn "overrides" by sponsoring recruits who are so successful at recruiting or selling, or both, that they become "breakaways" and buy products directly from the company. In some, such as Mary Kay Cosmetics, where everyone buys from the company, commissions are paid for recruits who develop their own "units" by reaching defined sales and recruiting goals. Overrides or commissions encourage direct sellers to motivate and train recruits to high levels of activity as distributors.[23]

The second important, and related, characteristic of network DSOs is the presence of "recognition levels," a formal status hierarchy. If our hypothetical Martha achieves stated levels of recruiting and selling success, she can receive a series of honorific titles and perquisites such as foreign travel and luxury goods. If she reached the top she could become a national sales director in Mary Kay, a master coordinator in Shaklee, or a crown ambassador in Amway.

Recognition levels and titles are not authority levels; as Martha moves "up" in level she has no more authority over other distributors than she had when she started. In fact, since all are independent contractors, no distributor has authority over any other, and recruits often achieve higher recognition levels than their sponsors. But as Martha achieves new titles that reflect her successes, she achieves new status and prestige. As she climbs the status hierarchy she will probably be invited to speak to groups of other distributors about how she has achieved her success and the techniques she uses for "building" and "managing" an "organization" of independent contractors.

The language of business used in network DSOs, including "building," "managing," and "organization," is borrowed from the larger world of firm enterprises. But the terms do not, indeed cannot, have the same meaning in a social order where there are no bureaucratic relations. A distributor "builds" not by hiring people to work for her, but by convincing them to enter into an independent contractual relationship with the company. She "manages" not by controlling or directing, but by passing on ideas and motivating action. Her "organization" is certainly organized in that there are patterned relations among members, but each person is legally independent of every other person.

This legal independence is mitigated, however, by the

very real financial dependence that exists within lines of distributors. Individuals cannot succeed by themselves. Higher levels of status and income can come about only with the success of the downline, and active distributors become involved, even obsessed, with the work of their recruits. These financial relations become overlaid, in time, with social relations, and distributors often regard their lines as "family."

There are many large and successful direct selling organizations, such as Electrolux and Encyclopaedia Britannica, that do not have networks of this type. These tend to be older companies and more frequently have professional sales forces (recruitment criteria, formal training programs, full-time workers).[24] Although much of what I have to say about network DSOs applies to all direct selling organizations and some bureaucratically organized sales forces, I have limited my analysis to network DSOs, the newest segment of the direct sales industry that has grown rapidly in the past two decades. It is the industry segment most likely to appeal to part-time workers and to women. I also believe that, rooted in this country's recent past, it is the segment with the most to say about the social and organizational possibilities available to people today.

CHAPTER TWO
The Economic History of Direct Selling

Direct selling is an ancient form of enterprise. For thousands of years peddlers have toted wares on their backs and in carts for sale to consumers; and for thousands of years peddlers were largely men, mostly itinerant, and independent of each other. In the past hundred years in this country, however, direct selling has become nearly the opposite: today direct sellers typically travel no farther than their own community; they are largely women, and the industry is highly, if flamboyantly, organized.

Direct selling went through three important stages of development in the United States. It began as a population of independent Yankee peddlers who hawked their goods throughout the colonial economy. When new forms of mass merchandising developed in the mid-1800s, peddling declined. But manufacturers, displeased with the new retail outlets, organized direct sellers into sales forces to promote their goods. Organized direct selling spawned new variations after World War II, including network DSOs and the "party plan," a form of selling that exploits distributors' social networks. The latest developments were less a response to problems of distribution than a creative adaptation to a newly regulated environment and a new supply of workers—suburban women.

Direct selling rose and fell, became organized and reorganized, with changes in transportation, urbanization, the economic health of the larger society, and federal activism in employment matters. In the following pages I explore the historical record leading up to network DSOs and the conditions that made the industry's personalistic approach to economic organization viable. In chapter 3, I examine the post–World War II working conditions that sustain the industry today.

UNORGANIZED DIRECT SELLING: YANKEE PEDDLERS

Colonial peddlers—salesmen who sold tools, tea, and liniment from door to door—were the forerunners of today's distributors. These itinerant merchants, often from northern European backgrounds, were frequently based in Connecticut near the colony's developing manufacturing center, thereby earning the title "Yankee peddlers." They were subsequently joined by Jewish immigrants from eastern Europe, many of whom worked the southern colonies. In both instances peddlers brought goods, services, information, and social contact to a rural population with limited access to the small retail shops in towns and cities. Until the 1840s peddlers were an important distribution channel for both farmers and general stores. In the next two decades, however, the development of the railroad and the telegraph changed the way most goods moved between producer and consumer.[1]

A nation-spanning rail and canal system and improved communications enabled manufacturers to locate and supply larger markets. Country storekeepers, who had been dependent on peddlers, could now order goods from distant cities with real assurance that they would arrive safely and reasonably on time. Reliable supplies of merchandise spurred the establishment of more retail outlets, particularly in areas of the country, such as the South, where there had been few.[2] Many peddlers, in fact, became shopkeepers. According to Alfred D. Chandler, "The new stores, along with improved transportation and the rise of the modern wholesaler to supply them, all but ended the peddler as an instrument of distribution in the United States."[3] New techniques of mass marketing, including department stores, mail order companies, and chain stores, reduced the independent salesman to a minor economic figure.[4]

Although reduced in importance, direct selling continued as a form of enterprise in the latter decades of the nineteenth century, but its character changed. Direct salesmen were increasingly organized, not self-directed peddler-entrepreneurs. Early peddlers picked up merchandise from manufacturers, through importers, at markets and auctions, and through barter. But after the Civil War salesmen typically sold only the goods of a single manufacturer or wholesaler, becoming the first direct selling sales forces.

ORGANIZED DIRECT SELLING: THE SALES FORCE EMERGES

The reason for the resurgence of peddling in its new loosely organized form was an ironic one: the success of department stores.[5] A number of manufacturers did not want their products to have to compete with the cornucopia of goods in the big emporiums. They preferred to rely on salesmen whose financial success depended on selling their products and only theirs. In addition, some believed that a sincere personal appeal or knowledgeable demonstration would show the goods to better advantage. Manufacturers tried to recapture the advantages of personal selling in an era of mass marketing, but under conditions that gave them some measure of control. Direct selling is still a strategy for marketing products whose features are apparent mainly through demonstration.[6]

As late as the 1920s direct sellers believed they could compete favorably with retail establishments, particularly outside the cities where the turnover of a merchant's goods was slow. According to the president of one Cincinnati direct selling company in 1926, "The retail merchant cannot give service. He cannot give style. He cannot give quality or freshness of goods. He cannot give what the small town and rural person is looking for."[7] Household products and gadgets, religious books, textiles, shoes, hosiery, and personal care items were among the items sold by direct salesmen at the turn of the century.[8] Even automobiles were sold through direct selling distributors until World War I.[9] Direct selling, in this organized form, competed with retailers on the basis of its product advantages, convenience for the customer, and the specialized knowledge of its distributors—claims that are still made by the industry.

Several of today's direct selling companies, including the giant conglomerate Avon Products, trace their origins to the late nineteenth-century period of urban growth and economic expansion. It was an era when cities were becoming the glamorous cultural centers of the Gilded Age. City ways and modern products held appeal for country folk who felt passed by as the nation rapidly industrialized.[10] Just like Yankee peddlers, the new direct sellers distributed goods, and perhaps as important, they distributed urban ideas and culture in an era of rapid social change.

> The agent, peddler and drummer traveled from the city to the rural areas carrying products representing the urban manufacturers and wholesalers. To the rural youth he was the representative of the CITY par excellence, and in a period when mobility and success pointed to the urban areas, the traveling salesman become an instructor, a guide, and a handbook of city life and manners to all those anxious to cleave from their rustic background.[11]

If the traveling salesman was the exotic representative of slick city style, with his fancy suits, polished manners, and glib speech,[12] he also provided a realistic model for emulation to rural boys wanting to escape the farm. Manufacturers often preferred to recruit the hardworking country youths rather than more knowledgeable city sophisticates. W. T. Wright of the Chicago Portrait Company explained in 1924 to an audience of direct selling executives why farm boys were easier to control than urban recruits:

> You cannot do anything with [an experienced] man who thinks he knows a lot about another line [of products]. He spends too much time trying to tell you about how to run your business, instead of listening to you. A short time ago I built an organization of 160 men. They were mostly school boys and country school teachers. . . . They were ambitious but were not making any money. . . . We taught these men and boys. Not only showed them how to sell but took them out of the country environment and taught them our business. . . . You know you can take them away from the country but you cannot send them back without making them dissatisfied.[13]

But farm boys required instruction in city manners if they were to be successful, he continued. "I have sat and taught them not to put their knife in their mouth. How to act around a hotel. How to get out of a hotel. . . . I conveyed the idea that

I was really teaching something."[14] Even today, DSO executives claim to be a source of mobility and personal growth for distributors. But now the likely targets are not farm boys but people stuck in offices and at home.

The W. T. Rawleigh Company, today a manufacturer of spices and household products, was started by a Wisconsin farmhand discouraged by the hard work and meager wage of $20 a month for farm labor. Rawleigh wrote volumes of memoirs at the turn of the century that described the appeal of a career that promised unlimited financial rewards and a wider view of the world. He recalled the inspiration that led to a direct selling career.

> Mr. Jim Davis of Richland Center, Wisconsin, a medicine salesman, called at the farm one evening. After selling some Liniment, Conditioning Powder and Extracts to the family, he took supper, collected the amount of his bill and went away. He was there less than an hour, got his supper and $1.50 in cash and left a small bottle of Extract in exchange for his meal.[15]

In 1889 at the age of seventeen, with the assistance of a blind horse named Old Bill, Rawleigh began peddling unguents and patent medicines for a midwestern manufacturer. He made sales of $100 to $150 a week and, even paying his expenses, earned in a few months what his father made in an entire year of farming. In 1895 Rawleigh moved to town and became a manufacturer, concocting his own line of medicinals in his kitchen with his wife Minnie. By 1910 the W. T. Rawleigh Medical Company was established in fifteen midwestern states.

"HOME OFFICE" AND
"BRANCH OFFICE" DSOs

Rawleigh's firm, like many manufacturers relying on a direct sales force at the time, solicited distributors through circulars and advertisements in newspapers and magazines. The companies promised travel, independence, and riches. An aspiring salesman would order products through the mail and sell them when and as he chose. Occasionally he would be assigned a territory. The salesman kept the difference between what he paid for the merchandise at wholesale and the price he got from the buyer. He paid all his own expenses, including travel and lodging. Some salesmen representing publishers, or manufacturers of relatively expensive or extensive product lines, showed consumers samples they could order. These "canvassers" usually took a deposit and forwarded the order to the firm. The deposit became the salesman's profit; the firm received the balance when the consumer paid C.O.D. charges.

This loose, barely organized form of direct selling was known as a "home office" operation because the home office was the only contact the salesperson had. Salesmen received training in neither selling techniques nor product features except what could be sent through the mail.

Alfred C. Fuller, who in 1906 started what became for a while the largest direct selling company in the world, the Fuller Brush Company, recalled the response to his first advertised call for salesmen as "a frantic period of three months" when he "became the employer, so to speak, of two hundred men, most of whom I had never met."[16] Fuller Brush grew overnight from a basement manufacturer with a handful of local salespeople in New Britain, Connecticut, to a home office company with a nationwide sales force. Fuller attempted to coordinate and control this far-flung addition to his organization through mimeographed messages. He exhorted the men to "maintain impeccable deportment." He passed on hints, for example, to wear rubber boots a size too large on rainy days for ease of removal on the doorstep, "for any awkwardness at the door is disastrous."[17]

In 1915 the Fuller Brush Company, overwhelmed by its recruiting success, reorganized as a "branch office" company. In a branch office operation a company established local offices (branches) that recruited and trained salespeople and assigned them territories. The branch manager was sometimes an employee of the company but often was an independent salesperson who received a percentage of the branch's sales as compensation for managing the office, in addition to profits from personal selling. Branch office companies incurred the cost of maintaining and administering field facilities in exchange for better control of recruiting, training, and management of the sales force. Some companies had roving field managers who made contact with the salesmen in their local communities—something of a cross between the home office and branch office organizations. Today slightly fewer than half of Direct Selling Association members are organized as branch office DSOs.

THE 1920S: ENTRENCHMENT

By the 1920s organized direct selling was an established form of enterprise. There are no accurate figures on the number of direct selling distributors in this period because the United States Census enumerates only workers' primary occupations. Then as now, direct selling was a secondary occupation for many, if not most, distributors. A reasonable estimate from several historical sources suggests, however, that there were at least 200,000 persons selling door to door in 1920, double the number in 1900. Retail store clerks were rapidly outstripping direct distributors both in absolute numbers and as a proportion of the selling occupation, but direct sales had a firm hold on its place in the economy. Door-to-door salesmen were everywhere selling brushes, silk hosiery, and the new aluminum pots and pans. Table 1, although it greatly underestimates the number of direct sellers, gives at least an indication of the patterns of growth and decline of sales occupations. Most direct salespeople fall into the "huckster and peddler" category as defined by the census.

The industry was aided in the 1920s by at least three factors. It was an era when women were interested in applying scientific techniques to labor in the home and in laborsaving devices—products ideally suited to direct sellers' demonstrations. The "scientific homemaking" movement sought to bring to the domestic sphere the same techniques of efficiency being used in factories and offices by the followers of Frederick Winslow Taylor's scientific management movement. As Julie Matthaei has written, "Just as the manager learned and applied the scientific principles of economics and natural science to his business in order to achieve success in the business world, a homemaker needed to learn and apply these same scientific principles of business to her homemaking."[18] The new "home economics" demanded the use of both modern techniques and the new laborsaving technology being produced for the home. The trained "specialty agent" of many branch office DSOs was ideally suited to teach women, in the comfort of their kitchens, how modern appliances could transform their tasks, freeing them for nurturing and leisure. Major appliances, including washing machines and refrigerators, were sold by distributors who demonstrated their features and proper use in consumers' homes.

A number of extant door-to-door household product companies were formed in response to this new market opportunity. For example, West Bend, a manufacturer of high-quality cookware, was established in 1911, and Electrolux, maker of an expensive vacuum cleaner, began in 1924. Alfred Fuller, with a brush to meet every cleaning need, attributed his success to the scientific homemaking movement and to labor-force changes that affected middle-class women.

> This was the age of woman's emancipation. As she swept out into a world wider than her own home, she sought short cuts in her housekeeping, for which Fuller products were a ready answer. As women entered office and factory employment, maids became scarce, forcing women to do their own housework. A wife who was indifferent to the brushes and mops her servant used was particular about the quality of her own. The times were with us.[19]

The direct selling industry was also the beneficiary of the post-World War I labor oversupply and of excess industrial production capacity. Men were looking for jobs, and manufacturers were looking for markets. Addressing the National Association of Agency Companies in 1925, a predecessor of today's Direct Selling Association, association president Frank B. Jennings surveyed with satisfaction the state of the industry that had benefited from financial dislocation:

> During the war, when under the pressure of necessity we learned the meaning of intensive production, application of real efficiency methods and elimination of waste led to doubled and trebled outputs with the same expenditure of effort. Naturally when demand swung back to normal the producer met them with greatly reduced man power, resulting in a wave of unemployment. To forestall further curtailment of production, de-

Table 1: Number of Selected Sales Workers in the Labor Force, 1910–80

Group[a]	1910	1920	1930	1940	1950	1960	1970	1980
Hucksters and peddlers[b]	103,390	69,930	127,912	163,610	37,500	82,482	165,525	222,709
Wholesale and manufacturer's sales reps[c]	163,620	179,320	223,732	253,006[d]	727,140	987,731	1,066,912	1,301,246
Sales people in stores[e]	1,262,076	1,537,350	2,388,921	2,554,912[f]	2,510,730	2,724,313	2,830,185	5,169,758
Total number of sales workers	1,755,000[g]	2,058,000[g]	3,059,000[g]	3,450,000[g]	4,014,210	4,801,341	5,432,633	8,674,772
Total number in labor force	37,271,360	41,236,185	48,594,592	53,299,000[h]	58,550,700	68,006,553	80,071,130	104,057,985

Sources: Unless otherwise noted, data presented in this table are derived from the following sources:
1910–40: A. M. Edwards, *Population: Comparative Occupational Statistics for the United States, 1870 to 1940* (Washington, D.C.: United States Government Printing Office, 1943), United States Bureau of the Census, *Sixteenth Census of the United States: 1940* (Washington, D.C.: United States Government

1960: United States Bureau of the Census, *United States Census of Population: 1960*, Final Report PC(2)-7A, *Subject Reports: Occupational Characteristics* (Washington, D.C.: United States Government Printing Office, 1973).

1970: United States Bureau of the Census, *Detailed Occupation of the Experienced Civilian Labor Force by Sex for the United States and Regions: 1980 and 1970*. Supplementary Report PC80-S1-15 (Washington, D.C.: United States Government Printing Office, 1984).

Note: Estimates in this table exclude managers, professionals, and officials whenever possible if it appears their primary activity is not sales. Because these figures represent only those whose primary occupation is in a specified category, they may greatly underestimate numbers of persons in a particular category when a significant proportion are engaged in the activity as a second job.

[a]Occupational classification systems used by the United States Bureau of the Census vary greatly over the period 1910 to 1980. Decisions on which occupational classifications present relevant data were made by referring to United States Bureau of the Census, *Alphabetical Index of Occupations and Industries: Sixteenth Census of the United States* (Washington, D.C.: United States Government Printing Office, 1940); United States Bureau of the Census, *Classified Index of Occupations: Fifteenth Census of the United States* (Washington, D.C.: United States Government Printing Office, 1930, 1940, 1950, 1960, 1970, [five decennial volumes]; United States Department of Commerce, Office of Federal Statistical Policy and Standards, *Standard Occupational Classification Manual*, 1980 ed. (Washington, D.C.: United States Government Printing Office, 1980).

[b]Hucksters and peddlers are defined as relatively autonomous retail salespeople not working in stores.

[c]Wholesale and manufacturer's sales representatives are employed sales agents who sell primarily to anyone except the final consumer.

[d]Estimated: cited by Raymond Edward Ries, "The American Salesman," Ph.D. diss., University of Illinois, 1958, p. 20.

[e]Retail salespeople employed to work mainly in stores.

[f]Ries, American Salesman," p. 20. Probably an overestimate; appears to include managers, professionals, and officials along with sales employees.

[g]United States Bureau of the Census, *Historical Statistics of the United States: Colonial Times to 1970*, bicentennial ed. (Washington, D.C.: United States Government Printing Office, 1975), part 1, p. 142.

[h]Adjusted figure, comparative occupational statistics for the United States, 1879 to 1940, ibid., p. 12.

mand had to be bolstered, new demands created. Demand presupposes buying and these producers reasoned that people would buy, IF THEY WERE SOLD.[20]

Jennings described the appeal of direct selling to manufacturers in an era of consumer apathy.

Acting upon this reasoning, that the ultimate consumer was not buying to the extent he would if he were really sold, they decided it was up to them to get their products presented more forcibly to him. . . . Personal solicitation to the consumer was the answer and specially trained salesmen the means of this solicitation.[21]

An independent survey of 250 businesses published in 1929 by the editor of *Dartnell Sales and Advertising Magazines* confirmed that in "talking with both the jobber and the manufacturer we find unprecedented interest attached to the question of direct selling."[22]

Direct selling was only one of the new techniques being employed to stimulate the consumption of consumer goods. It was the era of advertising and public relations men, the new professionals whose job was to whet Americans' appetites for goods. Direct selling itself used the new advertising techniques to support product sales as well as to attract recruits more effectively.[23] Indeed, DSOs were such important clients that advertising agencies belonged to the industry association and were represented at annual meetings. Direct selling executives debated the relative efficacy of advertising for salesmen in general-interest publications such as the *Saturday Evening Post*, whose readers would see that they were paying the markup that companies promised would enrich salesmen, or in the several popular magazines of the time devoted exclusively to selling, including *Salesology, Independent Salesman, Opportunity, Specialty Salesman Magazine*, and *How to Sell*. Advertisements promised the opportunity for substantial income and a release from salaried labor, precisely the appeals that are made today. In the 1920s, though, most direct sellers were men, and advertisements often showed a man.[24]

THE INDUSTRY ORGANIZES

If the 1920s were expansionary years for direct selling, the industry's growth did not go unchallenged. Retail merchants, especially in small towns, were hurt by the flood of door-to-door peddlers and canvassers swamping the countryside. Merchants waged campaigns, often successful, to cast doubt on distributors' honesty. In 1925 one executive lamented:

> Retailers claim we misrepresent; that we employ dishonest sales agents; that we are unreliable; that our goods are not honestly guaranteed to be satisfactory; that when a guarantee is given, it will not be made good; that we do not sell at low prices; that we do not and cannot give good service; that most sales agents are advance agents for burglars, and other untruths that would take a long time to tell.[25]

Retailers and local Chambers of Commerce waged war against direct salesmen by a variety of means. They proposed ordinances requiring each distributor to purchase a business license (a retail establishment with a number of clerks could operate under one license), to submit to physical examinations, and to post bond. Particularly for part-time distributors, the financial requirements were hardships. Merchants campaigned in support of these ordinances through editorial pressure on local newspapers, in which they were important advertisers. In 1925 in Dayton, Ohio, for instance, the secretary of the Retail Merchants Bureau of the Chamber of Commerce gave talks to Parent-Teacher Associations claiming that 87% of sales agents were dishonest and the rest of them suspect. In response, all the direct selling firms in Dayton, of which there were several, resigned from the Chamber. The Chamber, alarmed at the loss of members who gave "unsparingly of their time and money" squelched the campaign.[26]

Under organized local pressure, direct selling companies responded by organizing themselves to wage "the peddler's war," as it became known. Ten home office companies had created the Agents Credit Association in Binghamton, New York, in 1910 to discuss their relations with sales agents, particularly in matters dealing with collection of accounts and credit extended to salesmen they knew only through the mail. The association was renamed several times in the next fifteen years, but in 1925, in part in response to attack, it reconstituted itself as the National Association of Direct Selling Companies (NADSC). Ninety-one firms were members that year, including branch office companies and suppliers to the industry.

Organization at the industry level clearly aided the cause of direct selling. In 1927 the NADSC general counsel opposed 164 state and local ordinances and reported "killing 111 of these bills."[27]

Some battles were lost, however, including an important one in Green River, Wyoming. A 1932 Green River ordinance prohibited unsolicited sales presentations without prior invitation of the homeowner. NADSC fought this battle to the United States Supreme Court, where the constitutionality of the local law was affirmed. Green River laws, as they are generically known, were vigorously opposed by NADSC wherever proposed, and they continue to be opposed by its successor, the Direct Selling Association.[28]

EFFECTS OF THE GREAT DEPRESSION

When the Great Depression hit the United States in 1929, direct selling was a mature, organized industry with a modest but significant place in the economy. The depression upset this stability in two countervailing ways. First, it meant the demise of a number of direct selling firms—one account claimed that half of an estimated 6,000 DSOs went bankrupt.[29] NADSC reports show a modest decrease in membership in the early 1930s, with some members' dues in arrears. Direct selling firms failed for the same reasons other businesses failed. An advertising agent for the industry explained the bankruptcies. "Conditions such as we are having always take a heavy toll; firms that are improperly managed or insufficiently financed are swept away; articles whose appeal has been getting weaker and weaker will finally give up the ghost—but direct selling will go on."[30] Direct selling did indeed go on, but in favor of branch office operations that employed personal recruiting in the field, rather than advertisements, to attract distributors.

A second, mitigating effect of the depression was the new ease of recruiting. Direct sellers were finding it much easier to interest unemployed and underemployed persons in the idea of door-to-door sales when alternative forms of work were eliminated, a countercyclical effect that persists today. An executive of Better Brushes declared in 1930 that "today you can hire three men in one-half the time you could a year ago."[31] Moreover the quality of recruits was higher, reflecting the industry's ability to select from a better-educated, even middle-class, applicant pool.

> The modern agent [is] letter-perfect in his sales talk, well groomed in appearance. One came to my door the other day [in 1932] to deliver a brush my wife had ordered. He drove a car, and in appearance, personality and general ability would compare favorably with salesmen calling on the store trade. There is a great contrast from five years ago, when so many agents were old Civil War veterans or men who had made a failure at everything and turned to canvassing as a last resort.[32]

Although many DSOs failed a number prospered, perhaps because of the improved skills of the distributors. Well-managed companies selling staples, such as Fuller Brush, continued to find a market. According to Fuller "our sales, only $5,000,000 in 1932, rose at the rate of about $1,000,000 a year" until 1939.[33]

A number of companies were started during the depression, too. Frank S. Beveridge, an executive with Fuller Brush, struck out on his own in 1932 and founded Stanley Home Products, a company whose innovations were to become critical to the development of modern DSOs. The *Encyclopaedia Britannica*, which was sold ineffectively by its then owner, Sears, Roebuck and Company, through its catalog division, was made the sole product of a new branch office direct selling firm in 1933.[34] Financially pressed companies, or companies merely looking for a low-overhead distribution system, turned to direct sales.

THE INDUSTRY CONFRONTS THE STATE

The election of Franklin Roosevelt to the presidency in 1932 and his subsequent New Deal economic reforms influenced the development of direct selling in several ways. The "First New Deal," the package of legislative and regulatory programs enacted until 1935, was mostly concerned with issues of relief and recovery, including the Federal Emergency Relief Act, the Civilian Conservation Corps, the National Employment Service Act, and the National Industrial Recovery Act (NIRA). The last, NIRA, was designed to encourage employment by stimulating business.[35] An important, if contradictory, principle of the NIRA was that industries should be competitive and self-regulating under the careful eye of the federal government.[36] Fair trade codes specifying ethical business practices, many of which were drawn up by industry associations in response to the formation of the Federal Trade Commission in 1914, if approved by the National Recovery Administration (NRA), were given the force of law. Trade codes typically had two types of provisions. One specified fair business conditions, including output levels, prices, and ethical trade practices. The other concerned fair labor practices such as wages, hours and conditions of work, and collective bargaining. Industries failing to voluntarily self-regulate could be made to follow codes proposed by the president.[37]

The direct selling industry also sought to bring its members in line with government-dictated standards. In 1928 the NADSC president described the situation to members:

> You all know of the existence of the Federal Trade Commission and have some impression of the activities of that body. Recently they have been becoming active in the direct selling field and want to know all about it. They have some ideas of their own and are not at present actively unfriendly to direct selling. But it is known among the competitive lines of business that the Commission is looking into direct selling and you can bet that very shortly they will be furnished enough ammunition by people who desire to hurt this kind of business so that the Commission will be inclined to do something active about it. What the Commission can do has been seen in other cases. They can lay down a code of practices, rather than a code of ethics for any business.[38]

Industry executives felt they had a good chance to shape the regulatory environment if they acted quickly.

> There is a way to head [the Commission] off. If an association
> will write a code of ethics which is to be followed by all mem-
> bers of this association and will then offer it to the Federal
> Trade Commission as a transmittal of the practices we follow in
> our business, it is a ten to one shot that the Commission will
> adopt our viewpoint. If we show them that we intend to keep
> our skirts clean, clean our businesses and do what we consider
> the right thing with our customers and salesmen and public
> generally, the Commission will quite likely say that is the
> proper spirit and will rule in our favor, or will do nothing at all.
> One thing is certain, that if we don't do it first it is going to be
> done to us.[39]

Even before the threat of government intervention, some association members had been interested in policing the direct
selling industry and established a code of ethical practices. Because of the low investment and overhead necessary to set up
and maintain business, at both the distributor and company
levels, direct selling attracted many unscrupulous persons
happy to make a fast buck. "Fly-by-night" aptly described canvassers who took deposits and never delivered goods, as well
as companies that conveniently disappeared when promises of
service and quality cut too far into profits. Unlike retailers
with substantial capital investments and a fixed business location, dishonest DSOs could not be run out of town—they
themselves ran to the next unwitting community. One dishonest distributor in a neighborhood ruined the business environment for all DSOs for years to come.

In the early 1920s the National Association of Agency
Companies had a "Vigilance Committee" to investigate com-
plaints of dishonest practices, and NADSC later passed a code
of ethics in response to government pressure. Although the
National Industrial Recovery Act provision giving associations'
codes legal standing was overturned by the Supreme Court in
the 1935 case *Schechter Poultry Corp. vs. U.S.*, the industry's
self-interest prompted them from time to time to maintain
a consumer protection stance, to cooperate with regulatory
agencies, and to act against unethical DSOs.[40] Indeed, as early
as 1936 the direct selling trade association's Anti-Propaganda
Committee proposed enlisting the FTC's aid in combating the
perennial editorial campaigns against door-to-door selling. The

committee report stated, "If the Federal Trade Commission can be convinced [that] the propaganda in question works direct hardship on Direct Selling Companies, and is actually unfair business practice and restraint of trade, some action by the Federal Trade Commission may be secured."[41] Even today, companies applying for membership in the Direct Selling Association assume a one-year probationary standing while their business practices are investigated by the DSA's legal staff.

If the NRA's pressure for a code of fair business practice was acceptable to the industry, the Social Security Act of 1935 was seen as a clear threat to the industry's survival. Whereas the "First New Deal" had attempted to repair the damage of the depression, the "Second New Deal" programs attempted to create conditions for preventing the future collapse of social welfare. The Social Security Act provided for the care of the unemployed, the elderly, the dependent, and the sick. The Social Security Administration was to be financed by mandatory contributions of employers and workers through payroll taxes. Moreover, a minimum wage was being proposed for employees.

Today we understand the word "employee" to represent both a social role and a work relationship that has quite specific meanings. Before the advent of Social Security the legal relationship between the distributor and the DSO was not a significant question. Whether a DSO referred to its distributors as "employees" or as "independent businesspeople" was a matter of company preference in the use of language, not a legal distinction. Both terms are used in reports dating from the era. There had been a few instances where states tried to get DSOs to pay workmen's compensation insurance for distributors as employed workers, but the various state supreme courts had handed down conflicting rulings on the matter that DSOs could hide behind. In any case, the issue did not seem important because the costs were not substantial.[42]

With the industry still bearing the effects of the depressed economy, the proposed 3% payroll tax to be paid by the employer, plus a 3% tax to be taken out of the employee's earnings by the employer, seemed onerous to many DSO executives. It posed a particular burden for home office companies that delivered goods C.O.D. The distributor took his profit from the deposit collected with the order; the proposed Social

Security Act would make the DSO legally responsible for collecting 3% of the deposit even though it never had control of the money.

Not all DSOs were equally concerned about Social Security, however. Some felt they could readjust prices and commissions to maintain profit levels. One executive encouraged the industry to look at the larger benefits of the legislation. "We forget that at the same time [it costs us something] that the Social Securities [*sic*] Act will probably help to re-establish anywhere from ten to fifteen million people as a consuming power and whatever little we might lose in paying an extra tax we will easily gain back by having better business."[43]

Thornier, in fact potentially devastating, was the threat of a minimum wage. Direct selling was, and continues to be, a very inefficient industry by the standards of bureaucratic organization. Many distributors worked part time and had competing interests, such as another job or family obligations. There was high turnover, as much as 100% or more a year, making recruitment a perpetual concern and reflecting the failure of DSOs to substantially engage the commitment of much of its sales force who sold products "on the side." Moreover, direct selling organizations had very little control over the quality and quantity of the selling behavior of even their active salespeople. Dispersed workers, particularly those not tied to a salary, evaded easy supervision.

The logic of direct selling, however, allowed even poorly skilled, less-than-committed workers to profit a company as long as overhead was kept low enough. Many DSOs required only that a distributor maintain minimal sales, such as an order every three months, to remain active. Even if the average distributor contributed only $10 a month profit to the DSO, enough distributors added to a sales force at sufficiently low cost could result in a highly profitable business. A minimum wage law, which was predicated on the bureaucratic organization of work where the employer had the undivided, supervised, and presumably productive time of employees, threatened the viability of direct selling, which was based on a different economic logic.

Retailers must have recognized with glee what a minimum wage would do to their archrival, and they lobbied to get "outside salespeople" covered by minimum wage laws. General Hugh S. Johnson, head of the National Recovery Administration, held hearings on the matter in Washington. NADSC's general counsel reported:

> It was apparent at the hearing that the retail code authority and the labor board were working hand in glove on this proposition, and to me it was apparent that the benefits that might come to the salesperson were a secondary consideration and that the real object was to put [the direct selling] industry on trial and to demonstrate, if possible, that we were an uneconomic unit in distribution and couldn't compete at that time with retailing under the conditions under which retailing had to operate.[44]

If covered by minimum wage laws, the direct selling industry would have had to fundamentally reorganize. Minimum standards of productivity would have been necessary to justify the expense of a salary, and more controls would have had to be instituted. The free wheeling, sell-if-you-can approach would no longer have been economic.

At the hearings NADSC was represented by its general counsel and by some of its member firms, including Real Silk Hosiery, Fuller Brush, and the California Perfume Company (now Avon). In addition, the refrigerator, sewing machine, vacuum cleaner, and tea and coffee industries, many of which sold direct to consumers but did not belong to NADSC, sent representatives.

The direct selling lobby attacked the proposed minimum wage for outside salesmen in two ways. First, they conceded that some outside salesmen in fact had an employeelike relationship to the company distributing through them—that is, they were under the control and direction of the company. They argued, however, that these were mostly the traveling salesmen known as "commercial travelers" who were manufacturers' representatives selling largely to industrial accounts for resale and who, not incidentally, were represented by another trade association. The direct sellers, who sold only to consumers, argued that they were fundamentally different: "We lack the element of control that the wholesale house or manufacturer who sells through a commercial traveler has over that man. He knows what that man is doing. He is not a

competitive seller. He is an order taker calling on regular customers. We have men out whom we cannot follow. They never
report to us."[45] It became clear at the hearing that DSOs that
sold products to the distributor for resale, as some home office
companies did, were probably exempt from the proposed
minimum wage laws; the distributor was in fact a customer of
the DSO who sought other customers. But DSOs that sold direct to the consumer with the distributor as an intermediate
agent were exposed to regulation, according to NADSC's general counsel: "If you have any strings on it, fixed territory,
terms or conditions of sale or re-sale, or do any other controlling thing, then you are considered an agency house . . . and
these people are your employees."[46]

The second argument that the industry presented to
General Johnson was practical and political and not at all involved in the legal niceties of how much control constituted an
employment relation. The industry argued that should it be
forced to pay a minimum wage some 250,000 to 300,000 distributors would be put out of work in the midst of a depression.
NADSC's representative at the hearing reported that General
Johnson expressed concern at this figure, and he predicted
that the National Recovery Administration would rule in the
industry's favor.

The twin issues of Social Security and the minimum
wage created by the New Deal awakened DSOs to the importance of defining their relationship with distributors. General
Johnson's hearings became moot when the National Recovery
Administration lost support for its activities, including minimum wage proposals, in the wake of continuing depression
and with an unfavorable Supreme Court ruling on key National
Industrial Recovery Act provisions. By 1935 the NRA was "vir-
tually moribund."[47]

The idea of a minimum wage, however, did not die. Many
of the labor protection provisions of NIRA were transferred to
the new National Labor Relations Board in 1935. The passage
of the Fair Labor Standards Act of 1938 extended labor protections, including a minimum wage, to all workers engaged in
interstate commerce. The Hour and Wage Division of the Department of Labor held appeals hearings to determine whether
individual firms were exempt from minimum wage laws.

By then, however, a number of DSOs had legally re-defined their relationship to their sales forces by adroit maneuvering. The debate, however, had raised disquieting employment issues that DSOs were anxious to resolve, issues that would resurface with the success of network DSOs in the 1970s.

THE INDEPENDENT
CONTRACTOR SOLUTION

Industry archives have preserved the moment when direct selling organizations discovered an escape from the encroaching grasp of the state. After a lengthy discussion about the likely effect of employment regulation, a member asked the general counsel a question at the 1935 annual meeting: "How about [the direct] sales person as an independent contractor? . . . If we changed our form of application and specified that this man buys the merchandise from us for resale?"

One can imagine the growing pleasure with which the counsel considered the arrangement. He responded, "That, of course would let [us] out entirely. There would be no question about [payroll tax] then."[48] There would be no further question of a minimum wage, workmen's compensation, state and federal unemployment insurance, benefits, or tax withholding.

Declaring distributors independent contractors in fact became the direct selling industry's solution to government's attempts to influence working conditions then and in the future. Increasing numbers of DSOs made it clear to new recruits that they were in business for themselves and paid all the costs of doing business, including transportation and the purchase of samples and promotional materials. The DSO/distributor relationship was codified in a signed contract specifying the legal independence of the direct seller. The legal and financial necessity of making distributors independent contractors became a virtue: a cheaper labor supply.

Although the "independent contractor solution" freed DSOs from the burdens of the employment relation until it was vigorously challenged by the Internal Revenue Service in the 1970s,[49] it was not a solution without costs. In earlier years DSOs had attempted to control distributors by prescribing such matters as how and where they were to go about selling. That most such attempts at control were only modestly effective did not stop DSOs from trying. To be free from the charge that they were in fact employers, DSOs now had to refrain from dictating retail prices, selling methods, and hours of distributor selling. Nor could they prohibit distributors from selling for other DSOs. In exchange for the low overhead of the nonemployed distributor, the DSOs had to eschew the bureaucratic controls employed by other forms of selling, including retailers, commercial travelers, and departmental sales divisions. Many of the techniques being developed by the increasingly sophisticated profession of sales management, such as call schedules and routing plans, were now legally beyond their reach. In fact, however, almost all DSOs made the exchange. By the 1980s distributors of all but one were independent contractors, legally free from control of their selling (although some branch managers were employees).

THE EARLY MODERN ERA

The record of the direct selling industry in the 1940s is less clear than for the years before and after, but at least three developments appear to have occurred during that decade: branch office DSOs supplanted home office operations as the dominant form of direct selling organization; the party plan marketing technique was invented and popularized; and the first network DSOs were formed.[50]

Home office operations were the first form of organized direct selling, and it is clear from transcriptions of trade association meetings that they dominated until the 1920s.[51] Direct selling advertisements, most of which carried recruiting messages for home office companies, reached their zenith in billings in 1927, giving evidence of home office decline after that year.[52] Several factors probably played a role in the changing form of DSOs. First, high-ticket items such as encyclopedias, sewing machines, and vacuum cleaners achieved wider acceptance as commodities and were sold more effectively by trained branch office salespeople. Second, in this era systematic management techniques were more generally used in business. Techniques of recruiting, training, motivating, and rewarding salespeople could be practiced effectively only where there was personal contact, as in a branch or a bureaucratically organized sales department of employed workers. Although one might imagine that the more organized and managed branch form of DSO would be avoided after the employment relation problem, branch training and motivation activities were not necessarily controlling in an authoritative way (they encouraged self-control) and hence were not subject to the charge that branch distributors had an employment relation. More likely, according to an industry executive, many branch office executives were simply not sophisticated enough to understand the regulatory implications of their management actions; they merely saw that organizing in branches gave them more control over distribution and sales, and lax enforcement of employee "status laws" permitted them to flourish. Undoubtedly, too, some made the calculation that it was unlikely they would be subject to a federal audit and hearing. By the 1980s home office operations, the first organized form of direct selling, accounted for only about 5% of all direct sales.[53]

THE PARTY PLAN

The "party plan" was the second important development of the 1940s. Anecdotal history attributes this marketing innovation to Frank S. Beveridge, the former Fuller Brush executive who founded Stanley Home Products.[54] Beveridge reputedly was interested in learning why one distibutor in Maine was so successful. He found that the distributor was demonstrating the products to groups of women in private homes and was closing a high proportion of sales. Whether or not he originated this innovation, Beveridge certainly perfected what became known as the "party plan," soon widely copied by other DSOs.

A Stanley distributor would ask a "hostess" to invite friends to her home for a "party." The party often involved simple parlor games to create a friendly atmosphere and promote interaction among the guests. After a few icebreakers the salesperson began showing products, often inviting guests to comment on them or to demonstrate their features. Frequently a drawing was held for a surprise "gift." At the end of the party guests were invited to purchase the products and to enjoy refreshments provided by the hostess. A hostess was usually credited with a percentage of the party's gross sales, which she could apply to her own purchases.

The party plan was an important innovation for the industry for several reasons. First, it allowed the salesperson to be more efficient in the use of his—and now more frequently her—time.[55] Rather than being addressed to one prospective customer, the sales demonstration was delivered to a roomful, sometimes as many as fifteen people. The hostess, moreover, did much of the work. She issued the invitations, served the refreshments, and provided the location. Not only were the prospective customers brought together by the hostess, they were screened for interest in buying.

A more important reason the party plan was such an important innovation was that it skillfully blurred the social and economic spheres.[56] An essentially economic function, the demonstration of consumer goods, was transformed into, or at least confused with, a social function. The cues for social behavior—a friend's invitation, a gathering of acquaintances, a private home—set the stage for mannerly conduct and the fulfillment of social obligations. For many of the guests good manners seemed to dictate that one help the hostess/friend have a successful party. Success seemed to require that one show interest in the ostensible purpose of the gathering—the chance to inspect products—through at least a modest purchase.[57]

The party plan was characteristic of the new type of salesmanship growing up to accommodate twentieth-century business needs. C. Wright Mills described the evolution of the American salesman as the role changed with the needs of capitalist enterprise, an evolution mirrored by the changing forms of direct selling. When demand exceeded supply, the salesman had only to bring goods to a waiting consumer. This was the situation of the Yankee peddler. When demand and supply were in balance, the salesman served an information function by demonstrating product features. This was the specialty salesman of the pre–World War I era. But when the industrial capacity of the country substantially outstripped real needs, the salesman's role was to stimulate demand "not by lowering prices but by creating new wants and more urgent desires."[58]

High-pressure techniques, associating consumption with aspirations such as love and popularity, and the invasion of the private sphere became the tactics of a glutted marketplace. As Mills wrote, "The bargaining manner, the huckstering animus, the memorized theology of pep, the commercialized evaluation of personal traits—they are all around us; in public and in private there is the tang and feel of salesmanship."[59] The party plan was characteristic of the increasing commercialization of social relations and the direct selling industry's contribution to a much larger trend. Today about 25% of goods sold by the direct selling industry are sold at parties.[60]

THE FIRST NETWORK DSOs

If the party plan was an effective way to take pecuniary advantage of social ties, it was also a limited one. A distributor could only infrequently go back to a hostess as a party sponsor, and a hostess could invite her friends for only an occasional party. But another innovation dating from 1941, network direct selling, made deeper, more intense and sustained use of social networks for financial gain.

Yankee peddlers and organized distributors made money by taking a markup on goods sold, pocketing the difference between the wholesale and retail prices. Sometimes they were paid a commission. Network DSOs provide another income opportunity: a royalty on the sales made by a distributor's recruits to the DSO.

The first network DSO was probably started by a psychologist, William Casselberry, and Lee Mytinger, who sold Nutrilite XX vitamins through what they called the C&M Marketing Plan.[61] They had been selling the products of the California Vitamin Company directly since 1934, but in 1941 they established a new scheme by which distributors could earn a bonus of 3% of the sales of people they personally sponsored into the organization. When sponsors (and their recruits) had sold $15,000 worth of products, the sponsors could set up their own profitable wholesaler relationship to the people "below" or "downline" from them in the recruiting chain. New wholesalers were called "breakaways" because they had broken from the sponsor's organization to create their own wholesaler relationship to the company. To encourage sponsors to develop successful breakaways (though they would lose profitable wholesaling business), C&M Marketing gave them "override" royalties on the sales of a breakaway's organization of recruits. All of the distributors were connected financially to the people who sponsored them and to the people they in turn sponsored.[62]

A network of financial relationships, while new in this configuration, had antecedents. First, branch office companies sometimes paid a "finder's fee" to a distributor for locating a new salesperson. In 1929 one DSO executive described his company's attempts at using existing salesmen to recruit new distributors not for a fee, but on a "friendship basis." More successful, however, was the following practice, which clearly presaged network DSOs.

> We originally put it on the so-called friendship basis. We feel our men are very close to the organization, but they are very busy during the daytime and sometimes at night, and it makes it rather difficult to ask them to take a certain amount of their own time without some compensation. However, when we offered a five dollar prize for each man who obtained another who signed up and paid his deposit [on a sales kit], plus a very small percentage of that man's gross sales for the first sixty days, what did we get? We got a new man who paid his deposit, and we received the vital interest of the salesman who obtained that man, to help the new man along the rough spots during his spare time, so that the original salesman would obtain a certain amount of additional recompense by virtue of the gross business done. Of course, there is a minimum that man would have to do before that gross goes into effect, but it is so small that a man has to be a very poor salesman, indeed, in order not to qualify.[63]

In addition, the memory of a fraudulent form of financial network must surely have been circulating during the time network DSOs were developed: the pyramid scheme of Charles Ponzi. Ponzi claimed he could make a profit by buying and selling international postal reply coupons in different countries because of the substantial rate differences after World War I. Starting with only $150 of his own money, Ponzi offered to let others share in his investment strategy. He sold notes payable to investors promising return of principal and 50% interest in ninety days. In fact, he returned the money as agreed to early investors within as little as forty-five days, building up confidence in his scheme. But Ponzi never bought the coupons, merely used the money of later investors to pay off earlier ones, much like a chain letter that he manipulated. Between December 1919 and August 1920, when a bankruptcy petition was filed against him, Ponzi received more than $9 million.[64]

Whether the idea of a pyramid of financial links between individuals in fact inspired the formation of network DSOs probably can never be known, but the legacy of Ponzi's pyramid scam remains even today with the direct selling industry. Many members of the public equate network DSOs with pyramid schemes, and in fact the Federal Trade Commission in 1979 held hearings on whether Amway's network constituted a pyramid. Pyramid schemes involve the use of paper profits to continue financial speculation in a chain of transactions. In fraudulent network schemes it usually involves selling someone an "investment opportunity" in which no goods or services are sold; the payment grants only the right to sell someone else the opportunity to "invest."

The network character of the financial relationship, according to the FTC's determination in the 1979 investigation of Amway, is not illegal. What is illegal is payment for which no product or service of value is anticipated. Pyramiding, according to the FTC, is a type of gambling. Network DSOs look a lot like pyramids in that they involve recruiting and structure recruits into a chain of levels. But as long as the DSO pays a royalty only on the *sales* of recruits, not for merely bringing the recruit into the organization, they are legal businesses.[65]

C&M Marketing prospered using the network form of organization until the late 1950s when management problems threatened. One group of Nutrilite distributors in Michigan, headed by sponsors Rich DeVos and Jay Van Andel, formed the American Way Association and sent representatives to California to company headquarters. DeVos and Van Andel decided that, though they would continue to sell Nutrilite, the supply of the product was too precarious. They began to manufacture goods for their downline recruits to sell. In 1959 they incorporated Amway—a contraction of American Way—which is now the world's largest network DSO.

Even before the formation of Amway, other DSOs began to copy C&M Marketing's organizational innovation. Stanley Home Products became a network DSO, and subsequently several successful Stanley distributors went off to found their own network companies. In the 1950s and early 1960s former Stanley distributors Mary Kay Ash, Mary Crowley, and Brownie Wise founded respectively Mary Kay Cosmetics, Home Interiors and Gifts, and the Tupperware sales force.[66] Some branch office operations, including the venerable W. T. Rawleigh Company, switched organizational forms, although many, such as Avon and Encylopaedia Britannica, continued as branch office companies.

By the late 1950s the network DSO form looked essentially as it does today, with its sponsorship lines, status hierarchies, and emotional and familylike character. This form of direct selling, like the earlier Yankee peddler, home office, and branch office forms, was a conjunction between the interests of manufacturers and individual distributors within a given set of economic and social conditions. As conditions changed in the decades to the present, direct selling grew from a modest industry to an extraordinary social phenomenon. In 1976 8% of families in this country included an active distributor, and one family out of every four said it had had one in the past.[67] Although all forms of direct selling grew in this period, it was network DSOs that grew the most and grew the fastest.

CHAPTER THREE
Changing Conditions of Work and the Growth of DSOs

Phyllis, a self-described direct selling addict, distributes for Shaklee, Tupperware, Avon, and Princess House. Her enthusiasm for direct sales is in marked contrast to her feelings about her previous work: "I was a receptionist, but I was also doing a lot of typing, filing, answering the phones, waiting on customers. That type of thing. And the pay scale for that type of job—I mean you get a raise once a year if you're lucky, and you might get ten cents an hour. That didn't do you any good at all."

Not only was the pay for clerical work low, she found the working conditions poor: "I would say in the eight-to-five job you have all these horrendous pressures. They want things done now, and they don't accept reasons or excuses why they are not done now."

Direct selling, on the other hand, gives her a greater sense of control and lifts the limits on her income-producing possibilities. "In this [direct selling] job you don't have the pressure. The pressure you have is your own. To get a raise, you give yourself a raise, because if you want more money, you go out and do more shows. You see? And so if I can earn $90 a night and sometimes more, why should I work an eight-to-five job?"

Phyllis's decision to give up a clerical job that she found harried, financially unrewarding, and subordinate to the control of others was, of course, an individual reaction to a particular situation. Her choice, however, can also be understood in a more generalized way as a response to the bureaucratic organization of work and to the career opportunities that firms offer people of her social class, educational credentials, and sex. Phyllis's decision was at once a response to social struc-

tural conditions as she understood them and a small incre-
ment of change in the larger social world she reacted to.

DSOs AND THE
CHANGING ENVIRONMENT

This larger social world is usually referred to as the "environment" in organizational analysis. The environment is the
social, political, economic, and historical context in which organizational action, including individual action, takes place.
It includes regulatory conditions, competition, interorganiza-
tional networks, and available technology—those things outside the organization that influence how it goes about its
business and how successful it is likely to be.[1] It also includes
the more subtle, but no less important, social understandings
about the "right" way to conduct business, for example, what
constitutes a "good" employee and the ethical bases of business activity.[2]

In this chapter I take seriously the idea that one must
understand the environment in order to understand the development, persistence, and even internal operation of any given
organizational form. It seems to me, however, that focusing
only on large-scale structural factors, important as they are,
obscures the fact that social structure is created and acted
upon by people. It is the everyday wants, experiences, understandings of interacting individuals, like Phyllis, that create
the social arrangements we call the "environment." At a given
historical moment, at a given social structural location, the
environment represents an array of constraints and possibilities that people interpret and act (or fail to act) upon.[3] It is
people's experienced material conditions of life, as well as
their aspirations, that make certain choices more plausible
and attractive—or more grimly necessary.[4]

Direct selling attracts recruits because their understanding, and frequently their experiences in the work world, leads
them to view the industry as a viable and attractive possibility
given their perceived alternatives. Direct selling has many different appeals, including the sense of control over work, being
rewarded for performance rather than social characteristics,
ease of entry, the tax deductions of an independent business,

and the familylike nature of network relations. These appeals must be understood not as abstractly attractive, but as attractive when viewed against a given set of economic and social alternatives. It is the relatively poor alternatives, according to my interviews, that have made many people choose direct sales in recent years.

Although accurate industry statistics were not collected before the DSA solicited the first study in 1974, data confirm that by the mid-1970s 2 million Americans were pursuing direct sales (table 2). Data about several large network DSOs also show a pattern of strong growth at this time (table 3). In 1976, overwhelmed by the industry's recent explosive development, the Direct Selling Association commissioned Louis Harris and Associates to perform a national survey of the industry.[5] The Harris poll asked members of a representative sampling of United States households if they had ever worked in direct sales. Nearly 16% of of the respondents had tried direct selling, and in 8% of the households someone had been active in direct sales that year.

The profile of direct sellers drawn by the Harris survey depicted someone resolutely "middle American." Eighty percent of direct sellers were women. They were more likely than the general public to have completed high school yet less likely to have a college education. They held more conservative political views and were more religious than the average American. Their median household income was $13,840, somewhat above the 1976 national average of $13,040. The ethnic distribution of direct sellers closely paralleled the ethnic distribution of the public. Thus the people who were rushing toward direct selling in the 1970s were largely women who embraced traditional beliefs. They were persons of modest education and few credentials in families of middling income.

Why were these people drawn to DSOs? Three factors, especially, were cited by my informants as reasons for their involvement in direct sales. Although not directly comparable to the Harris survey responses, the nonrandom, intensive interview data I collected in the 1980s suggest reasons for the growing attraction of direct sales a decade earlier. The reasons reflected the changing composition of the labor force and the changing conditions of work. Distributors cited, first, women's

Table 2: Direct Selling Industry, 1957–85

	1957[a]	1962[b]	1964[b]	1974[c]	1975	1976	1980	1981	1982	1983	1984	1985
Sales (billions of dollars)	2.00	2.50	3.00	5.00	5.30	5.60	7.50	NA[d]	8.50	8.58	8.64	8.36
Distributors (millions)	NA	NA	1.50	1.80	1.93	2.00	4.90	NA	4.93	5.11	5.81	5.12

[a]Frederick Taylor, "Door-to-Door Sellers Rack up Sales Gains—With Help from Slump," *Wall Street Journal*, 12 August 1958, p. 1.
[b]Alfred Law, "Door-to-Door Selling Expands: More Firms, New Items Enter Field," *Wall Street Journal*, 8 January 1964, p. 1.
[c]Data for 1974–84 are from the Direct Selling Association and include all forms of direct selling organizations, but not insurance companies that emply direct selling.
[d]NA = not available.

Table 3: Sales (in Millions of Dollars) and Distributors (in Thousands) for Four Direct Selling Organizations, 1969–85

	1969	1970	1971	1972	1973	1974	1975	1976	1977	1978	1979	1980	1981	1982	1983	1984	1985
Avon Products[a]																	
Sales	665	759	873	1,005	1,150	1,260	1,295	1,434	1,647	2,014	2,377	2,569	2,613	2,710	2,607	2,605	2,407
Distributors	NA[b]	NA	NA	NA	NA	NA	800	990	995	1,080	1,200	1,250	1,280	1,340	1,400	1,365	1,300
Stanley Home Products																	
Sales	117	126	144	155	176	150	151	158	166	192	213	233	239	235	277	333	327
Distributors	NA	NA	NA	NA	NA	NA	NA	NA	NA	NA	NA	NA	NA	NA	NA	NA	NA
Mary Kay Cosmetics																	
Sales	6	8	12	17	22	30	34	44	47	53	91	166	235	304	323	277	Leveraged Buy-out
Distributors	NA	NA	NA	NA	NA	NA	NA	NA	38	43	57	94	134	173	195	173	Privately held
Shaklee Corporation																	
Sales	10	19	44	61	75	79	101	169	247	275	314	411	454	471	538	459	406
Distributors	NA	NA	NA	NA	NA	NA	NA	NA	NA	NA	NA	NA	NA	NA	NA	NA	NA

Note: Because DSOs have very low overhead, most of them never go to the capital markets for funds and are therefore scarce. Data for these large publicly held companies are an indicator of growth patterns in the 1970s.

[a]Avon is not a network DSO.

[b]NA = not available.

need and desire to work and their concentration in service-sector jobs. Second, they described the rationalization and in-security of corporate life. A third factor was mentioned by industry executives: the heavy burden on management of maintaining the employment relation in a period of economic slowdown. Not surprisingly, these three "microresponses" mirror "macrochanges" in the environment.

Direct selling, a modest industry in the 1950s, was ide-ally poised to take advantage of changes in the 1960s and 1970s. Its promise of status, freedom, and friendship was at-tractive to new workers who found conspicuously little of those in their jobs. Its promise of self-control and indepen-dence appealed to workers buffeted by economic recession and dislocation.

WOMEN IN THE LABOR FORCE

The economic expansion of the 1950s and 1960s created 22 million new jobs in those two decades,[6] and 17.2 million more originated in the slow-growth period of the 1970s.[7] Although new workers came from all parts of the population, including minorities and immigrants, the most dramatic increase was in the ranks of women. Women's labor-force participation jumped from 33.9% in 1950,[8] to 45.5% in 1980.[9]

Many of the new workers were married women, a group, with some exceptions, that historically did not participate in the paid labor force in significant numbers. Substantial pro-portions of widows and single women have always worked, but married women had been expected to live on the income their husbands provided. By 1980, however, more than half of all married women were working, many of them mothers of small children.[10]

Economic Needs and Desires

Wives and mothers entered the postwar work force for several reasons. First, married women, like the population at large, were influenced by the accelerating consumption of the 1950s. They aspired to the cornucopia of mass-produced goods for themselves, their families, and their homes. Although their husbands' real income grew in this period, families' aspirations outstripped that growth. Homemakers in the 1950s, as today, were being pulled by what economic historian Julie A. Matthaei calls "their mandate to fill the family's expanding needs." Women's traditional role as caretaker was redefined to include taking care of the family's consumptive needs as well as its physical and emotional needs.[11] The process began with a few women, then snowballed: "As more homemakers enter into the labor force, moving their families up in the income hierarchy, they raise average consumption standards, putting pressure on their fellow homemakers who stay at home."[12]

Women also work because they have no husbandly providers, or because the husband's income is clearly insufficient to meet basic needs. In 1980, 73% of working women were single, widowed, divorced, or separated or had household earnings of less than $15,000. Increased rates of divorce in the 1960s and 1970s led women to the workplace.

The economic downturn of the 1970s, when men faced layoffs and reduced workweeks, put pressure on women as secondary wage earners.

According to the DSA's Harris survey, the need or desire for income is the reason many people are initially attracted to direct sales.[13] My interviews clearly reflected the larger picture drawn by statistics.

> My husband's in construction, and we had a baby. We were real behind on the bills, and we needed some money real fast. And I didn't have any money to start on anything. Tupperware doesn't take any money to get started, and you make money right away.

> My husband taught for seven years in this Christian school [where the pay was low], and meanwhile our finances went downhill. Shaklee held us together.

> [I started Amway because] we just needed more money. And I never went to school, so I don't have any of the degrees that they want so you can get a decent job over there [at the local university].

There is evidence, too, that in recent years women have worked outside the home because they enjoy the independence and attaining a sense of self apart from domestic roles. Women enjoy having money, including the power it gives them at home.[14] A 1970 United States Department of Labor study found that about half of all women holding blue- and pink-collar jobs would work even if they could afford not to.[15]

Working Conditions

Women, like men, work both because they want to and because they have to. When they work, however, they do not stand beside men either figuratively or actually. Women workers inhabit low-status strata in the economy, and when they work in the same organizations as men, they largely occupy occupational ghettos with other women.

When women entered the labor force in recent decades, for the most part they took "women's jobs," occupations that were segregated by sex. Four categories of jobs, especially, drew women to their ranks: clerical, retail, peripheral manufacturing and trade, and health and education service jobs. These four categories accounted for 95% of all female employment in 1970.[16] Whenever women dominate an occupation the pay is lower than for jobs held by men with similar skills—the reason behind the press for comparable-worth laws—so changes in the "integration" of jobs for men and women are an important indicator of how well off women workers are.

Unfortunately for most women, even as they have entered the labor market in large numbers, the sex segregation of the United States labor force has remained remarkably stable over the past thirty-five years, sustaining the gap between men's and women's wages.[17] It is true, though, that jobs taken by relatively well-educated middle-class women have become less segregated. More women have entered well-paying and formerly male-dominated managerial, professional, and technical occupations, although they stay clustered at the lower reaches of those "good job" categories.

A number of women distributors who worked in management or other "good jobs," however, gave frustrated aspirations as reasons for trying direct sales.

> I had great ambitions to do engineering. My employer sent me to school, and I worked hard and got straight A's in all the

courses, but they still wouldn't promote me. I had my review in January and they tell me I'm doing a good job, but they don't give it to me in money. Mary Kay is totally opposite. Every single step you take you are rewarded.

Teaching is very structured, it is very security minded. Everything is planned out, you know, the bells ring. People program their lives that way, and I think that was what I was fighting. I was [also] on top of the salary scale. I just had the typical burnout syndrome and just did not know what to do.

I was assistant vice-president [at a savings and loan]. Now the reason they gave me the title and a salary was that then they didn't have to give me extra money [for overtime].

Though middle-class women have had expanded, if limited, opportunities, lower-middle-class and working-class women have not fared so well. They have not entered the high-paying craft union occupations of their husbands in significant numbers, and they have been relegated to less-skilled and more insecure job categories. "Going to work" for these women means going to an assembly line, a fast-food outlet, a typing pool, or some other low-pay, low-prestige, and low-security position.

Many women in direct selling cited the poor conditions of pink- and blue-collar work as reasons for trying direct sales.

[I started direct selling because] I was laid off from my job. The owner of the company passed away, and they hired a new office manager. I'd been there seventeen years, I had done nothing wrong, but they wouldn't even give me a recommendation. A year later they fired both of the other girls who were working there, at Christmastime.

One thing that did attract me to Shaklee was the thought of being able to get out of the beauty shop full time. I was getting tired of standing behind a chair working forty hours a week.

Internal Labor Markets

The "better" women's jobs—better because of clean and safe working conditions, employment stability, and benefits—are often found in large organizations in stable "core" industries. Although women workers are better off in core organizations than they are in less stable "peripheral" ones, they are not as well off as men in the same firms. Sociologists James N. Baron and William T. Bielby have demonstrated that men and women in these businesses actually occupy different "internal labor markets," that is, they enter organizations at the bottom (or middle) of different career ladders. The career ladders for women lead not to the top, but to relatively less prestigious and less well paid positions.[18]

In direct selling, income and status are almost always tied only to sales and recruiting success.[19] There are no social barriers and usually no need for approval by a superior in order to achieve higher recognition levels. For people with few credentials such as a college degree, a firm's internal labor markets limit their income, status, and sometimes, self-worth.

> Three of us [women] in the office quadrupled sales, but my salary did not quadruple, or even double, or even increase 10 percent. It was ridiculous. So I thought I certainly could be building my own business [in Shaklee], my own future, rather than somebody else's business.

> When I put a great deal of energy into [Amway] I get a greater response, and when I put no energy into it I get no response. I like that very much. No matter how hard I worked when I had my salaried position I would get a fixed amount of money. If I worked or I didn't work very hard at all I still got the same amount. That is dumb.

Even when women are not segregated with other women in organizations, when they in fact enter occupational categories with men, they do not have the same advancement opportunities as men with comparable qualifications. A special 1986 *Wall Street Journal* report reviewing recent labor studies found that "today women fill nearly a third of all management positions (up from 19% in 1972), but most are stuck in jobs with little authority and relatively low pay. Even those few women who rose steadily through the ranks eventually crashed into an invisible barrier."[20]

Theorists debate the reasons for women's segregation into low-pay, low-prestige occupations. Some blame women's individual characteristics such as education and work experience, while others see sex-role stereotypes as limiting women's occupational opportunities. Yet others explain the differences as serving the economic interests of employers, who sustain sex segregation through employment practices.[21]

What theory best explains women's labor-force position may be debated, but the character of women's work experience is clear: women disproportionately occupy jobs that are insecure, low pay, and low status. Even when they work in organizations with relatively good conditions, they are less well off than male co-workers. They are likely to be subordinate clerical workers or, if managers, to have limited opportunities.

Household Labor

The reality of paid work is often matched by the difficulty of unpaid labor in the home. As women have entered the labor force through need or desire, they have not shed their role as principal caretaker in the home. In two-earner families women still do most of the housework and child care. The nine-to-five character of most job schedules makes caring for sick children and meeting other unexpected family needs difficult. Women must juggle two jobs in a world where work schedules were designed for men with wives at home, and where the child-care needs of women workers have little public support.[22]

Direct selling is infinitely flexible. Distributors sell when they want to, and as much or as little as they need or desire. Many women sell at night when their husbands can care for children, and they value being able to work around pregnancies and family illnesses.

> Although I had the desire to move ahead in business, most people are not thrilled about hiring pregnant women. So this was something I could do and move as fast as I wanted to—be pregnant and have my family and business—all at the same time.

> When I deliver [Tupperware] on Thursdays I take my kids. That's our going-out-to-breakfast day. I bag [products] when they're home in bed, and I talk on the phone at naptime.

Being able to care for family needs and work at the same time serves both the material and the emotional needs of women. Child care is expensive and claims a large portion of women's paychecks. A number of women also spoke of the pleasure of being able to accommodate their children's schedules. They cited the relief of not having to lie to employers when they took time off to care for sick children.

Service-Sector Work

Several institutional shifts have had important effects on the organization and experience of work in recent decades, especially for women. Perhaps the most important has been the rise of the service sector.[23] As a share of the gross national product, services grew from 36% in 1945 to almost 50% in 1983.[24] But as a percentage of employment the service sector increased beyond the halfway mark, from 46% of jobs in 1948 to 55.7% in 1976 (the difference reflects the service sector's lower productivity).[25] Moreover, service-producing work is projected to account for almost three-quarters of all new jobs created between 1982 and 1995.[26] Indeed, from 1970 to 1980 more than 700,000 new secretarial jobs were created—more than any other job category—and the increase is projected to continue.

Early evaluations of the shift to services were enthusiastic, for example, Daniel Bell's *The Coming of Post-Industrial Society*.[27] Bell saw the growth in demand for technical and professional workers as an improvement over a manufacturing-dominated economy. More recent accounts, though, are more sober. Economist Thomas M. Stanback, Jr., finds that "contrary to much that has been said, the service work force is not, on average, better paid or more highly skilled than the nonservice work force." Instead, the service sector is characterized by "a larger proportion of workers at the lower end of the earnings scale, by a higher proportion of women and minority workers, by higher percentages of part-time employment, and by fewer structural and institutional arrangements that enhance job security."[28]

Women in this study cited the character of service work as a motivation to try direct selling. For example:

> I had done secretarial work. I hate it. I hate sitting in an office nine to five looking out the window, wishing I was outside. When I was a secretary I was doing all the work and he [the boss] was getting all the big money for it.

[In Mary Kay] I just feel better about myself. I have more self-confidence. In my forty hour a week job, well, I had a real bad attitude. It's a dead-end job, and I dreaded getting up in the morning. I used to be depressed all day Sunday because I had to go back to work Monday. In the back of my mind I know that [now that I am doing direct sales] I am not going to be stuck there for the rest of my life. I can put up with this [job] for a few more weeks—that's my attitude.

As office technology has advanced to include word processors and computers, clerical work has become increasingly routinized or "deskilled." The work of a typist or computer operator today is often, despite the middle-class setting, more akin to routine manufacturing labor with its mechanized and specialized character.[29] Direct selling, with its freedom of schedule and movement and its self-paced character, gives women an accessible alternative to offices.

LIFE IN THE CORPORATION

"Men's jobs" in offices, whether filled by men or women managers and professionals, have also been transformed in the postwar decades. The beginnings of the transformation were described by two best-selling books of the 1950s, C. Wright Mills's *White Collar* and William H. Whyte, Jr.'s, *The Organization Man*.[30] These authors wrote about work in the large organizations that accompanied the postwar economic boom and the effect those organizations had on the managing classes. They noted, especially, the ability of organizations to shape not only the world of work, but the person, family, and community of the middle-class worker. In Whyte's words, the organization man (and in the 1950s managers were men) was the critical new economic actor. "They are the ones of our middle class who have left home, spiritually as well as physically, to take the vows of organization life, and it is they who are the mind and soul of our great self-perpetuating institutions."[31] Even the popular culture of the period reflected the new manager who shaped himself to the needs of the firm: the best-selling novel and long running Broadway play *How to Succeed in Business without Really Trying*[32] parodied a generation of young men throwing themselves into corporate life.

Michael Maccoby's replication of Whyte's study in the 1970s found that the organization men were no longer the cheerful positive thinkers of a generation earlier, perhaps reflecting the economic climate of the time. They were still products of the firm, but now they were more serious and manipulative corporate players. He titled his book after the quintessential manager of the seventies, *The Gamesman*.[33]

Competition

Men in direct selling, especially, speak about the competitive pressures of bureaucratic life and their unwillingness to mold themselves to it in order to achieve corporate mobility.

> One of our distributors is a young man who has just left Aerojet. He's a very young man, twenty-five years old. He used to draw on the board a diagram of Aerojet: here it is way up here [on the board], and he was one of these way down here. He's very bright, very articulate. It didn't matter what he did, he isn't going to get up there until all these guys [above him] crawl up the ladder. So if he was lucky he'd be sixty years old and they might make him something.

> Shaklee answers a lot of people's needs. If someone is unhappy with what they've been able to achieve because they've been an employee, because they have to wait to move up the corporate ladder, because they don't like going to lunch and going on vacation when somebody else tells them to, or not having enough money, Shaklee offers them an opportunity.

Status Degradation

Scholars point out that professionals, the elite of the work force, are increasingly employees subject to bureaucratic authority, not self-directed, autonomous workers.[34] Although professionals do not represent a substantial proportion of direct sellers, they have been a target of recruitment in recent years by DSOs including Mary Kay Cosmetics and Tupperware. A Tupperware executive described how his company has benefited from the erosion of professionals' status, particularly in professions dominated by women.

> We have had a significant shift since the late 1970s of people coming out of the underpaid, underappreciated professions. I'm

going to specifically mention nurses, dental technicians, school teachers. [They were attracted to Tupperware] perhaps as much [as anything] by the fact that these professions were continually being degraded in their status in the community, in terms of appreciation and recognition for their professional characteristics. [These professionals] were looking for a new place to land, if you will.[35]

Shaklee and Amway have stressed the labor-intensive nature of professional work in appeals to professional workers:

The physicians that we talk to, they maxed out at what their income can be. They are finding that to make more they are going to be there twelve hours a day. They take a vacation, and there's no pay coming in. So they see Amway as a way out.

One substantial line of Amway distributors is composed almost exclusively of professionals who have recruited each other using such appeals.

Corporate Instability

Another recent institutional transformation that has upset the middle classes is a tidal wave of mergers and takeovers. According to Paul Hirsch, "During the past decade, professional managers have been sharply reminded they are hired agents for the owners of the corporation. [They] have experienced a loss of power and autonomy to set the firm's future course."[36] Top managers, while no longer in certain control, are the frequent beneficiaries of golden parachutes and silver handshakes. Middle-level workers, though, are often out of a job, demoted, or rearranged to accommodate new ownership. As the *Washington Post* noted, "Middle managers, the staff people long thought essential to a smooth-running corporate operation, are becoming increasingly expendable because of the rapid rise in office automation and a new corporate emphasis on pushing decision-making far down into the operations."[37]

Several distributors spoke about the real or feared insecurity of corporate life, for both themselves and their families, as a precipitating factor in their attempting direct sales.

To be quite frank, at the time the company I was working for, under a particular manager—it seemed like when I went east [he said] I should have gone west, and when I went south, I was supposed to go north. I was putting in long hours on my job. One of the things about A. L. Williams was that I could control, more or less, the effort I put in and be my own boss.

[In this area] the women seem to be very strong in the [Amway] organization. They're building their organization quicker than the couples [usually recruited by sponsors]. They see something that can have some meaning for them, give them some kind of security that a lot of women realize they're never going to have. Who knows, when you're sixty you may be let go, and what have you got then?

I don't ever want to think of something like losing my husband or my house or my finances, but if you were to strip me of everything that I have and put me on the street, I could survive. That is what Mary Kay has done for me, and to me that is priceless.

The comfortable, uninterrupted employment career that many middle-class families have traditionally depended upon, while perhaps still the norm, is no longer inevitable. At the least, the threat of a takeover has changed the psychology and career-planning strategy of the middle classes.[38]

Certainly, of course, not all clerical workers occupy mind-numbing positions, and not all managers selflessly submit to the rationalized requirements of an insecure corporation. No doubt, too, there are workers in low-status, low-pay occupations who are happy with their jobs for reasons that may have nothing to do with status or pay, or their status and pay may meet their expectations. But clearly, social conditions are influencing a substantial number of unhappy and uncertain workers, especially, though not exclusively, women.

CONSTRAINTS ON EMPLOYERS

After the depression employers had a reliable and skilled work force whose activism was largely confined to getting a bigger piece of the pie. As long as the pie expanded, generous wage and benefit increases did not threaten a satisfactory profit level. For example, the cost of benefits such as retirement, sick pay, and paid vacations was less than 5% of payroll in 1929. By

1981 indirect compensation represented more than 37% of the payroll for all industries and was even higher for heavy manufacturing.[39] Although many benefits are voluntary contributions or negotiated as part of a labor agreement, a substantial proportion are the result of state mandates—for example, to Social Security and workmen's compensation insurance funds.

Employer Obligations

Indeed, the state became increasingly active in supporting workers' interests in the postwar era, both through legislation and through the judicial process. Philip Selznick argues that until the end of the nineteenth century employment law relied on the model of "master and servant," with the employer acting paternalistically in the role of master and the employee obediently fulfilling his status as subordinate, often in the master's household.[40] There was no thought that either party should negotiate the terms of their relationship, merely that each should uphold traditional standards attached to each role. At the turn of the century, with the rise of individualism as a social ideal, employment law began to reflect the view that both employee and employer were self-willed individuals who voluntarily entered into a contract whereby one party exercised authority over the other in return for a wage. The presumption was that each party could terminate the agreement "at will," by firing or by quitting. The "at will" doctrine, though apparently fair in treating both parties to the employment contract equally, in fact codified an unequal relationship: "By the end of the nineteenth century the employment contract had become a very special sort of contract—in large part a legal device for guaranteeing to management the unilateral power to make rules and exercise discretion."[41] Its most important effect was to enable employers to lay off workers when business fluctuated.

The passage of the Wagner Act in 1935 opened a new era in labor law and employment law. Government legislated that both labor and management had the right to negotiate their relationship to each other, and that management in fact was required to submit to negotiations with duly recognized unions. In the area of employment law, government increasingly encroached on management prerogatives in its pursuit of social policy and an expanded vision of social welfare. Today government-directed restrictions on management are sweeping and include the civil rights of female, minority, older, handicapped, and pregnant workers in hiring and firing, voluminous health and safety requirements, permissible hours and schedules of work, and the management of pension funds. These and other requirements are so extensive and so detailed that they have spawned legal subspecialties to interpret the daily changes in legislation and case law. Personnel offices, once charged largely with hiring and firing, are now quasi-legal operations in businesses of any size.

The point in this discussion is not to argue either that these developments are necessary protections to vulnerable employees necessitated by the past record of abusive businesses or that they constitute excessive and irrational limitations on reasonable management practices. Rather, it is important to understand that just as conditions of the postwar era have been ripe for producing frustrated workers, they have been similarly ripe for frustrating employers. Management cannot hire, fire, schedule, promote, demote, or otherwise rearrange its work force without consulting a growing body of employment law. Moreover, the generous wages and benefits negotiated in a period of economic boom represent the heavy weight of precedence. Although there have been much publicized union "give backs" in some newly deregulated industries, some employers find the existing level of benefits difficult to roll back even while it is difficult to afford.

Independent Contractors

The low overhead of a sales force of independent contractors is an increasingly attractive option for manufacturers and wholesalers. Indeed, in 1977 the Direct Selling Association estimated that if distributors had been employees, in that year DSOs would have had to pay $500 million in mandated payroll taxes. Not surprisingly, an executive with Electrolux—the only DSO with an employee sales force—said, "In all candor, I can't say that if I were to start a direct selling company today I would treat my salespeople as employees. It's quite expensive."[42]

All types of employers have been searching for alternatives to the regular employee work force. Temporary employment agencies have boomed to fill the demand for nonemployee workers. In fact the growth of these agencies has posed a challenge to recruiting for direct selling. An industry executive described the situation:

> We are now competing with employers—traditional employers—for the first time in a great way. A decade or two ago, the housewife who wanted to work part time basically could have gone into real estate perhaps, or direct selling. We now see traditional employers and the use of temporary employment agencies rising dramatically in terms of their utilization of women by providing flex-time and part-time opportunities. It's generally minimum wage type opportunites. It's generally without any fringe benefits, and it's usually without any impact on [a company's] pension plan. . . . These are changing the nature of the possible recruiting universe out there for our companies. It's a major concern to us.[43]

Collective bargaining, elaborate grievance procedures, and government constraints, along with high levels of compensation, have increased the cost and reduced the flexibility of maintaining a work force of employees. Moreover, apart from financial considerations, management finds it difficult to sustain high levels of commitment among educated workers in large, depersonalized work organizations. An entire industry of consultants and pop management writers offers seasonal formulas for motivating workers, from "get tough" to "warm culture" strategies.[44]

The simultaneous growth of organizational power over workers and workers' invoking of legal limitations on management does not necessarily constitute a contradiction. Rather, as workers are subject to impersonal, systematized conditions, often with the introduction of new technologies, they may be inclined to invoke their "rights" as workers, to make increased use of grievance machinery, and to seek legal redress against management.[45]

DILEMMAS RESOLVED: THE GROWTH OF DIRECT SELLING

The rise of large-scale, rationalized workplaces as an important location of work, the movement of women into the labor force in largely low-status and low-pay occupations, the increasing insecurity of employment, the degradation of much professional and managerial work, and the increasing costs of sustaining the employment relation represent substantial changes in the conditions of workers and organizations.

Moreover, social changes other than explicitly economic and organizational transformations have influenced what workers seek and do and the environment in which employers must recruit and manage. For example, the women's movement accompanied the increasing labor force participation of women and most certainly derived from it, at least in part. The sustained wage gap between men and women provoked protest, but so did the *experience* of working in organizations that employ a sexual division of labor. As Manuel Castells reminds us, "Women not only provide cheap labor but are also considered as particularly skilled for certain types of jobs such as secretaries and receptionists and for certain fields such as advertising and public relations where their skills in handling social relationships and their sex appeal can be used to sell products."[46] Work organizations that patronized and stereotyped women unwittingly spurred a new feminist consciousness.

Women in the past thirty-five years have been under increasing economic pressure to work. Not surprisingly, social values have changed to accommodate economic neccessity. In 1950 working women, particularly mothers, were under strong pressure to remain at home. By 1985 work outside the home was not only accepted but expected, particularly for educated, middle-class women. Women who worked by choice or by necessity no longer had to search for excuses. Now, however, women who could afford to devote full time to child rearing bear the stigma of a society that devalues homemaking.

The changes described here, and others, contributed to ecological conditions from which new forms of social relations and social organizations emerged. These conditions did not in themselves create organizations, but they changed the settings in which people worked and lived, the experiences they had, and the values they held. New forms of organization—or old forms rediscovered—could take on new importance if they were able to solve emerging problems for workers and management. DSOs are one of several organizational innovations that emerged in the postwar era because they solved a set of problems for management and for particular types of workers.[47]

DSOs, first, give manufacturers and wholesalers of a wide variety of products a distribution outlet far less encumbering than a retail operation or a sales force of employees. Direct selling distributors pay their own way. They work out of their homes, and they bear the costs of promotional materials, sample cases, and even the gasoline for trips to sales meetings and parties. Because they are not employees, most government regulations do not apply to their relationship to the organization. Distributors are a cheap, flexible source of labor.

Second, DSOs solve a variety of problems for a variety of workers. Direct selling appeals to people for different reasons, and there is evidence that its appeal is changing with time. For women needing to work, direct selling, like conventional employment, is a source of income. Just as other industries have attracted women workers, so too has direct selling.

Direct selling, however, appeals *especially* to women because it resolves problems that women routinely encounter in bureaucratically organized work. As self-employed persons, distributors work when and as much as they choose. Schedules can accommodate the needs of children, and hours can expand and contract with family needs and life-style changes. Direct selling accommodates the reality that women are primary caretakers in the home.

As employees, women are largely subordinates. They work for other people, usually men, who control and evaluate their activity. Their movement up the corporate ladder, a ladder constrained by internal labor markets, depends on the positive evaluation of a supervisor. As one Mary Kay beauty consultant put it, "The ideal thing about [direct selling] is that a woman can do it on her own time and she doesn't have to, pardon me, kiss a man's butt in order to get [ahead]."

Distributors are their own bosses. They move ahead in DSOs, achieving more status and income, according to their own ability to sell and recruit. There is no "invisible barrier" to prevent them from reaching top levels of success. Indeed, many people in the industry believe there are more women making $100,000 a year in Mary Kay Cosmetics than in any other corporation in the country.[48] One DSA executive estimates more women make $40,000 or more in direct selling than in the next several industries combined.

Direct selling also appeals to men and women with no credentials and little wealth. Bureaucratically organized work rewards people who have degrees and experience. Most self-employment requires at least a modest investment. Direct selling, however, provides an income producing opportunity for people who could never aspire to a well-paid, high-status job in a firm. It lets people have a business of their own, however modest, with almost no entry cost. Just as in the Great Depression, out-of-work people today can try their hand at direct selling in the hopes of making a go of it.

DSOs paradoxically appeal both to people who have what are ostensibly good jobs *and also* to people who have little desire to work. Like social movements, DSOs provide "opportunities for meaning, community, identity, a sense of personal power, and other gratifications" to distributors who apparently have sufficient sources of income.[49] For some women who do not need the income from a job but need the social approval that comes from working, or access to adult interaction, direct selling provides a self-paced entrée into the marketplace.

Direct selling in the 1980s, though it has roots in the colonial past, is thus a wholly modern phenomenon created and sustained by the social and economic conditions of the day.

CHAPTER FOUR
Family, Gender, and Business

An Amway distributor described the usual separation between people's work lives and their family lives and the problem he saw with that arrangement:

> In today's structure, the man goes to work here, and the woman goes to work there, and they come home at night and they're tired. It's been a long day, and a lot of the time they can't even share what's going on in each other's day because it's so different. There comes to be a separation between the husband and wife.

His network DSO, on the other hand, promises an alternative relationship between work and family.

> With the Amway business you have continuity, and both people can work together to achieve a goal that's going to benefit them and their family. And the kids too. They like to come around and serve cookies at the meetings, or clean the products on the shelf. So there's a real strong moral attitude in this business that everyone [in the family] should become involved.

Most businesses today, as this distributor described, exclude workers' families from the place and process of work. People in the United States now generally accept that bringing one's personal life into the office is improper and disrupts the efficient conduct of business.[1] Moreover, firms often have nepotism rules about employing members of the same family. Corporations fear that selection and promotion on merit might be compromised if employees are related to each other. Businesses can also lose control of important processes: members of a family can favor each other or band together in decision making. The impersonal, economically efficient running of firms is predicated on the separation of work from family—if not absolutely, then as an ideal.[2]

This separation of the public sphere of work from the private sphere of domestic life is a strategy for managing the tension between two powerful, commitment-seeking units. Although work organizations cannot make employees give up all outside commitments (as a convent or military organization can), they can require that employees leave their families behind when they walk through the door at work. Rosabeth Kanter describes the compromise that modern business organizations exact from workers: "While you are here, you will *act as though* you have no other loyalties, no other life."[3]

Network DSOs, however, though they have no less need for members' loyalty than firms do, employ a radically different strategy for controlling the tension between work and family: *they manage the family*, making its powerful emotions and social unity serve organizational ends or actively manipulating the pull of family ties. The affective bonds and authority relations of the family are directed toward profit-making ends.

I discuss two overlapping topics in this chapter. First, I analyze the means by which network DSOs manage the family, either through its integration into business practice or by directly overcoming it as an obstacle. I suggest how the strategy represents a break from the recent past of family/work relations. Second, I examine the relation between gender and organization in direct selling. I argue that the integration of family, both in reality and as metaphor, creates a "feminine" form of organization qualitatively distinct from "masculine" firms. Finally, I consider how women's interests are, and are not, served by organizing in a feminine manner.

HISTORICAL BACKGROUND

Although the separation between one's private life and one's life as a worker is commonplace in this country today, this was not always so. In fact there have been several different work/family arrangements and a number of different forms of the "typical" family. Many scholars, though, recognize three relationships between the economic and domestic spheres that were important in the push toward modernity: a unified family economy centered in the home; a transitional period where family members worked together both inside and outside the home; and a separation between economic life and family life.[4] Direct selling organizations claim to offer an alternative to the model of separate spheres.

In this country's preindustrial economy of largely agrarian and craft workers, the family represented an economic unit. In this first arrangement, parents worked closely together and children were important contributors to families' livelihoods, for example, as farmhands and apprentices. As Ann Oakley writes, "The [preindustrial] unit of production is the unit of kin relationships, and life is not divided into what one does to earn a living—called work—and what one does the rest of the time."[5] Modern distinctions between work and play, adulthood and childhood, were very much blurred.

Seventeenth-century American families, typical of pre-industrial economies, often had a sexual division of labor: men and women typically performed different household and money-raising tasks. This division was very flexible, though, as pointed out by Rosalyn Baxandall and her colleagues:

> In the Colonial Period the husbands of poor or middling women were usually farmers, artisans or small shopkeepers, and in these cases the men did their work at or near home also. Craft or retail shops were usually part of the home, and women often assisted in their husbands' work. Furthermore, the closeness of communities and absence of mechanical devices made sharing and cooperation, even in housework tasks, necessary.[6]

Even where work was divided by sex, the contributions of both men and women were understood to be critical to their mutual livelihood. Men's labor produced income while women's work conserved money that otherwise would be spent in the marketplace on goods and services.

A second work/family relationship came about with the rise of early industrial capitalism from about 1770 to 1830. In this period a few early factories were established in urban areas. More frequently, women took in piecework manufacturing in their homes. Organized production, both in the first

American factories and by home-workers, began to produce for the marketplace goods that previously had been made only for personal consumption. According to Alice Kessler-Harris, "By 1800 [the family] had begun to turn to manufactories for some of its essentials. In an uneven pattern, beginning in the settled northeastern areas about 1790 and extending west and south over the next fifty years, manufactured products—yard goods, candles, brooms—began to replace those formerly made in the household."[7]

The transition from an agrarian economy to an industrial one was spurred in part by the demand for goods produced only laboriously at home, such as textiles, and for laborsaving farm machinery. These purchases required money—scarce in a barter economy.

Families, taking advantage of the new implements and manufactures, no longer needed the labor of all their members all the time. Moreover, they needed the cash that wage labor would bring to service new debts. During this transition from a preindustrial to a fully industrial economy, women and children were especially important sources of wage labor, both in factories and as pieceworkers at home. They worked for cash while some men worked at their traditional occupations. Over these decades more men entered the factories as full-time workers.

In this early industrial era the family was still the important economic unit, even as members moved outside the home to work. Rosabeth Kanter describes the system in which "spinners in textile mills chose their wives, children, and near relatives as assistants, generally paying them from their own wages. Children entering the factory at eight or nine worked for their fathers, perpetuating the old system of authority and the traditional values of parents training children for occupations."[8] Families performed many of the tasks we associate with management today: recruiting, supervision, and discipline.[9]

By the 1890s the spilling over of the family onto the factory floor was becoming less common, and a third work/family relationship developed. The rapidly growing industrial economy created more opportunities for men to earn income off the farm, and capitalist ideology urged the movement of young men into the wage-labor force. In this period approaching the turn of the century, Janet Clark says, men's "success or failure was identified with their skillful ability to support their own nuclear family."[10] Men were expected to be "good providers" to their wives and children.

Professional management increasingly replaced kinship as an important means of labor discipline. Unmarried and widowed women continued to work in the factories, but the new norm for middle-class families became the wage-earning husband and the wife at home.

It was the blossoming of industrial capitalism that produced the separation of spheres we associate with the modern family. Men went "out into the world" to earn a wage, and middle-class women were pressured to stay at home, largely isolated from the public world of politics and the economy. Just as an important ideology sustained men in the "good provider" role, new ideas developed in the Victorian era to justify women's new place. The "cult of true womanhood" supported the notion that women were a critical counterbalance to the harsh public life of industrial capitalism. Women were seen as uniquely able to provide nurturing and respite for men, and they were expected to cultivate the moral and spiritual realms for their families. Though women were understood to be men's moral superiors, they became legal and economic inferiors. Although less affluent women continued to perform wage labor, a new social ideal denigrated their work outside the home.

The domestic labor of married middle-class women, now frequently aided by employed domestic workers, made it possible for men to enter the paid work force. Middle-class women's privatized and unpaid labor, however, lost status in a now moneyed economy. Women became dependent on men's wages, while their own labor became economically invisible.[11]

Although this arrangement served industrial capitalism well for decades, it had substantial drawbacks for both men and women, at least viewed retrospectively. Women lost marketable skills and the psychological benefits that accrue from publicly recognized work. They lost economic and social independence; the course of their lives was determined by making a "good" marriage. Men now had the entire economic burden of the family on their shoulders. More than that, a man's entire selfhood was dependent on his success as a bread-winner. "Success in the good-provider role came in time to define masculinity itself," says Jessie Bernard, and men were less valued for their performance as fathers and mates.[12] Men, as economic heads of households, encroached on women's decision making in the domestic sphere, often conserving the right to control the purse and to make other significant household decisions.[13] Sociologists have debated whether, on balance, this role served men's interests, but it certainly further undermined the unity of the family.[14] Moreover, the entire family lost the subtle benefits of closeness, of joint effort in securing their livelihood.

This separation of spheres characteristic of industrial capitalism began to break down in the 1940s and 1950s when increasing numbers of women entered the "men's world" of the labor force. By the 1970s more than 40% of American women were in the public sphere of work. The transition since then to a new, more egalitarian model for work and family may be emerging to accommodate this economic shift, but if so, it is only in fits and starts. As women enter the public sphere they expect their husbands to assume domestic chores and to perform some of the emotional labor in the family. Numerous studies show, though, that even as women enter the work force they continue to do most housework.[15] While a more caring role model for men may be developing, it is at best half-formed. For many men, giving up the good provider role means giving up self-control and control of the family.

Network DSOs grew at precisely the moment when a family/work relationship predicated on a separation of spheres was under tension. Direct selling organizations offered an alternative vision of work and family to a population seeking new solutions: an *integration* of the domestic and economic spheres reminiscent of preindustrial America. Direct selling offers flexible work arrangements to women and sometimes allows them to work and care for children at the same time; it lets women "have it all." In network DSOs that attract both men and women, direct selling promises a shared work life and the emotional benefits to marriage that ensue from economic partnership. For women whose entry into a firm-dominated labor force has been less than happy, DSOs promise working conditions that emulate the nurturing character of the domestic sphere they are familiar with. The promise and the reality, however, are not always the same.

A FAMILY BUSINESS

The preoccupation with "family" among network DSOs is nothing less than extraordinary when compared with the whole of American business. All the DSOs I studied expressed concern with the effect of work on family. Many of them have an ideology of family participation that permeates their literature and public meetings. An A. L. Williams distributor told me that "as a company, there's no question that A. L. Williams is absolutely committed to producing more successful families than any other company in the history of the world," not only through product sales, but through organization.

Many network DSOs integrate the family into the business of selling, using its powerful emotions and authority structure to serve economic ends, not unlike the factories of the 1800s. In some instances DSOs manage the obstacle that competing family ties present. Unlike most firms, network DSOs recognize the power of the family and attempt to harness or actively divert it. Not all DSOs stress the work/family linkage to the same extent, and they vary in how they solicit family participation or acceptance, but four family-management strategies are common in the industry.

1. Network DSOs encourage the recruitment of family members. The "family tree" of a DSO line is often filled with actual relatives who have sponsored each other into the business. Nephews, sisters, brothers, and cousins are prime targets for sponsorship. There are many mother and daughter units in Mary Kay Cosmetics. In DSOs where both men and women sell, such as Amway and Shaklee, there is very strong pressure for spouses to build an organization together. Recognition awards and promotion through status levels are often given to couples, not individuals. Attendance at meetings by only one spouse raises eyebrows in some lines. The Amway and Shaklee house organs are filled with pictures of couples who have achieved success together. An A. L. Williams distributor described his preferred recruits:

Although we have some very successful single people, we try to stay away from single people. A lot of times, if they want to become involved, they do so. If we're going to pick and choose, we will pick people who are married and have similar lives, families.

A Shaklee distributor, a divorcee, described her status in that organization:

[As a single person] I'm looked at as kind of rare. In fact, the home office has called me and had me talk to a group about what it is like to build a Shaklee business as a single person.

Recruiting people with whom there is an existing social bond, such as relatives, creates a good basis for business relations in direct selling. When mothers encourage daughters and cousins support each other in their selling, the act reproduces their nonbusiness relations. Support in selling appears to spring from a long-term foundation of caring, and the financial self-interest of sponsors is obscured. In fact, for distributors who are committed to the ideology of direct selling, there is no separation between the interest of the loved one and self-interest: they truly want to share their commitment with those they love.

Recruiting spouses utilizes the emotions and authority relations of marriage for business purposes, as I discuss further below. However, even in DSOs where only women sell, husbands are sometimes a co-optive target of the organization. In Mary Kay Cosmetics, for example, gaining husbands' support is an explicit corporate goal. Husbands are invited to attend Seminar, the annual meeting for beauty consultants, and are given a parallel three-day schedule of activities. They are briefed by the company's executives, paid a visit by Mary Kay Ash, and treated to a recreation program that may include a top sports figure such as Arnold Palmer. Winners of the sports competitions, including a bowling tournament with pink bowling pins, are given recognition at a ceremony not unlike those for beauty consultants. One distributor described the purpose of including husbands in Seminar:

They are treated so royally and so wonderfully that they want their wives to belong to this organization. So that is kind of a psychology on Mary Kay's part. These men are really treated with kid gloves. I mean, you couldn't imagine how it must make them feel for Mary Kay to say how wonderful they are.

Husbands who do not attend Seminar are not neglected. Mary Kay Ash sends a telegram to the husband of each participating woman thanking him for, as one beauty consultant put it, "eating scrambled eggs and frozen dinners" and taking care of the children.

The president of another DSO said it is crucial to gain the husband's acceptance of his wife's work and is an important management strategy in direct selling.

> A lot of [our talk to husbands] is very casual, but it's very direct. It starts with top mangement, and [then] our regional managers see how we handle the husbands. So when they start recruiting people, one of the first things they do is bring the husbands in. They take them to dinner. They bring them to sales meetings and make them a part of it. At a high-level convention or meeting with top-level awards, we call both husband and wife up, and we let [the audience] know that this woman could not be successful without his support and backing.

This same company uses the husbands of successful distributors to explain to the husbands of new recruits how they can assist their wives. The subliminal message is that other "real men" accept their wives' selling. "And so they begin to realize, 'Well, gosh, that's no big deal if I baby-sit and fix dinner. Sure, I can do it.'"

Husbands' approval is critical in companies such as Mary Kay and Tupperware. Much selling takes place at night, and husbands must handle child care alone and accept the absence of their wives.

2. *Network DSOs espouse an ideology that claims family is more important than work.* For many people who feel guilty because their work leads them to neglect spouses and children, an industry that encourages the subordination of work to family seems worthy of commitment. Mary Kay Cosmetics, Home Interiors and Gifts, A. L. Williams, and a number of other DSOs support the aphorism "God first, family second, career third." This phrase was recited frequently in interviews. For example:

> I want to succeed financially. That's not the most important thing in my life. My God's first, and my family is second. My wife knows that I could quit A. L. Williams in a minute if it meant losing her and my family.

DSOs' professed support of this formula for organizing one's life is comforting to people who believe its tenets. The reality does not always match the formula, however.

> There was a time there when I was going crazy with Mary Kay. That's all I thought about. I ate it, I drank it, I slept it. Everything, OK? And things were getting just crazy for me. I was feeling guilty. I was feeling like I was taking time away from my family.

> Sometimes it is hard to put Mary Kay third, sometimes the others get shoved down the line a bit. . . . It is just a continuing effort remembering to put it third instead of first.

It is not clear that distributors, especially committed ones, organize their lives differently than they would if they had other attractive occupations.[16] Direct selling is seductive, and for some distributors it becomes the center of their lives. That revered founders such as Mary Kay Ash and Art Williams profess commitment to families, however, is comforting to distributors struggling to reconcile work and home.

3. *Network DSOs argue that a commitment to direct selling can strengthen marriages.* The promise of a closer marital bond is an important recruiting point in some DSOs, including Amway. What direct selling can do for a marriage is "a big carrot," as one distributor put it. "The greatest marriages, the most absolutely blissful relationships I have ever witnessed, have been in this business." DSOs hold out the possibility of a shared enterprise that will bring not only riches, but emotional closeness.

Even DSOs where only women sell promote direct selling as healthful for marriages. Women who become entrepreneurs are described as more interesting to their husbands. These wives have another way to strengthen the marriage bond. A number of women, in fact, said their husbands took an interest in their businesses. One woman described how her Mary Kay business gave her some influence with her husband:

> We have a new line of communication. We got to talking the other night about customer service and were just sitting there really going at it. I have a little more clout. If I had talked to him about customer service five years ago, I didn't have a lot of clout because where was I coming from? You know, I might have been on the tennis court all day long.

The breakdown of the good provider role has left many families struggling both with the problem of generating new income and with maintaining the "face" of husbands whose paychecks are insufficient for family needs. This problem is widespread, but most corporations treat it as a private concern. A number of DSOs, however, deal with this emotional issue quite openly, although they vary in how they manage it. Some urge recognition of pressure on husbands to recruit wives into selling. Direct selling becomes a way of expressing wifely love.

> Mary Kay says there's a lot of men out there who are going to go to their graves earlier because they have to work so hard. What's wrong with helping your husband out and sharing? In this day and age most women work, so why not work and get the most out of it, plus have time for your family?

Some companies, particularly those that recruit women largely from blue-collar families, such as Tupperware, downplay the "career" character of direct selling. Selling is presented as a way to make money that does not threaten the essential position of the husband as head of household.

Yet others actively attempt to preserve the good provider role for families that fear its loss. These companies, including to varying degrees Amway, A. L. Williams, and Shaklee, maintain an image of the family as one with the husband in control and the wife as a submissive helper. A sexual division of labor is encouraged within the couple's direct selling business: men go out to demonstrate the business opportunity to prospects, while women do the inside work of managing product sales and demonstrations. Women are supposed to encourage their husbands to greater efforts, to help them be "winners." Stephen Butterfield, a former distributor, described an Amway leadership seminar that included separate lectures for husbands and wives trying to build successful businesses:

> The male leader told the husbands to be gentle and considerate in their sexual approaches to their wives; the lady should be wooed with furs, jewelry and candlelight dinners in expensive restaurants. The female leader told the wives to submit to their husbands cheerfully, even if they thought it was unpleasant sometimes, because a man needed to feel like a winner in the bedroom as well as out in that livingroom showing the Plan. The year was 1980. I wondered if I had been caught in some time-[warp].[17]

As Butterfield describes it, some DSOs attempt to stop the clock of social change at a familiar, reassuring time while maintaining the modern rhetoric of economic partnership.

Direct selling organizations are aggressive in attempting to manage families, but they are not always successful. Those with women distributors routinely fail at co-opting husbands, according to my interviews. A Tupperware distributor, a Mary Kay sponsor, and an industry executive spoke of how husbands posed significant hurdles to achieving business goals:

> My husband, the only way he supports me is baby-sitting and helping me spend the money. Otherwise I get no support from him at all. That's a real drain. I'm always just running, trying to get everything done so he doesn't have anything to complain about when I leave. I don't know if I'm going to get to go to Jubilee, [Tupperware's annual meeting], because if he throws too big a stink about it, it's just not worth the fight.

> The consultants who are doing well, they're either single and don't have a husband, or if you're married, you've got to hope that your husband is supportive. It's that middle husband, the one who is insecure himself, the one who has to have dinner on the table at five and never wants to baby-sit [who is a problem]. There are a lot of men who are like that, and there are women who cater to that.

If a husband is the type where his ego needs the glory, the applause, and he has to be center stage with the spotlight on him, it won't work. Because all those [downline recruits] are there because of her, not him. What will work is if the guy is smart enough to realize that he has to keep her in the spotlight. She's the number one, and he sits back and gives her tips.

A wife's absences from home and her business success are sometimes tolerated by otherwise recalcitrant husbands because of the income she earns. Mary Kay Ash has a much-repeated saying for beauty consultants: "If you want to keep your husband excited, stay thin and make bank deposits."

4. *Children are a fourth way DSOs solicit distributors' commitment.* All stress that flexible work arrangements allow parents to put their children's schedules before work. Some distributors like being able to work with their children present—for example, when they deliver products, or solicit business. One Mary Kay beauty consultant approaches women with her young son:

My little boy, he got so used to me approaching women at the shopping mall that he would ask the ladies first, "Do you use Mary Kay cosmetics?" He was only four years old at the time. Of course I would bring my card out and I would say, "Could I have your name and number?" And he would say, "Address, too." I had to calm him down a bit.

Women, especially, cite the ease of integrating their roles as mother and worker as a reason for doing direct sales. For some, particularly blue-collar women who treat direct selling as a sideline and not a "real job," they can have the happy combination of making money and being an "at home" mother. One Tupperware dealer put it this way:

I was driving my son and four friends to a birthday party, and I heard them talking in the back about their moms working. And one of the kids says, "Say, does your mommy work?" And he goes, "No." That's what I want. I don't want them to think I work. They don't even think that I have a job because I'm not gone from eight to five.

Network DSOs that recruit husband-and-wife teams usually try to integrate the children into the business in some way. Children sometimes attend meetings held in parents' homes and are occasionally included at conventions and other events.[18] Many children of Amway and Shaklee distributors are paid to deliver products, take telephone orders, and otherwise participate in their parents' business. The ideology of a family business is realized in some homes, with all members participating in some fashion.

In DSOs with strong entrepreneurial ideologies, the parents' continuing commitment is often sustained because of their belief in the importance of teaching their children the moral principles of capitalist enterprise. This is not unlike parents' going to church because it sets a good example for their children. A father and a mother spoke about the influence of direct selling on their children's development:

> I have a ten-year-old son. He's my partner. Most of our social life revolves around either his school or A. L. Williams. He's very, very supportive. As a matter of fact, for a ten-year-old, he's one of my best recruiters. He'll talk to his friends about asking if their parents could use extra money. . . . It's teaching him how to set his goals and what he wants out of life.

> I have bought a division under Avacare for my daughter and have it on ice because she's only twenty. But I figured when she gets older she will have that division. I have sponsored my son into another multilevel marketing company, and I'm helping him develop that business. . . . What I'm doing with my children is much more than earning money [for them]. It's teaching them. They will be totally self-sufficient by the time they get married. They will never go on welfare. That would just break my heart.

Some DSOs actively encourage parents to see their selling as a critical part of their children's moral education. One Amway tape, for example, encourages children to be their parents' paid helpers and to view unearned allowances as "welfare for children."

The inclusion of children in the business is sometimes more illusory than real, however. Although children may perform some business-related work at home, by its very nature direct selling requires parents to be away from home a lot. Direct selling is also hard work, and active distributors find it demanding. Some parents spoke of this problem:

> I'm not there all the time—I can't be. I've got to work harder now than I've ever worked in my life. But when I do take off I spend quality time. I don't go home and watch television like I used to do five years ago. I can afford to do some things and spend time that the kids are going to remember.

> A lot of beauty consultants have kids. . . . I sort of have this uncomfortable feeling. . . . I don't know. There is sort of that superwoman consciousness about it all. You can do it. You can look beautiful and sell products and work full time and get home on time.

Children are actively co-opted by some DSOs. Amway, for instance, encourages parents to let children choose an item from their product catalog as a "goal." The picture of the item is taped to the refrigerator, along with a calendar. Each night that their father goes out to show the business plan to a prospective recruit, the children check off a space. When enough spaces are checked, they receive the item. The parent's absence is made to serve children's material interests. As an Amway distributor put it, eventually "there will be freedom for us from jobs, and we'll be able to be together as a family," but in the meantime "there are rewards for them." [19]

Direct selling's flexible schedule does make it possible for family needs to be accommodated. As more wives and mothers enter the labor force, part-time jobs, flex-time, temporary work, and other new work arrangements are appearing. Corporate America is beginning to recognize and make some adjustment to the nonwork lives of its employees. Most firms, though, offer these new arrangements not so that the barrier between family and work can be lowered, but so that it can remain high. [20]

Direct selling uses a very different strategy. It begins by recognizing the pull of family obligations and certifying them as real and important. In some instances it uses those ties to serve business purposes, for example, by encouraging the recruitment of relatives and sustaining commitment for the children's sake. The industry even uses the desire to be with loved ones to urge work outside the home. The contradiction inherent in this ploy may be blatant, but the appeal is effective precisely because of the strong commitment people feel to their families. In an industry that cannot rely on bureaucratic controls, harnessing the emotions, aspirations, and fears of families is an important business strategy.

THE METAPHORICAL FAMILY

By integrating the family into business activity, direct selling organizations use existing social ties for economic purposes. The industry also does the reverse, making the economic ties of sponsorship the basis for familylike social relations. DSOs are "metaphorical families." The result of both strategies is to create a double-stranded bond far stronger than either one alone. Moreover, pecuniary self-interest and affective interest in the other are indistinguishable.

Metaphorical expressions of kinship, what anthropologists call "fictive relations," are widely employed in network DSOs. The expressions vary by individual and by organization, but distributors commonly understand themselves as "family" or, in Tupperware, as "close friends." For example, Mary Kay Cosmetics is a "sisterhood."

Whereas individuals employed by firms tend to describe their positions in the organization by function or level, such as "accountant" or "supervisor," in DSOs people use kinship terms to describe their place. Lines in companies such as Amway and Shaklee are often spoken of as branches on a "family tree." People trace their "genealogies" by identifying their upline sponsors. Amway lines have "family reunions." Women in Mary Kay are "sisters," but Tupperware distributors are "daughter dealers" to their "mother managers." In Cameo Coutures, a recruit's sponsor is likewise her "mother," and the mother's sponsor is the recruit's "grandmother." When a Mary Kay distributor has enough recruits to form her own unit, she becomes the "offspring" of her director. Movement up the director ranks is measured in part by the number of offspring a woman gives birth to.

The overlay of a metaphorical family on top of blood ties and marital bonds creates some interesting organizational relations. For example, one Mary Kay beauty consultant's real sister is her "offspring." Her mother remains in her unit as a consultant. Thus all three are "sisters" in the larger enterprise.

Family metaphors also describe organizational activities. In Amway and a number of other DSOs, recruiting people to set up their own businesses is called "duplication." Duplication means doing exactly as the upline does, but it also refers to an organizational growth strategy reminiscent of biological asexual reproduction. Tupperware uses the terminology of courtship to describe securing appointments for home parties: these are "dates." "Dating" future hostesses is understood to be a crucial job at a party. In Shaklee and some other DSOs, a distributor whose line becomes inactive is known as an "orphan." There are "adoption" rules that regulate the incorporation of orphans into active lines.

Family metaphors refer not only to positional relations and activities, but also to the *content* of ties between distributors. "Family" establishes an ideal of loving, nurturing relations between distributors; the metaphor establishes normative expectations. For example, distributors assume familylike obligations toward each other in their conduct of business. The obligations typically extend beyond the economic sphere, too. Amway and Mary Kay distributors described this situation:

> I found a family I had never had. There was a tremendous amount of support to achieve. I went through a divorce about five years after I got into the business, and I took five years off from actively building my organization. In that time period I was never forgotten. I would get postcards once in a while, and it made me feel like I was still part of something. There was a tremendous amount of love and acceptance, support in growing.

> There is a sisterhood charisma between all the consultants. I have been stranded at airports and know for a fact [it's true]. One time I was stranded two days in Denver because of a storm. All I did was look in the phone book under "Mary Kay Cosmetics," and the [local] director came over to have lunch with me.

I know that anywhere I go I can call up a sister consultant and I'll be taken to her home.

"Family" provides a powerful model for intraorganizational relations. It is a satisfying conceptualization for distributors who are welcomed into a network of emotional ties and not seen merely as "workers" or financially significant "recruits." There is a preservation of personhood in some DSOs that is conspicuously absent in many corporations. "Family" also provides a well-understood model for interpersonal relations, especially useful to people without significant paid work experience. Direct selling puts them in familiar interactional territory by importing the logic of one institution—the family—for use in another—business.

"Family" has distinctive management advantages.[21] In an industry that cannot oversee intraorganizational relations very effectively, the metaphor provides a flexible guide to relations for distributors. For example, while all distributors are formally competitors for sales to consumers and all believe in free enterprise and competition, the notion of "family" mutes destructive competitive practices. "Mothers" do not compete with "daughters." Internecine warfare is thwarted by distributors' embracing family norms. Caring relations are typically interpreted to mean helping each other to be successful—that is, generating profit for the individual and the company.

The management of Mary Kay Cosmetics discovered the force with which the family metaphor is held when it completed a leveraged buy-out. Mary Kay Ash and her son Richard Rogers, cofounders of the company, bought back all publicly owned stock in 1985, returning the company to family ownership. The company had faced a decline in the period just before the buy-out, and management was concerned with the beauty consultants' interpretation of the financial transaction, hoping they would not understand it as an act of weakness. One executive described how the family metaphor provided a useful interpretive vehicle for the sales force:

The word "family" in Mary Kay means something. People consider themselves part of the family. All of a sudden they're asking, "What does this buy-out mean?" [They've come up with

the answer]: "Everything's back and owned by the family." All
of a sudden they feel like—I don't know what's going through
their minds—"We weren't family before, but now we're back?"
"All of those outsiders had stock, we got rid of them?" If I've
heard it once, I've heard it a thousand times, "It's great to be
family again."

A family strategy, in both its "real" and its metaphorical
forms, utilizes strong emotional bonds and social patterns to
inspire and channel economic activity. It also sustains an
interactional character within the industry that is wholly
distinctive.

A "FEMININE" ORGANIZATION

The organization men described by C. Wright Mills and William F. Whyte in the 1950s were rational beings, outwardly
calm if inwardly anxious. While the prototypical white collar
worker of the 1980s may inhabit a looser corporate culture
and exhibit a friendlier mien, today's corporate worker is
clearly a descendant of the forebears Mills and Whyte described.

The character of corporate workers, then and now, is
shaped in important part by the world of work they inhabit.
Bureaucratically organized corporations establish norms for
interaction that flow from their roots in economic rationality.
Workers are urged to be analytic and results oriented. Interpersonal relations are typically impersonal and segmental;
people relate to each other primarily in terms of the positions
they occupy. The hierarchical ranking of positions makes everyone aware of even subtle power differences, discouraging
collegiality. Promotion on the basis of merit pits employees
against one other and supports an atmosphere of aggressive
individualism. Individual success in firms is a zero-sum propo-
sition: if I win the promotion to manager, everyone else loses.
These conditions combine to create a work environment distinctive to firms. Not surprisingly, as Mills put it, workers'
"very self-images, what they do and what they are, are derived
from the enterprise."[22]

This corporate world is a man's world in more than one
sense. The valued pattern of relations is "masculine," as we
understand that concept in this society. Social action among

bureaucratic officials is characterized by aggressive individualism and instrumentalism; the structure of the firm rewards independence and competition. These are social traits that we associate with men. Paul Hirsch's fascinating study of the history of takeovers and mergers in the United States shows how the standards of business activity have changed in the past twenty-five years "from the world of a gentlemen's club toward that of a streetfighter's brawl."[23] Though changed, it remains a man's world.

The character of relations mirrors and supports the structure of power. If possessing "masculine" interactional skills is critical to making it up the ladder of success, then women are clearly disadvantaged. If men control the top positions in corporate America—and they do—they can maintain the conditions that sustain their dominance. Feminist scholars have argued, in fact, that bureaucracy is inherently patriarchal, not a neutral tool for getting work done. They argue that the structure of firm organization, including its patterns of control and its reproduction of men's culture, excludes women as a class. Numerous studies show that women workers tend to inhabit occupational categories that do not lead to important decision making positions. They have "women's jobs," less-valued positions that utilize stereotypical female traits of support and nurturing.

Even if the evidence shows that women as a group disproportionately occupy lower-level, less well-paid positions, individual women have made it to top jobs. The number of highly educated young women with M.B.A. degrees has increased women's presence in managerial circles. Even such privileged women, however, face the choice of conforming to the machismo model of management or being branded as "soft," a corporate synonym for "inept."[24] Marilyn Loden, a consultant who has studied women executives, finds that some are resisting the pressure to remake themselves to fit male models of competence. "Many talented women find that the sacrifices required of them so outweigh the potential rewards that they decide to leave corporate life altogether."[25] The corporate world gives women a tough choice: use their womanly skills in the less-valued, subordinate "women's jobs," or act like men.

Some feminists have argued that if women are to achieve power in the economy it is critical to pursue a third strategy:

create organizations that utilize and value women's cultural preferences and competencies.[26] Such organizations would have minimal hierarchies, encourage participative decision making, and value intuitive as well as analytic approaches to work. Relations would be characterized as nurturing and co-operative rather than instrumental and individualistic. Indeed, some women's organizations, including *Ms.* magazine, have consciously adopted such organizational forms in an effort to empower women on their own terms.[27]

This feminist agenda for organizations parallels in important ways the reality of network DSOs. DSOs have a status hierarchy but no hierarchy of authority. While there is ideological support for the idea of the "independent entrepreneur," distributors in fact see themselves as connected in a network of social relations. There are strong norms in DSOs for encouraging others in both practical and emotional ways. A Tupperware distributor and an Amway distributor described this ethic:

> Everybody wants everybody else to succeed. It's not like competition that you get in some jobs where I don't want you to know what I know because if you do, then you can take my job. I want to share with you what made me successful, so you can be successful too.

> You don't find some one-star general encouraging some colonel to go ahead [of him] and say, "Hey, I'll help you and you can become a four-star general over me." No, you don't find that. But in this business we encourage people to go ahead of us. We don't care where they go. If they want to make eight times more money than I made, that's great.

The financial structure of direct selling does not result in zero-sum relations: one distributor's success may directly contribute to the earnings of upline sponsors. That distributors' mutual encouragement may be self-interested in no way negates the "feminine" character of relations that result, however. People applaud and are genuinely happy when others do well. There are hugs and kisses for even small successes. In DSOs tears accompany disappointment and pleasure without people's feeling shame or appearing weak. Cooperation is far more efficacious than competition as a form of economic action in DSOs. As a Tupperware dealer put it, "In this business you don't get to the top unless you take a lot of people with you."

Feminists, in urging the formation of organizations that celebrate and utilize women's skills, see this as a strategy of empowering women. Feminine organizations create a world of work where women are able to pursue success as themselves, not by adopting an alien masculine orientation. This strategy is an attempt to take the pattern of social relations that characterizes the domestic sphere, in which women are skilled, and use it to women's advantage in the public sphere of the economy and the polity.

Direct selling, with its stress on nurturing and cooperation, its absence of authority differences, is clearly feminine when compared with the bureaucratic firm. Indeed, it is in part the character of its interpersonal relations that attracts so many women: DSOs feel familiar, feel "right," to women distributors. Network DSOs' co-opting of the family and their creation of a metaphorical family reproduce to an extraordinary extent the social structure of the private sphere within an economic organization.

DOES DIRECT SELLING
EMPOWER WOMEN?

Is an organization that accords so well with women's experiences and abilities feminist? Does it lead to more power for women as individuals and as a class? The answer that comes from this study of the direct selling industry is clearly mixed. My interviews suggest that network DSOs empower women as individuals in significant ways. They also suggest that the industry does not challenge, and sometimes reinforces, the patriarchal structure of society.

Women distributors spoke of at least three ways direct selling gives them influence. First, they describe the power that an independent income gives them in marriage. This sort of power is not granted exclusively by direct selling, of course, but women who would not or could not do other types of work find DSOs a possible route to economic strength. As a Tupperware dealer put it, "My husband has this claw on the checkbook, and he doesn't like to share it. So having my own income gives me a little bit more freedom." She established her own checking account, an act of independence, at the encouragement of her "mother manager."

Although most women do direct selling part time and earn very modest amounts, it does provide a route to a good, even substantial income for very hardworking women with a talent for this form of business. The fifty-nine national sales directors in Mary Kay Cosmetics earn over $100,000 each—some two or three times that figure—and there are women in other established DSOs who have large incomes. The nurturing skills these women used to achieve success in direct selling would not have been valued in corporate settings.

Distributors spoke, second, of how their work in direct selling is a source of influence with their children. Many believe that direct selling allows them to be more than "just a mom" in a society that values economic achievement and allows them to be role models to their daughters. As one woman said, "[my daughter] sees me in a very independent role, yet whenever she needs me I'm always there."

Third, and perhaps most important, direct selling gives women the *experience* of being powerful. Women who have been in subordinate positions all their lives and, further, had seen other women only as dependents, spoke of the pleasure of being thought of as skilled and able. For many, direct selling gave them their first glimpse of their own sex in the role of competent adult. A Mary Kay beauty consultant described her first direct selling function:

> I couldn't believe it. [These women] were just bubbling. I had never been around a bunch of women who were not talking about their kids, not talking about so-and-so running around with so-and-so, you know, all the negative things and about household chores. You see, that's what I had been around because I had been home for a while. Housewifey things. These women were talking about *business*.

The entrance to the Mary Kay Cosmetics headquarters in Dallas, Texas, is an impressive sight for the thousands of women who visit each year. The vestibule has the requisite oil painting of the founders, Mary Kay Ash and Richard Rogers, in a prominent place. Where one would expect to find pictures of pin-striped male executives or corporate directors, there are large paintings of the national sales directors, the industrious women who sustain the sales force. The display of fifty-nine images of hugely successful women is jarring because it so thoroughly violates expectations. Women who see other women succeed begin to imagine the possibility for themselves.

Women's DSOs, such as Mary Kay Cosmetics, Home Interiors and Gifts, and Tupperware, celebrate women's abilities in business. They are unabashedly women's worlds where pink Cadillacs, fur coats, and warm hugs are as much a part of the organizational culture as aggressive individualism is part of a firm's. While they differ from one other, they all have the character of sororities: women's spheres where women enjoy each other and act "naturally." In DSOs where men also sell, the atmosphere is different but still familylike and expressive.

Although women distributors have been empowered personally and economically by direct selling, and though women's DSOs celebrate women's abilities as a whole, direct selling does not challenge existing social arrangements in which women are subordinate.[28] In particular, the model of the family that DSOs embrace includes a submissive wife.

The submissive wife role is expressed most overtly in DSOs that recruit husband-and-wife teams. For example, A. L. Williams recruits the whole family, but the expectation is that only the husband will sell insurance. The wife will do her part by giving her husband moral support and encouragement and by not complaining when he is out at night trying to bolster their income. A. L. Williams has a Partners' Organization run by Williams's wife Angela. Angela Williams is, like her husband, a gifted orator and tells a very moving story about how her support of Art's business was critical to his success against great odds. She urges the "partners" in rally audiences to do the same and, further, to participate in her auxiliary organization.

There are women A. L. Williams agents, but the model the organization supports is clearly that of the traditional family.

[Angela Williams] runs a great Partners' Organization, which is the wives' side of things. And we have some male partners, too. They get together for monthly meetings on how to support us. Next week they're doing a pep rally. They're going all out—they make costumes, pom-poms. So my wife is just loving the business too.

[My wife doesn't sell insurance], definitely not. She's not licensed. Some wives get licensed, just so they can talk about it a little more, but they don't have to be licensed. That doesn't mean they can't go out and actively crusade our concepts. They can recruit people. They can talk about what we do a little bit, and then refer them to us. But my wife's taking an active role in building up the Partners' Organization.

Amway, Shaklee, and United Science of America distributors similarly follow a sexual division of labor. The husband shows the business plan while women sell vitamins or cosmetics to their friends and keep the books.[29]

More than one woman said her husband paid no attention to her business at first, but after she began to make a good income he became involved. A Shaklee wife said it was not uncommon for retired husbands to take over the businesses their wives had built.

In fact, Tupperware has institutionalized this practice. Only women are dealers, the beginning level of distributor. Managers, the next level, may be single women or husband-and-wife teams. Such teams, in which a husband quits any other job, are called Total Tupper families and are regarded favorably by the company. The next level, a distributorship, for a long time could be assigned *only* to a husband-and-wife team. A woman's mobility was thus constrained by her husband's career choice. Although there have been exceptions to this practice in recent years, according to informants it remains the rule.

Occasionally, too, the Tupperware headquarters fills executive positions by recruiting from among the distributors. The husband always becomes the employee, although the wife may consider herself part of the team and travel with him at company expense. The paycheck, though, has only the husband's name on it. According to former Tupperware president Joe Hara, "We have to pay it to somebody. What we are trying

to do is decide what is in the interest of good marital relations. . . . I know of no situations that involve a gal who doesn't
want more free time."[30]

Even women's DSOs assume that a wife's duty is first to
support her husband's needs and only then to care for her
business. For example, Mary Crowley's book of aphorisms includes, "Don't marry a man you aren't willing to adjust to" and
"Let the husband be the HEAD of the household and the wife
be the neck. You never saw a head turn without the neck."[31]
Mary Kay Ash's advice to beauty consultants is less religious
and more witty. She is a sort of Erma Bombeck to working
women, convinced of women's extraordinary abilities but urging women to coddle their way to autonomy. Her autobiography is filled with tidbits on how to gain a husband's support
and manage a direct selling business so as to interfere as little
as possible with a man's life at home. For example, she says
she sometimes fooled her husband by putting a frozen dinner
on a plate and heating it in the microwave oven: "Mel used to
brag that I never served him a TV dinner, but I did sometimes—on a plate!"[32]

Mary Kay beauty consultants are urged to gain a husband's permission for a new recruit to begin work. A beauty
consultant described how she did this:

> Because it's a family business, there is no way I want to recruit
> a lady without talking to her husband. Because eventually she
> is going to have to go to him for money or guidance and there'll
> be customers calling and coming, so he's going to have to get
> involved. I ask her, "Do you feel I need to sit down and talk with
> your husband?" If so, we will stop the interview right there and
> set another time so I can go and talk with them.

In truth, Mary Kay urges women to recognize that social
realities such as divorce and the husbands' early death can
leave women financially and socially on their own. She prompts
women to learn to take care of themselves, but first to secure
their husbands' support for such an undertaking. As one former beauty consultant put it, "Everything [Mary Kay] says,
even listening to her inspirational tapes, is all directed to
women. It has an undertone of 'we are capable, but we still
have our place.'"

Traditional marital ties are also used to support profits in DSOs. Romantic love as the ideal bond between spouses emerged with the rise of industrial capitalism and the separation of spheres.[33] No longer tied by shared activities, husbands and wives were cemented by a new romantic model of mutual affection. Love is the critical social glue that holds the family together under the conditions of modern capitalism. There is an implicit exchange model in romantic love: women provide affection and sex, and men give their wives money and status.[34] Butterfield argues that the Amway line he belonged to exploited this exchange relationship and that sexual impulses, alternately suppressed and titillated, fueled economic activity:

> Despite their unintentional parody of Bible school sexual ethics, a great deal of subliminal—and perverted—sexuality goes on at Amway functions. Audiences are led in mass denunciations of soap operas dealing with the theme of adultery, husbands and wives are instructed from the stage to kiss and hold hands. Dexter Yager jokingly refers to the "other woman" in his life, who turns out to be his daughter; the wife of a prominent Diamond [-level distributor] calls the ladies to Christ by describing Jesus as a wonderful "hunk" of a man. But just beneath these comfortably square plugs for the monogamous "Christian" nuclear family lurks the tail of the serpent: the men strutting in their suits, leaving business cards on the chairs like dogs peeing on fire hydrants to mark their territories; the women arrayed in alluring and expensive costumes, turning heads as they pass; the equation of attractiveness with pin level ("I'm so glad my man is a *Winner*"); [and] the salacious play on the word "excited" (Are you *excited*? Show me how *excited* you are!).[35]

According to Butterfield, Amway distributors are encouraged to read books about preserving love in marriage.

Historians and sociologists who study the development of the family over time have debated whether the separation of spheres served women's interests.[36] Many agree that, at the least, the domestic sphere did create a world in which women could develop expertise and exercise a degree of independence and authority. It was a world in which women's values and culture were preserved. This arrangement, while to an extent liberating, did not threaten the essentially patriarchal character of the economy or the husband as head of the family.

I think this judgment fits the direct selling industry too. Network DSOs give women a sphere in which they can develop competence, a degree of economic independence, and the opportunity to interact in ways that do not do violence to their sense of themselves as women. But DSOs, even one led by such an obvious booster of women as Mary Kay Ash, do not challenge the prevailing sociopolitical arrangements of society. In fact, it is probably the compromise direct selling represents that has made it attractive to so many women. They can be personally empowered—*feel* liberated and modern—without upsetting the traditional premises of their lives.

Whether a women's organization is feminist depends not only on its grounding in women's culture, but on its political and ideological bases. Women's DSOs might be characterized as *prefeminist*, celebrating womanly abilities and values but not challenging dominant social structures.[37] It is also clear that creating economic organizations that emulate the domestic sphere can be used not only to empower women, as women's organizers hope, but to maintain their submission.

A quick look at network DSOs might lead an observer to conclude that they are an anachronism, a throwback to a preindustrial model of social organization where husbands, wives, and children worked and played together. In fact, direct selling organizations are a product of today. They are a response to families' desire to be together in an economy that keeps them apart and to a world of work that disadvantages women in several ways. Network direct selling organizations are one industry's opportunistic response to the segmented and gender-divided arrangements of postindustrial society.

CHAPTER FIVE
The Business of Belief

Mary Crowley, founder and chief executive officer of Home Interiors and Gifts, opened the business meeting with a Bible reading from Proverbs: "Let's read what King Solomon told his sons about how to become leaders," Crowley said to the twenty-five women in the management training course. "If any group needs wisdom and understanding, it's management. And what is wisdom but seeing the world from God's point of view? Once you can do that, you just have to succeed at your mission—*our* mission. Which is ensuring that no home in America is ever dull or unattractive."[1]

At the time she spoke those words in 1983, Mary Crowley's mission was an unqualified success. She had 40,000 distributors, called "displayers," demonstrating merchandise at parties and selling $400 million a year in decorative accessories for the home—figurines, artificial foliage, and wall sconces. Home Interiors and Gifts, almost half of which was owned by founder Crowley and her son, probably netted more than $20 million after-tax profit on those sales.[2]

Mary Crowley's "mission" to improve America's homes echoes Art Williams's "crusade" to help the finances of American families. Both chief executives used religious metaphor and authority to voice their appeals, and both associated their products—decorative accessories and term life insurance—with "higher" values: the importance of an attractive home and financial security for family well-being.

Other American companies try to sell goods by associating their products with a variety of benefits, including good health and sex appeal. But direct selling organizations, in an extraordinary number of instances, go much further. Many network DSOs are founded on *organizational ideologies*, holistic belief systems in which products and the act of selling are merely manifestations of a superior way of life. These ideologies, and the products that are often their expression, are claimed to have the power to transform lives in physical, emotional, and spiritual ways.

In chapter 3 I considered the material circumstances that have grown to favor direct selling, such as the need for women to work, the increasing insecurity of a corporate career, and the expense of maintaining the employment relation. Direct selling succeeds, however, not only because of its financial rewards and flexible work arrangements, but also because it appeals to the values, beliefs, and aspirations of many Americans.

In this chapter I consider the ideological bases of direct selling. Material circumstances may constrain and prompt economic behavior, but ideas and beliefs can transform economic necessity into acceptable, even desirable and exalted social activity. Conversely, people's beliefs and values can form the basis of economic pursuits.

I follow up this argument by first discussing the usual ideological basis for business organization—economic rationality. Second, I describe the quite different ideological underpinnings of network DSOs, which are enterprises rooted in substantive or value rationality. I argue that value rationality, expressed as a belief in entrepreneurialism and the transformative powers of products, provides a viable basis for organizing large-scale enterprises. Finally, I suggest how the values espoused by direct selling organizations simultaneously serve the material and ideal interests of distributors and management.[3]

BELIEF AND ORGANIZATION

All organizations—corporations, Girl Scout troops, the president's cabinet—are based in part on beliefs.[4] Beliefs may legitimate organizational arrangements, such as who is in a position of authority and who has to take orders. Beliefs may also provide a basis for "associative relations," that is, relations among people who share ideas and interests.[5] Beliefs and ideas are a sort of social magnet that take potentially chaotic interactions among people and give them direction and order by providing a common orientation.

Organizational analysts who study modern corporations rarely discuss the role of beliefs in ordering intraorganizational relations. That is because economic rationality is so pervasive and so unquestioned a basis of relations that it is understood to be present.[6] Economic rationality is expressed in modern business as a systematic orientation to profit and efficiency. Long-range planning, goal setting based on cost/benefit analysis, accounting systems, hiring for expertise—the entire panoply of modern management techniques is adopted to further the profitability and efficient running of the enterprise. The depersonalizing of relations and the establishment of bureaucratic routines promote the sort of stability necessary for long-term investing and systematic growth.

Economic calculus characterizes not only business decisions but social decisions in the firm. In its purest expression the firm subordinates the individual and social needs of workers to considerations of financial utility. Moreover, economic rationality supports a preoccupation with the efficiency needs of the "system" rather than concern with the actual ends the system is put to. This depersonalizing of relations and the failure to consider more than the financial returns of decisions may result in a well-known pathology of modern corporate life: a sense of meaninglessness, of being a cog in a machine with no higher purpose than to make money.[7]

Assiduousness in the pursuit of gain, however, is what makes the firm an extraordinarily effective instrument for achieving economic ends. Indeed, a major theme in Max Weber's writings, the foundation of modern organizational analysis, is the importance of economic rationality in the movement of the preindustrial West to industrial capitalism.[8] This movement toward modernity, as Weber's work makes clear, could not have happened, first, without the development of economic rationality as a widespread social orientation. Second, it was the formation of bureaucratic firms in the economic sphere and bureaucratic state agencies in the political arena that has made possible the capitalist world economy we know.[9]

VALUE RATIONALITY

Although economic rationality, and its expression in bureaucracy, clearly dominates organized life today, it is not the only ideological basis of organization.[10] Value-rational organizations are familiar in the modern world and represent many of those groups people feel most strongly about.

Value rationality is a belief not in efficiency or profitability, Weber says, but in a substantive ideal or goal such as "duty, honor, the pursuit of beauty, a religious call, personal loyalty, or the importance of some 'cause' no matter in what it consists."[11] Organizations based on values exist to enact and further a systematized set of norms or an ideology.[12] A central ideal serves both as a source of commitment to members and as a guide to action within the organization.

Religious organizations are prototypical value-rational organizations, with their orientation to otherworldly beliefs. Protestant church members, for example, embrace the teachings of Christ, try to act "Christian" in their lives, and organize their church activities to celebrate and spread their beliefs.

It may seem obvious that churches are based on values, but a wide variety of secular organizations are also based on beliefs that their members try to uphold and put into practice. Bennett Berger described a belief in "American pastoralism," an affinity for nature, community, and self-reliance, as the basis for founding a northern California rural commune.[13] Philip Selznick studied a Bolshevik political cell and described how its fanatically held political ideology turned members into "an organizational weapon."[14] My own study of the United States president's personal staff shows how intense personal loyalty is the basis of staff organization.[15] Professional associations, fraternal orders, social movement organizations, and many voluntary associations are based on value rationality.

Although economic organizations are usually based on economic, not value, rationality, this need not be so. Traditional forms of enterprise, such as small family firms and craft guilds, are often directed toward more than profits and may have a value orientation. For example, they commonly retain a concern with traditional ways of performing work, even if inefficient, and by their nature are highly personalized. Alternative organizations, such as collectivist food co-ops and free medical clinics, usually subordinate economic considerations to political and social goals.[16] Howard Aldrich and Robert Stern show the tension between populist ideals and economic individualism in producer cooperatives.[17] Extralegal economic pursuits such as piracy and dealing in contraband may be oriented toward adventurism as well as gain and typically must eschew many of the efficiency-enhancing strategies firms employ (e.g., they may select not for expertise but for loyalty and may embrace opportunism rather than long-range planning).[18] By their nature they are highly risky. Indeed, most exceptions to enterprise based on economic rationality tend to be unstable and marginal in a market economy where they must compete with more efficient firms.

Network DSOs are unusual, maybe unique, in today's economy because they are large capitalist enterprises founded on value rationality. Although DSOs, with their typically high turnover, do not have continuity of personnel compared with similar-sized firms, some DSOs have maintained a very large size for decades (largely by routinizing the turnover problem and making recruiting a perpetual activity). Moreover, DSOs are hardly economically marginal. They can be extraordinarily profitable—or as one DSO executive put it, "a money machine."

Network direct selling organizations are based on one or both of two substantive values: a belief in entrepreneurialism and a belief in the transformative powers of products. "Entrepreneurialism" and "products" might at first consideration seem to be part of an economic rationality. Both are clearly "economic," the first referring to economic activity and the second to commodities. But entrepreneurialism and products as conceptualized in DSOs are not only instrumental, not merely a means of profit. They are infused with moral and social meanings that transform their purely economic character into a value-laden, even transcendental stance.

Indeed, by pursuing moral and social ends *through* economic activity, direct selling simultaneously resolves problems inherent in both economic and value-rational enterprises: by infusing values into economic pursuits distributors have a sense of meaning that escapes many bureaucratic workers, and by making the economic a central ideal, DSOs overcome the financial distress that value-rational enterprises typically encounter.[19]

THE ENTREPRENEURIAL ETHIC

The notion that ideas and economic activity intersect in an entrepreneurial morality is the topic of Max Weber's famous and much-debated book *The Protestant Ethic and the Spirit of Capitalism*.[20] Weber's study of Calvinist townspeople in seventeenth-century Europe argues that religious ideas encouraged and shaped their economic pursuits. Although Weber's burghers (people who lived in towns or burghs) are widely separated in time and space from the direct selling distributors of contemporary America, the logic of their situations has some parallels and suggests reasons for their common adherence to an entrepreneurial ethic.

Weber wrote *The Protestant Ethic* in part to challenge Marx's idea that one's social class, or place in the economy, determines one's consciousness. Weber wanted to refute Marx's economic determinism by showing that ideas or consciousness can also influence economic behavior.

Seventeenth-century adherents to ascetic Protestantism, particularly Calvinists, attracted Weber's attention because they represented an important break with the past. Traditional economic units, such as feudal manors and craft guilds in towns, practiced what Weber called "budgetary economizing," or taking care of traditionally determined needs. When basic needs were satisfied workers took time off for other pursuits; there was little interest in efficient methods or working harder to produce a surplus for sale in markets. Most people were not oriented toward amassing riches.[21] Indeed, an interest in earthly wealth was considered immoral in an era dominated by religious ideas.

During the sixteenth and seventeenth centuries, however, political and economic changes, including the production of a surplus on manors, were beginning to support the growth of markets.[22] Towns became market centers for an emergent rural capitalism, and traders and master craftsmen benefited from the increased economic activity in urban areas.

A burgher class of prosperous businessmen, a historically new social grouping, took to the new economic conditions with a prodigious dedication of effort. They worked hard, lived frugally, and reinvested all their surplus. Weber's intellectual task was to explain this feverish entrepreneurialism, given traditional notions of "budgetary economizing" and the otherworldly orientation of the era.

Weber argued that new religious ideas that came out of the Protestant Reformation, particularly ascetic Calvinism, served to justify and spur on the activity of the burgher businessmen. Calvinists believed in predestination—the idea that God had "elected" certain people to be saved and to join him in heaven. People could do nothing to change God's decision, but earthly prosperity was taken to represent God's favor. Riches, however, were not for one's pleasure but were to be reinvested and made to multiply in the service of God's will. Discipline, frugality, and the notion that work is its own reward and one's occupation is a "calling" are all central tenets of ascetic Protestantism.[23] Calvinism therefore both justified entrepreneurial activity as morally correct and supported investment over consumption, the latter furthering the development of a capitalist economic system.

Gianfranco Poggi's analysis of *The Protestant Ethic* thesis suggests, in contrast to some other interpretations, that Weber was not arguing that ideas (Calvinism) *caused* capitalism (entrepreneurial activity).[24] Rather, the Protestant ethic gave meaning to economic activities and beliefs *already being pursued by the burghers.* The importance of Calvinism lay less in providing new ideas than in providing moral justification that spurred on and gave direction to capitalist fervor by such practices as saving and reinvestment. The intersection of the material and ideal interests of burgher businessmen in the Protestant ethic at a historically propitious moment reinforced and channeled a transformation that was already under way.

THE AMERICAN ETHIC AND
THE SPIRIT OF CAPITALISM

The Protestant ethic was an ideology that created a climate for and justified material desires. Moreover, its tenets were sufficiently specific to channel desires into particular practices. This "spirit of the age," then, served as both context and conduit of individual choice.

The direct selling industry also rests on an ideology, an "American ethic" that creates and legitimates a desire for material wealth. The American ethic, like its Calvinist forebear, directs individuals toward a materialist orientation and specific activities in the pursuit of gain.[25] Not surprisingly, the activities support the direct selling organizations that articulate the ideology.

The "American ethic" is an amalgam of economic, political, and social beliefs widely shared by people in this country. Like the Protestant ethic, it is nothing less than a worldview, an orientation to oneself and one's society. Unlike Calvinism, which represented a relatively defined ideology, however, the American ethic is loosely formulated and varies substantially across DSOs. Its centerpiece, however, is relatively constant: a belief in the moral virtue of entrepreneurialism. Not surprisingly, entrepreneurial virtue as articulated in the American ethic can be traced back to its expression in the Protestant ethic some three hundred years earlier.

The original Protestant ethic created a social ideal—a pious and self-reliant entrepreneur—that suited the needs of an emerging capitalist economy throughout the West. The ideal spread to America, but it had changed somewhat by the nineteenth century, when wealth was no longer seen as a signal from God. Riches were now regarded as the reward of individual accomplishment and a sign of character. This revision of the Protestant ethic stressed initiative, competitiveness, and perseverence and was consonant with the rise of industrial capitalism. Rags-to-riches stories and biographies of the captains of industry who put together industrial empires were popular best-sellers in the 1800s.

The social ideal changed yet again with the rise of large corporations as important places of work. Rather than stressing independent success and competitiveness, the new ideal suggested that working one's way up the corporate hierarchy by getting along with others was an acceptable alternative.

The Protestant ethic of hard work, accumulation of wealth, and individual effort, while changed from its origins in

Calvinism, is very much a part of contemporary American culture.[26] In the direct selling industry the ethic is entwined with other American beliefs, especially a belief in meritocracy, the idea that status and social rewards are distributed according to individual accomplishment—that people who are successful deserve their success, while people of modest achievement are less worthy. Meritocracy is founded on the conviction that it is possible for people to control their lives in important ways, that they can pull themselves up by their bootstraps if they will only try. Because status and financial rewards in direct selling are in important ways a reflection of one's selling and recruiting success, the meritocratic ideal has the force of experience within the industry.[27] But distributors believe in meritocracy in a general way, as a political philosophy that helps them explain "success" and "failure" in all spheres of life, both within and outside the industry. As one distributor put it, "I don't think of people who leave [Amway] as bad people. I think of them as people who, for whatever reason, chose not to be successful." Success is almost universally defined as financial freedom from wage labor, although most DSOs indicate that money can translate into leisure, family time, and various items of value.

The meritocratic ideology puts great pressure on individuals to succeed. Success represents not only material wealth but a certification of self. One distributor described how the meritocratic ideal is understood in his DSO:

> You are as good as your work. [Our organization's philosophy] is very heavily materialistic; everything we stress is about the things you want. I mean, it's easy to say "I don't want a Mercedes Benz" or "I don't want a big house" because you can't get one. People [in my DSO] are saying, "You can get one. Why not have it?" They're saying that everybody else isn't philosophically against it, it's more like sour grapes. And I think that's possibly true. So what it comes down to is enjoy the good life, enjoy American technology.

Although corporate success is highly valued, the independent entrepreneur remains the meritocratic ideal, and because everyone in direct selling is an independent contractor, they all lay claim to being entrepreneurs.[28] Being a direct selling entrepreneur, however, means more than simply being in business for yourself. Like many other Americans, distributors associate entrepreneurialism with initiative, self-reliance, and other culturally valued character traits.

Distributors also associate entrepreneurialism with a host of American political values and symbols: it is bound up in ideas about patriotism, equality, freedom, and free enterprise. Most DSOs espouse the idea that all people, no matter what their race, religion, age, education, or sex, can succeed as long as they are guaranteed the freedom to try.[29] One woman described the importance of this egalitarian philosophy to her.

> [The founders of this business made it] possible for anybody, no matter whether they had education, no matter what race they were, no matter if they had money or not, there were no criteria that would prevent them from having the American dream. And it sounds corny to a lot of people, but I felt very much that way because I never had the opportunity of an education. It wasn't corny to me at all. I thought it was just wonderful.

As expressed in many DSOs, entrepreneurialism is as much a political view as an economic activity. As one person put it, "I believe in this country 100%, and therefore I believe in this business and what it's about." In some DSOs the political vision is subtle, but in many it is nearly a caricature of American cultural symbols, a celebration of a national success ideology. The names of a number of DSOs invoke American-isms. For example, Amway is a contraction of "American Way." Similarly, United Sciences of America, Incorporated, a vitamin company, contracts its name into "U.S.A., Inc." American Dream International is a California DSO whose corporate logo is a bald eagle. The names of the Fortunate Corporation and Total Success similarly associate the concerns with the idea of success.

Many speakers at rallies and meetings employ patriotic rhetoric. Even the DSA's 1986 annual convention for top industry executives began with a nationalistic celebration. Eight attractive young men and women sang and danced to a medley of patriotic tunes. At the end of their forty-minute performance celebrating the American way of life, hundreds of executives stood up and sang "America the Beautiful."

While most DSOs I studied subscribe in some way to a

belief in the moral virtue of entrepreneurialism, not all of them make overt association with patriotism. In fact some find the patriotic fervor objectionable. The vice-president of one company rejected such appeals as hype and said her DSO made "no false promises wrapped in American flags." Likewise, the president of a cosmetics concern said there were "no religion or so-called Americanisms and flag waving in this company."[30] Such rejections simply confirm that much of the industry infuses nationalistic symbols into its business practices.

As the latter executive suggested, in some DSOs the American ethic becomes entwined with religion as well as patriotism. Religion is usually nondenominational, simply an encouragement to keep God in one's life, including one's business life. Mary Kay Ash and Mary Crowley both encouraged distributors to keep "God first, family second, career third." Drinking and smoking are prohibited at both companies' activities. Several DSOs include the New Testament's Golden Rule in their formal corporate philosophies: "Do unto others as you would have them do unto you." A number of DSOs open meetings with prayer and sing hymns, often with the lyrics changed to reflect organizational philosophies.

MANAGEMENT AND MORALITY

Religious and patriotic ideas serve at least three functions in direct selling. First, they support the notion that direct selling is more than a job—that it is a way of life that encompasses the spiritual and civic realms as well as the material. In direct selling one can work and serve God and country at the same time. Indeed, it is but a small leap to understanding that if one wants to serve God and the nation a commitment to direct selling is an important step toward those ends. Direct selling, in many distributors' eyes, is a quasi-religious, quasi-patriotic activity: God and the nation are served by the pursuit of direct sales. In this way the American ethic contributes to a generalized desire to go out into the world and make money.

Clearly, of course, for some distributors the material rewards are more important than the ideal, but the industry is structured so that both are possible. One Tupperware distributor described two of her fellow dealers:

> Nina is very religious. [Her husband] John lost his job very
> shortly after she started in Tupperware, and she supported her
> family for a number of months. She [had planned] to go into
> Tupperware, to put her kids in Christian Academy. After it sup-
> ported the family for as long as it did, she decided that she
> wanted to become a manager. And that's why she named her
> unit "Genesis," because it was a new beginning for her family.
> Now Melanie's unit is "Mega-Bucks," because her bottom line in
> getting into Tupperware is money.

Second, religion and patriotism are occasionally used to manage selling activity and structure organizational practice. The
Southwestern Company, Home Interiors and Gifts, and other
DSOs use prayer and religious readings to help distributors accept rejection and persevere in the face of difficulty. A woman
distributor of cosmetics similarly spoke about the importance
of "some type of faith in God":

> Sales are up and down and you've got to be able to roll with the
> punches. You can't let the lows get you down so bad that you
> blow the highs that are coming around the corner. So you need
> to be able to lean on some faith.

Third, by associating direct selling with a transcendental morality, religion and nationalism channel individual action by
supporting moral relations among distributors. Distributors
see themselves as part of a community sharing common beliefs. Prayer, singing, and pledges of allegiance celebrate those
beliefs. Because bureaucratic controls are weak or nonexistent
in DSOs, moral controls may serve the important function of
mediating competitive relations among distributors.[31]
    The severe asceticism of the Calvinist burghers who
practiced self-denial while they accumulated wealth has no
counterpart in the materialism celebrated by DSOs that hap-
pily give away jewelery and cars. But in more important ways
the Protestant and American ethics serve similar functions:
they give meaning to the economic pursuits of people entering
the economy in new ways. The burgher businessmen found
justification for breaking with traditional orientations to
work. Direct selling distributors—mothers, underemployed men
and women in salaried jobs, underappreciated professionals—

likewise find support in knowing that being an entrepreneur is a worthy calling, particularly if outsiders question the appropriateness of their selling or if they perceive no better alternatives. Having a business of one's own is, to many, a much-needed sign of status and self-worth. The power of entrepreneurialism as a calling lies in its ability to draw on and affirm beliefs already held: individualism, meritocracy, patriotism, religion, community. If one is committed to those, as many Americans are, a commitment to direct selling easily follows. One distributor stated this well:

> It's not like [the DSO] is forcing you to do anything. I guess it's kind of reinforcing all the things you learned as a kid in elementary school. You know, the things that were good and the things that were of value.

Direct selling organizations have taken the things that are "good" and "of value" and built an industry on them.

PRODUCT IDEOLOGIES

While most DSOs support an entrepreneurial ethic to some extent, not all of them have product ideologies, the second ideological basis common to the industry. Product ideologies are a belief that the goods or services the DSO sells are special and have the power to transform their users in important ways. Many marketing strategies try to get consumers to believe that a product will confer status, attractiveness, or some other benefit on users, of course, so direct selling is not unique in this regard. But some direct selling organizations are distinctive in associating products with a larger set of beliefs, particularly beliefs articulated by a founder. The products are often a manifestation of the founder's ideology: if one believes in the founder's ideas, then using the products is a means of practicing belief, and selling to others becomes a form of proselytizing.[32] It is the beliefs that are central to sustaining commitment and directing activity, but the products are their material manifestation.

In DSOs where there is a strong belief in the virtue of entrepreneurialism, such as Amway, product ideologies are weak or absent. Amway distributors, for example, believe that their products are "good," better than what one can buy in a supermarket, but the products do not have a central place in the thinking or emotions of distributors. Rather, the "business opportunity," the chance to be an entrepreneur and to extend that chance to others, is the critical organizing force. In a sense the business opportunity is the product in Amway, American Dream International, and other DSOs that stress entrepreneurialism. Commodity sales simply give access to the socially and financially valued status of entrepreneur. In these DSOs distributors sell the "dream," and product sales flow from that.

In DSOs such as Shaklee, where products have a central focus, customers are sold first on the efficacy of the products, often without mention of the advantages of being a distributor. People are encouraged to develop a commitment to the products and perhaps the ideology behind them and only later, when committed, are urged to sell to others. Many distributors of Shaklee products, for example, follow this routine.

Direct selling organizations vary by how much they stress "opportunity" and "career" and how much emphasis is placed on the products. Some encourage one basis of belief over the other, while many combine the two in some manner. Even within the same DSO, distributors vary in which is more important to them. Moreover, the direct selling industry as a whole has varied over time in its emphasis. For example, executives agree that the women's movement has had an impact on what women distributors want from their participation in the industry, and many DSOs are responding to changing gender ideologies in their "opportunity" appeals.

> When I first joined Tupperware [in the early 1950s] I was not allowed to use words like "work" or "career." It was a part-time opportunity for women who were homemakers. That was the whole thrust of the company. I had some knock-down-drag-out [fights] with the then management of the company to try to modernize their thinking. I wanted us to view our prospective Tupperware dealers as businesswomen in their own right, [but management's] whole focus was the kitchen, the little lady at home.

Just as the range of entrepreneurial ideologies in DSOs spans "pin money" to careers, there is a range of ideologies that inspire commitment to products. Moreover, the diversity of products that are their expression is great, from water purification systems and candlesticks to eye shadow and prayerbooks. Three types of missions, however, are particularly common to network direct selling.

MISSIONS AND MARKETS

The first common mission positions the product as a health and life enhancer tied to an ideology of wellness or environmentalism. Network DSOs promoting health include Shaklee, Nutri-Metics International, United Sciences of America, Herbalife International, and Avacare ("Natural Source Products by People Who Care about You"). Shaklee, for example, is based on the beliefs and teachings of chiropractor Forrest Shaklee. Shaklee's philosophy was a vision of the proper relationship between man and the natural world, expressed in the corporate motto, "In Harmony with Nature."[33] He believed in an ecologically harmonious world where people do not upset the natural balance through the indiscriminate use of nonbiodegradable products. He felt that our sources of food were nutritionally deficient because they were developed for cosmetic and commercial reasons. Shaklee began his company by selling nutritional supplements, but the company now offers a mix of cleaners, personal-care products, and even a fertilizer. All the products are natural and reflect the founder's philosophy. In addition, they are intended to be integrated into an environmentally aware way of life that promotes individual health and social concern. Shaklee adherents brush their teeth, wash their hair, and clean their houses with the products. According to a company brochure, "A Shaklee home is different because it's filled with a sense of natural well-being. It's a home In Harmony with Nature."[34]

The second ideological theme frequently seen in direct selling concerns products as enhancers of the self—usually cosmetics, but also clothing, accessories, and other "beautifiers." Mary Kay Cosmetics is built on the ideas of Mary Kay Ash, a philosophy that combines belief in the value of entrepreneurialism and in the confidence one gains by looking one's best. It is a philosophy particularly tailored to women. Mary Kay Ash describes her ideas in her autobiography:

> We're not only in the cosmetics business, we're in the people business. And, as a people-oriented company, our goal is to offer women opportunity. And these women, in turn, fulfill the needs of other women by teaching them good skin care. In other words, our whole reason for existence is to give people the opportunity to enrich their lives.[35]

Some clothing companies attempt to build their product lines on an ideology too. For example, Cameo Coutures, a distributor of lingerie, is built in part on the antifeminist ideas of Marabel Morgan, author of *The Total Woman*.[36] Morgan advocates women's accepting the dominance of the husband in the home and being feminine in a traditional way. The company sells intimate apparel at parties and encourages its "couturieres" to begin with a story of women's "three moods" as wife, mother, and sweetheart. Purchasers are encouraged to buy a "uniform" for each mood. The company's cofounder suggested how its traditional vision of women is a basis for its sales technique:

> I mean, when she's in there fixing breakfast, she doesn't want on a slinky, sexy negligee. She wants a nice robe that looks just right. On the other hand, when her husband comes home from work and he's relaxed and she wants to cuddle up by him with the television, if he looks over at her and she's got the same robe she had on in the morning, it's got a little egg splattered on it. . . . he's thinking this is the mother of my children, instead of thinking about her as being a wife or sweetheart. And then, of course, there's always the time when the gals want to be the sweetheart. Excited and exciting and excitable. So we have pieces of lingerie that are like that, that help a man feel that way.[37]

Women whose views of themselves and their relationship with their husbands are reflected in this vision are the target of Cameo Couture's products and business opportunity.

A third common set of DSO ideologies concerns products as supportive of the family and home. Tupperware and some cookware companies, for example, stress that their products preserve nutrients and protect the family's health. A. L. Williams argues that converting from whole life insurance to its term insurance helps provide a family with financial security. Mary Crowley's home accessories are designed to create a warm and caring environment for family life. Crowley described how her products serve this function:

> Psychologists say people actually operate better in surroundings that have a certain amount of serenity. And educators tell us that the last thing a child sees before he goes to bed and the first thing he sees in the morning can influence his life. We encourage mothers to hang a pretty little plaque, a shelf and maybe a candle in a child's room. Saying prayers by candlelight can become a memory-making time.[38]

Crowley's philosophy, like those of the founders of Amway, Mary Kay Cosmetics, and Shaklee, is codified in a book that is widely read by distributors.[39]

MARKETING BELIEF

The products sold by network DSOs are not apparently different from those sold by other companies; nor is the DSOs' strategy of associating products with well-being an innovation. But when products and entrepreneurialism are joined to a larger set of beliefs, commodities and selling take on meanings beyond their utilitarian values: they become affirmations of an orientation to the world and a means of expressing support for ideas. This view complements the interpretation of Mary Douglas, particularly in her work with economist Baron Isherwood.[40] Douglas holds that goods are material culture whose meanings are socially constructed and have more than instrumental value. She emphasizes that the use of goods is a means of communicating to an audience. In direct selling I see evidence of goods and the "business opportunity" serving to construct a self. Products and entrepreneurialism help people to define a persona for self-definition, which of course is then communicated to others and becomes a basis for community.

Indeed, it is a critical management task to get people to understand the DSO's system of belief and organization as the "answer" to their "problems" of money, meaning, self-esteem, and community. Direct selling executives face much the same problem as social movement leaders in manufacturing discontent ("Are you happy with your job?") and in mobilizing commitment to the DSO's ideology.

Network direct selling companies are, in important ways, in the business of marketing belief in their crusades and organizations. As two DSO executives put it:

> Our job is selling. That's our whole job. We're constantly selling ideas. We're constantly selling the opportunity. We're constantly saying, "Hey, look. Here's what Mary Kay can mean to you." That's our job.

> It's important that a [direct selling] company has a mission, that a company believes in something besides making money and there's a comfort level between the salesperson and the company, between the salespersons and their customers, and between the salesperson and society in general in terms of their role. So these are a lot of intangibles that can't be quantified on the bottom line but are very, very important.

The conjoining of product, opportunity, and belief is effective because of its highly personalized nature. First, it is often the ideas of a founder that are being commodified. In most such instances DSOs actively support the image of the founder as a special person with an extraordinary vision. DSOs, for example, encourage a personality cult by printing the founders' writings, taping their words for distribution to members, and presenting them at mass rallies. Belief in the superiority of founders helps sustain belief in the products they support.

Perhaps more important, however, is the personalized way the product is presented, whether the product is an opportunity or a consumer good. Distributors who are committed to the products sell their beliefs to others through testimonials. Nearly all the Shaklee distributors I interviewed, for example, first told me how their own health and well-being had been restored through product use. In some instances the stories represented medical miracles, such as not needing sunglasses after taking vitamin A tablets. Even in less dramatic cases, the message was a sincere expression of well-being. Be-

cause much direct selling goes on among members with existing social relations, the message can be powerful indeed:
people are more likely to believe a friend than an impersonal
media message. One distributor talked about how she over-
came disbelief in the supportive environment of the organization through product use:

> I was hearing a lot of stuff about Shaklee, but I wasn't believing
> it. And I knew my friend would be honest with me, but I just
> figured he was brainwashed. I figured these people really be-
> lieved themselves, but they just weren't really aware. So when
> we began to experience things ourselves, of course we were im-
> pressed. . . . I have come to the conclusion, very strongly in my
> mind, that God brought me into it.

OBSCURING THE ECONOMIC
IN THE SOCIAL

The commercial exploitation of social networks as market opportunities might be expected to "turn off" potential customers, and in fact it sometimes does. Amway distributors, for
example, are instructed not to tell potential recruits whom
they represent until their sales pitch has been made. This
practice reportedly angers many unwitting friends and acquaintances. But some network DSOs effectively obscure the
financial transaction that in fact is taking place: they present
themselves as direct selling companies that paradoxically do
not sell.

For example, Mary Kay beauty consultants profess that
they do not sell cosmetics. Rather, they "teach skin care" and
the skillful use of cosmetics. Shaklee distributors do not sell
vitamins and soap, they "share products" that enhance good
health. As a company brochure describes it, some people simply use the products, "others share enough product to bring in
a second income. Still others take advantage of the major
earning and career opportunity in sharing Shaklee products
and training others to share them."[41] A. L. Williams agents do
not sell insurance, they "win" another battle against the enemy
whole life insurance industry. Other DSOs similarly use language that obscures the pecuniary relationship between buyer
and seller. By transforming selling into a nurturing function

such as "teaching" and "sharing," many distributors come to see their economic activities as primarily an act of caring. People who cannot imagine themselves selling goods through their social relations have no difficulty making a profit by nurturing others, often with some degree of passion. This is clearly understood by executives in the industry. One executive put it this way:

> It is my thesis that unless they believe in the product, whatever it is, women will not be involved in our kind of industry. They must have a loyalty to the products they are selling. There are exceptions, there are obviously women who, like some men, could sell refrigerators to Eskimos—supersaleswomen. But the backbone of our industry is the antithesis of a supersaleswoman. It's somebody who doesn't consider herself a salesperson and is sharing information about this product that she believes in. She has a strong positive feeling for the product.

But the power of belief to transform selling into caring is not limited to women. Art Williams spoke about his largely male, mostly part-time sales force of 155,000 agents. "I've got mayors, policemen, teachers, dentists and newspaper reporters—the kind of people who would throw up before selling typical life insurance."[42]

Because belief in the product or the opportunity is so closely bound up with the act of selling, most distributors I spoke with could not imagine selling "just for the money"; belief is critical. A Shaklee distributor, for example, described the importance of experience with the product as a basis for a sincere approach to others:

> I think you have to have a personal story, a personal experience. My back had hurt me for eight years, and nobody had helped me. You see, it was easy for me to sell it then.

An A. L. Williams distributor also described the importance of a belief in the organization's mission for business success.

> Most people who really understand the crusade end up building a large [downline] organization, but that's not their primary purpose. They may start out in the sales mode, but they don't stay there for long.

Belief in the transformative possibilities of Mary Kay cosmetics helps one distributor sell to women she believes cannot afford the products.

> Sometimes I walk away kind of guilty, [but a top director told me] if I put some sunshine in her life and if she's not going to go home and beat her kids because she feels better about herself, then I have done something really worthwhile.

People accept the qualities claimed for the products they sell and believe in fantastic income possibilities in part because of the socially supportive environment of the DSO; the testimonials of one's respected acquaintances and a revered founder carry great weight. This trust has made the industry susceptible to false or exaggerated claims. For example, Herbalife International, a 700,000 distributor company whose 1985 sales were reportedly nearly $500 million, has been repeatedly investigated by the Food and Drug Administration for making false claims.[43] The Herbalife diet regime of taking about twenty pills a day is supposed to promote weight loss while maintaining good health, according to founder Mark Hughes. But nutritional experts claim that the weight loss is due to the herbal diuretics and laxatives in the formulation and that such side effects as nausea and diarrhea are common.[44] In October 1986 Herbalife agreed to pay $850,000 in legal fees to the California State Department of Health Services for its investigation of the company's practices. Although admitting no wrongdoing, Herbalife agreed to limit claims, including the claims that its "Cell-U-Loss" will naturally eliminate cellulite and that its Schixandra Plus retards aging.[45]

Similarly, A. L. Williams settled out of court with a Prudential life insurance agent who claimed that A. L. Williams agents made misleading comparisons between whole life and term insurance. Also admitting no false claims, A. L. Williams agreed to issue a clarifying fourteen-point statement that addressed alleged deceptive practices.[46] Amway, Shaklee, and a number of other DSOs have also been challenged by consumer groups and government agencies.

The exaggerated claims are not always promoted by the founder or headquarters, and in fact most of the large DSOs actively discourage distributors from making wild promises about the effectiveness of their products or the amount of money one is likely to make in direct selling. One Shaklee distributor told me, in response to the company's clampdown, that she simply tells potential consumers what miracles the products performed for her, without promising they will do the same for everyone. Herbalife now encourages the same practice. But distributors sometimes become obsessed with the products and convinced that they have nearly magical properties. Shaklee's cleaning and fertilizer formula Basic H, for example, is employed in hundreds of ways by distributors who compete to find new uses for the formulation. Two reported uses include putting it in bread dough to encourage rising and feeding it to cows so they will yield better milk, neither use being promoted by the company.[47]

Mundane products such as Basic H and a philosophy of pecuniary self-interest like the American ethic hardly seem obvious ingredients for a missionary vision to change the world. But a number of informants in several DSOs spoke with great emotion about how their organizations are helping to shape society. They talked about believing their DSOs are spearheading a mission to serve mankind in some important—usually political or religious—way. Here are three examples from three different DSOs:

> With the poisoning of the earth that's going on, if you want to get macro, with people who are making noise about nuclear energy like "stop this madness now," and "let's stop dumping toxic waste into our environment" . . . we can do something about the level of violence in our culture, I believe, by becoming aware and eliminating the violence in ourselves. So [this organization] gets into my own personal philosophy. If I can stop dumping toxic waste down my drain in the shampoo and the soap dish and the laundry soap, and if you can magnify that—if everybody in the state would do that—we wouldn't have pollution.

> I think we are making an impact on the socioeconomic conscience of the nation. I think we are opening up new thoughts on how people can be not what they are, but what they can become—to the different ways they can contribute. For instance, there is no way we could ever get a handle on the numbers of people who have come into Mary Kay and found a way

back to church. Certainly we are not a religious entity, but through the positive inputs they get. . . . I know that sounds very Pollyannaish, but I just think that there are so many ways we are impacting this nation.

If there were Amway in every country, people wouldn't bomb each other, they're not going to kill each other. They'd be killing their own distributors—no way! [Laughs] But the whole feeling of Amway is free enterprise, to be economically independent and free. Freedom is the main word they talk about, freedom. So if that gets through the world it should help world peace and understanding. That is the mission, I think—world peace and understanding.

Not all DSOs encourage distributors to think of their product use and selling as contributing to worldwide harmony or some other universal good, but a number do. Nearly everyone I spoke to, however, including distributors and industry executives, talked about how the industry was able to touch people's lives by giving them opportunities for income and self-esteem and, in that sense at least, was an important force for the good.

All businesses, as I have suggested, have ideological bases even if they are merely understood and only rarely articulated. While there is much variation among direct selling organizations in the overt celebration of the American ethic and product ideologies, the industry taken as a whole stands out when compared with other businesses in this country.

STRATEGIC INTERESTS AND IDEOLOGY

So far I have analyzed the ideological structures of network DSOs apart from the interests they serve. Beliefs, though, are not only abstractions, personally held and privately contemplated, though they may be those too. Ideologies, especially those related to economics, usually serve interests by justifying people's pursuits and organizing relations among individuals. The American ethic and product ideologies likewise serve the interests of management and distributors and help to organize relations within DSOs. Ideology in DSOs, as in social movement organizations, mobilizes recruits to action. As Louis Zurcher and David Snow put it, ideology "provides both a picture of the world as it is and as it should be. It provides a guide for action by which the desired changes can best be achieved. At the same time it underscores what is wrong, attributes blame and responsibility, and addresses the Leninesque question, 'What is to be done?'"[48] How that question is answered serves the interests of participants in the industry.

Management's Interests

The American ethic, that amalgam including freedom, meritocracy, individualism, equality, and community, serves the direct selling industry by its very presence in society. Unlike some social movements or religious organizations, DSOs have little need to convert adherents to alien ideas. Rather, DSOs blend the American ethic with widely held beliefs, make them salient to recruits, and shape them to organizational ends.

For example, most Americans, like their Calvinist forebears, define success as earthly riches, although to Calvinists money was a sign of God's favor and for Americans it is a sign of individual character and ability. Direct selling organizations merely accentuate the existing social belief that success is money, though money is sometimes defined as the ability to provide security and pleasure or to otherwise control one's life. Direct selling organizations hold out the promise of income, if not riches, and publicly praise the biggest earners. If anyone doubted that money brought confidence and esteem, the doubt would be dispelled at any network DSO function. Top earners are lavishly rewarded with titles, luxury goods, and applause. They are invited to tell their stories to others who hope to emulate their success.

But while recruiting and selling may bring financial and social rewards to individuals, it also brings income to managers and owners. Equating success with money and establishing organizational practices to support that view clearly serves DSO profit making. If enough recruits internalize the equation success = money and see direct sales as the route to its achievement, a DSO can be a "money machine" indeed. Managerial profits rest on the cultivation of personal income goals.

A belief in equality, individualism, and meritocracy also serves managerial purposes. As expressed in direct selling, the organization provides "opportunity": the product, the selling routine, and organizational support. The rest is up to the individual. Clearly, some people have been fabulously successful at selling, so success appears attainable if only one tries. In truth, in important ways people do start out equally—who you know in the organization or who you are makes no difference; production is all that counts. However, objective differences that do exist—such as a saturation of direct sellers in some areas, the attractiveness of a given product line in various locations, and structural sources of inequality that have given some people better selling skills, for example—these are never discussed. Failure is attributable to the individual, not the organization, the product, or the setting. Unlike bureaucracy, direct selling's structure makes it hard to blame the organization. One cannnot point to a discriminating boss or a system of internal labor markets that limit opportunity. In direct selling, failure is privatized.[49]

Likewise, communal ideals in direct selling—commitment to the same enterprise and to helping each other succeed—serve management interests. The ideology, as translated by DSOs, means assisting each other in selling the companies' products.

Promoting entrepreneurialism also enhances profits. From the company's viewpoint soliciting "entrepreneurs" is a nearly costless way to distribute goods. Distributors act like members of a social movement: they recruit others with a passion because they are "convinced of the rightness of their cause and the inherent attractiveness of their message."[50] The fervor of committed distributors forms the basis for creating a sales force.

Although not as stable or controllable as an employed labor force, independent contractors have the great advantage of being cheap. Moreover, entrepreneur/distributors think of themselves as owners, not workers. They are doing in a small way the same thing as management—selling products. Ideologically, structurally, and legally this is a work force that cannot organize its interests in opposition to management.

Product ideologies, particularly where they exist in force, have important financial consequences too. Because products are believed to confer significant benefits, and because belief in the products is critical to selling and is enhanced by use, distributors (and their families) become significant consumers as well as distributors. In some DSOs, such as Mary Kay, personal consumption without selling is not encouraged by the organization. Others, however, including Shaklee and Amway, solicit distributors who consume but sell only intermittently. Even if there is only a weak product ideology, as in Amway, the network of distributors can be a powerful customer base for the DSO: giving distributors points toward bonuses and awards makes all kinds of products attractive to them. For example, the MCI telephone company solicited Sears, American Express, and Amway to sell long-distance services through their customer networks. Amway brought in 800,000 customers, more than Sears and American Express combined, presumably because many sales were made to distributors who were given bonus points for sales.[51]

Depending on the ideas of the larger society to provide a basis for business activity has drawbacks, however. When society is in a politically conservative mood, direct selling has a ready-made army of recruits. But when social ideas are different the pool of potential sellers shrinks. A social welfare ideology, in particular, poses a threat to the industry because it challenges the work ethic as well as the material need to work. An industry executive spoke of the threat:

> Over the years we've seen greater social welfare benefits being given, and that has affected the psychology of people going out to work. If you are receiving some sort of social welfare benefit, the system punishes you if you go out to work. You'll have a diminution of your benefits based on the income you earn, say, through direct selling.[52]

Direct selling has traditionally been countercyclical, doing well during recessions. But a social welfare ideology and an ideology of entitlement during recessions undermine sales.[53] The direct selling industry, which was threatened by the possibility of an expensive employment relation in the 1930s, tries to make a virtue of necessity: distributors are led to see nonemployed labor as morally superior and to view their selling as insurance against ever having to accept social welfare benefits.

Distributors' Interests

While it is clear that the direct selling industry is not merely a collection of enterprises committed to philosophical ends but comprises profit-seeking businesses, it would be a mistake to see entrepreneurial and product ideologies as serving only the profit interests of management. Distributors' interests, aside from income, are also met in direct selling in at least three ways.

First, substantive rationality—the centrality of values and an ideological worldview—is emotionally and intellectually satisfying to many distributors. In contrast to the usually separate spheres of family, work, community, and even religion, in direct selling these can be fused for committed persons. Many of the people I interviewed compared direct selling with life in firms or at home alone, the only alternatives most had known, and found direct selling a satisfying experience.

While employing "entrepreneurs" serves the profit interests of owners, being an entrepreneur serves important functions for distributors too. It allows them to take advantage of tax benefits from which workers are usually excluded, such as deductible lunches and travel. More important, though, it confers a socially valued status and grants the trappings of a business class many could never otherwise hope to enter. Informants spoke of the pleasure of saying they were in business for themselves, of having business cards to hand out in social situations, and of the possibility of a company car. Entering the world of business, in a society that values businesspeople highly, is important apart from financial rewards. That distributors' status is largely recognized only within the industry and not appreciated generally simply concentrates intraorganizational relations.

Perhaps most important, however, is that direct selling organizations utilize the cultural competencies of women that are underappreciated by the bureaucratic world of business. DSOs reward women socially and financially for the skills they in fact have—the ability to teach others, to nurture, to encourage, to share—abilities not so highly valued in firms. As sociologist Ann Swidler put it, "One can hardly pursue success in a world where the accepted skills, style, and informal know-how are unfamiliar. One does better to look for a line of action for which one already has the cultural equipment."[54] The direct selling industry employs the cultural equipment of women to make a profit and in turn rewards women financially and socially for those skills.

Direct selling represents an interpenetration of the material and the ideal. Its ideologies make attractive what material circumstances prompt men and women to do—make money. Conversely, it makes what men and women believe in—the American ethic and other social values—produce and justify material gain. Circumstance and ideology, for many Americans, meet in direct selling.[55]

CHAPTER SIX
Charisma and Control

More than 7,000 Mary Kay beauty consultants filled the Dallas Convention Center. They had flown from all over the United States, Canada, and Mexico at their own expense to attend the annual Seminar, a three-day event filled with workshops, information on new products, inspiring speeches, and top-name entertainment. Tonight was awards night, the formal-dress extravaganza that is the highlight of Seminar. On this evening the top performers of the Mary Kay sales force would be recognized and rewarded. It was an evening when normally anonymous women would step onstage, hear their names called out, and see their images projected on the Convention Center's two giant video monitors. Thousands of their peers would give them a standing ovation.

Many awards were given as the night wore on, enough for every member of the audience, it seemed. But the most coveted of all were the pink Cadillacs, the well-known symbol of achievement in Mary Kay. Each pink Cadillac winner stepped through an archway at the top of a golden staircase blinking with lights. At the sides of each step leading down to the stage stood men in tuxedos, an honor guard of two dozen Mary Kay Cosmetics executives who did homage to the top sellers.[1] As each woman was escorted down the stairs, music played and the audience roared its approval. Mary Kay Ash herself waited at the bottom holding aloft gold-plated car keys. Clouds of dry-ice vapor rose around the women's feet, creating the sensation that this was a happier world where dreams do come true.

This scene, which took place in July 1986, was staged three more times over a two-week period. Seminar is so popular an affair that 28,000 beauty consultants participated that year, too many to accommodate at a single convention. Rather

126

than turn women away, Mary Kay and her executives do four back-to-back performances, each as enthusiastic as the others. Even though beauty consultants pay their own expenses at Seminar, the glitzy and professionally executed production cost the company more than $5 million.

Mary Kay Cosmetics has a reputation for its skillful orchestration of "recognition ceremonies," including Seminar, but all the network DSOs have similar meetings. Amway has Rallies, Extravaganzas, and Family Reunions. Tupperware hosts an annual Jubilee. Shaklee has an International Convention. Recognition ceremonies are as common among network DSOs as they are infrequent in other types of organizations.

It might be tempting to dismiss these flamboyant meetings as silly parties, as journalistic accounts often do. The meetings are clearly partylike and enjoyable occasions for distributors, but they are not at all silly. Despite appearances, these ceremonies serve dead serious organizational purposes and are as carefully planned and executed as stockholders' and directors' meetings are in other industries. Seminar and Jubilee are occasions for celebrating important organizational values and for defining and acclaiming "success." In companies with living founders, like Mary Kay Cosmetics and Amway, they reinforce the image of the founders as special people and are opportunities for articulating the founders' philosophies. Elaborate meetings like Seminar are one important means by which network DSOs help sustain the commitment of distributors. They are one of an array of control strategies distinctive to direct selling, strategies that make sense only when examined "from the inside," that is, considering the logic of network DSOs.

This chapter is about network DSOs' strategies of control—those practices and arrangements, other than the purely financial incentives of work, that maintain commitment and social order. I argue for the usefulness of Weber's social system typology of charisma in understanding control and commitment strategies. And I argue that network DSOs are best understood as charismatic forms of organization and that the practices and arrangements distinctive to the industry flow from that. Finally, I analyze the three basic means by which social order and commitment are maintained in network

DSOs: creation of a new self, celebration of group member-ship, and becoming a stakeholder in the organization.

ORGANIZATION AND MEANING

All organizations, from corporations and armies to Little League teams and monasteries, seek committed individuals and a regulated social order. Successful organizations develop control strategies that create members who are, Kanter says, "loyal, loving, dedicated, and obedient."[2] In other words, or-ganizations hope to make people want to do what the organi-zation needs done.

Although all organizations need some amount of dedica-tion and order, strategies of control are diverse and reflect their varying purposes, the beliefs they are based on, and of course the interests they serve.

Corporate control strategies include time clocks, stock options, accounting systems, employee picnics, and the cur-rently fashionable executive retreat in the woods. Although diverse, all these controls serve the common purpose of soliciting workers' obedience to and acceptance of organi-zational routines. Sometimes they are designed to motivate work.[3] How can we usefully conceptualize so wide a range of strategies?

Weber asked the same question: "When and why do men obey? Upon what inner justifications and upon what external means does this domination rest?"[4] In questioning the sources of social order, Weber provided a clue to the answer: "inner justifications" and "external means" are the two conceptual categories he used for analyzing obedience in organized set-tings.[5] By inner justifications Weber meant the beliefs, values, and moral codes that appeal to people's emotions and intel-lect, such as the ideological appeals of DSOs discussed in chap-ter 5. By external means he meant organizational arrange-ments such as administrators and the material implements necessary for carrying out orders. In this category he also in-cluded appeals to personal interest, such as material rewards and honor.[6] In essence, Weber argued that control strategies fall into two groups—those that pull on the individual from within, and those that push the individual into complying.

There are many strategies of both types, but managers cannot simply select from a menu of control or commitment mechanisms. To be effective, mechanisms have to "make sense" to participants. Many popularized management formulas, however, advocate some new idea as the solution to gaining employees' dedication (and hence productivity) on the assumption that all organizations are alike. For a while in the early 1980s, for example, American executives were impressed with Japanese management practices and attributed Japan's superior productivity to quality circles, group decision making, and other facets of Japanese organization. American executives attempted to emulate Japan's corporations without regard for the different social system within which those practices were embedded. But what "makes sense" in running a Japanese company may have no meaning, or a different meaning, in an American corporation.

With myriad strategies possible, and recognizing that successful approaches must take account of the type of organization being considered, how can we create an analytic framework that examines diverse strategies of control yet is sensitive to organizational differences?

Probably the best intellectual tool for this task remains Weber's "ideal types" of social order.[7] Weber categorized authority structures into three fundamental types according to the principles of social control or domination they rest on. *Traditional* social orders are based on a belief in custom, "mores sanctified through the unimaginably ancient recognition and habitual orientation to conform."[8] Social action is based on piety toward traditional ways. *Charismatic* social orders are based on belief in an extraordinary leader such as a hero or a prophet—someone worthy of absolute devotion. Charismatic social action is based on a commitment to a cause or mission. Modern organizations are most frequently *legal-rational*, based on impersonal laws or rules. Bureaucratic organizations carry out tasks in conformity to regulations.

Each of these three principles is a set of beliefs about the proper relationships of people in a social system. Each is a justification for why some people should exercise power and others should obey. Members of a social order actively use these principles to gain acceptance—that is, to legitimate organizational arrangements and their actions toward each other. Each type of justification tends toward a characteristic form of organization, a typical structure for carrying out commands and the activities of the system.

Every social structure has, therefore, an authority or organizational structure as well as a related structure of meaning or belief. Both of these contribute to social control: organizational practices are those strategies that exercise control by means external to the individual, and structures of meaning control by getting inside people, by leading them to believe in and embrace the ideas the organization rests on. Both forms of control constrain action in ways that serve organizational ends.

Business organizations in industrial nations are fundamentally bureaucratic (see table 4), although they may display traditional and charismatic elements too.[9] Organizational practices in firms reflect concern with impersonal ideals, such as hiring for expertise and promotion for merit. Firms divide work functionally and hierarchically according to criteria of efficiency and effectiveness. Decisions are based on how they affect profitability, market share, and other economically rational objectives. Although all firms deviate from this characterization, it is at least mostly true or represents a public ideal against which firms style their actions.[10]

Although network direct selling organizations are, like firms, profit-oriented enterprises, the characterization above fits them poorly. They do not differentiate work, except between headquarters and the sales force, and they are not impersonal. They do not recruit people for their skills, and they have no hierarchy of authority. Moreover, they are oriented toward substantive values as well as profits.[11]

Although Weber's model of bureaucracy is not helpful in understanding DSOs, his model of charisma, I believe, helps explain their organizational arrangements, including such practices as Mary Kay's Seminar.

CHARISMA AND ORGANIZATION

In everyday language "charisma" refers to a magnetic personality, an aura of "specialness." In the 1980s Chrysler executive

Lee Iacocca and President Ronald Reagan were widely considered charismatic in this sense.

Weber used the term charisma in a far more restrictive way. Charisma, in his usage, has four distinguishing elements. First, charisma is a "gift of grace" or rare quality that resides in an individual. It is manifest as "supernatural, superhuman, or at least specifically exceptional qualities," an endowment "regarded as of divine origin or as exemplary."[12] According to

Table 4: Bureaucratic and Direct Selling Types of Organization

	Bureaucratic Organization[a]	Direct Selling Organization
Legitimation	Universal rules, laws	Mission: substantive philosophy of founder and belief in moral value of entrepreneurialism
Membership	Bureaucratic officials	Followers
Differentiation	Horizontal differentiation by function; vertical differentiation by expertise	Minimal differentiation of sales work; administration separated and may be differentiated by function
Stratification	Hierarchical distribution of authority, rewards, status	Undifferentiated authority structure joined to status hierarchy; administration may be hierarchical
Recruitment	Universalist appointment based on expertise and experience	Particularist recruitment for commitment potential, affective bonds
Compensation	Financial rewards, especially salary	Combination of material, purposive, and solidary incentives
Character of Tenure	Career	Way of life

[a]Adapted from Max Weber, *Economy and Society*, ed. Guenther Roth and Claus Wittich (Berkeley: University of California Press, 1978), pp. 217–26.

Weber, charismatics include heroes, messiahs, oracles, shamans, and others whom people believe to have a truly extraordinary ability or vision.

How can we identify a true charismatic? The "proof" of charisma, the second critical element, is the presence of a following.[13] If followers recognize the validity of the leader's claim, they have a moral obligation to submit to the leader's direction. People who are convinced of Christ's divinity, for example, have a *duty* to submit to his teachings. Charisma demands, third, that followers assume new selves and become converts or devotees. They must repudiate their former way of being in the world and take on a new orientation consonant with the leader's teachings. When Christians say they are "born again" they refer to the adoption of a new self. Finally, charismatic leaders typically must demonstrate their abilities to followers through miracles, the continued success of a mission, or other proofs.

In charismatic organizations that approach a "pure" or "genuine" type, a leader has a following whose interactions are "based on an emotional form of communal relationship."[14] The leader typically is aided by disciples or devoted aides. There is total concentration on serving the mission, and followers may withdraw from the everyday world, even from their families. They may give up their jobs, their possessions, even their sense of self.

This pure type of charisma is rare indeed, and even where it exists it cannot last long in this form. If they are to endure, charismatic organizations must prepare for the loss of the leader. As Benjamin Zablocki notes, "Charismatic leaders, however revered, get old and die. Others may get worn out in office or get corrupted by the potentially absolute powers of their position."[15] Charismatic orders must also become economically stable and turn from obsession with their mission to the mundane task of securing a livelihood. In fact, many charismatic communities solve neither the problem of succession nor that of economic viability and thus are short-lived.

There are notable successes, however, in the preservation of a charismatic mission. The Roman Catholic church is the archetypal example of the institutionalization, or transformation into organizational routines, of a charismatic social order. To Roman Catholics Christ's successor is the pope, designated by the cardinals, who are themselves in the line of apostolic succession. The Roman Catholic church has established routines that ensure continuity of the religious mission as well as economic stability. Institutionalized charisma integrates stabilizing elements of traditional or bureaucratic organization into a fundamentally charismatic base.[16]

In describing charisma and charismatic organization I have used the example of Jesus Christ and the Roman Catholic church because it is familiar and because it illustrates well Weber's conceptualization.[17] Charisma, however, is not restricted to the religious sphere and appears in many secular settings, usually in less intense forms. Edward Shils claims that charisma is present whenever an individual is understood to be connected with crucial questions of human existence.[18] This may be, but need not be, religion. For example, Nobel Prize winners and astronauts are charismatic in this sense and enjoy the admiration, if not adoration, of millions as they stretch the bounds of human knowledge and experience. Indeed, anytime someone attempts to deal with more than mundane, this-worldly affairs—to address questions of ultimate meaning and the workings of the universe—we have the potential for charisma.

This sort of charisma may attach to an individual, but it can also characterize institutions. Some organizations, because of their extraordinary power to shape the world and bring order out of chaos, have what Shils called "awe-arousing centrality" and Kanter referred to as "institutionalized awe."[19]

Are network direct selling organizations charismatic in the sense Weber described? No, not in the "pure," "genuine," or "intense" form outlined in his ideal type. The eminent Weber scholar Wolfgang Schluchter, however, argues that a "weakened" institutionalized charisma can come about with the transformation of any one, or all, of charisma's four critical elements.[20] For example, the mission espoused by the leader can be dissociated from the person and made part of an organization's crusade. Second, the "duty" to follow a leader can be made a voluntary recognition of the leader's vision. Such recognition, though, is the sign of a follower's enlightened or superior character. Third, the mission can embrace rather than repudiate the economic. In fact, the mission can be *proved* by its commercial success. And finally, the mission may be limited. Followers need not renounce the world or themselves in a totalistic way.

It is in this "weakened" sense that DSOs are charismatic. They have organizational ideologies that are missionary in character. Some, but not all, express the vision of a founding leader. Distributors see themselves as superior to their employed fellow Americans. Being an "entrepreneur," to them, is a morally superior way of being in the economy. They cite economic and ideological success of the organization as proof of the worthiness of leaders' crusades. While DSOs' missions are clearly limited when compared with those of some charismatic cults, they constitute an intense and encompassing experience when compared with other economic organizations. Direct selling organizations display a weakened, institutionalized form of charisma, but they are not weak in any absolute sense. In fact it is DSOs' relatively intense social, ideological, and personal experience, when compared with other forms of work, that appeals to many distributors.

Moreover, DSOs' organizational arrangements echo those of some charismatically based social movements. Typically, though not universally, they have a leader to whom a mass of distributor/followers is oriented. The small bureaucratic headquarters staff is usually there only to aid in sustaining the entrepreneurial mission; it does not direct the field in an authoritative way. Bryan Wilson's description fits network DSOs well:

> The modern charismatic leader displays the expected spontaneity, whimsicality, and unpredictability: but behind him stands not so much a circle of disciples as a trained cadre of officials, whose roles are well defined within a clearly articulated and relatively bureaucratic structure. Their concern is publicity and the projection of the charismatic image.[21]

Maintaining social order and soliciting commitment in direct selling organizations, because of their charismatic character, is very different from the bureaucratic controls used by firms. Firms control workers who have an employment relationship to the organization. Direct selling organizations control workers who are legally independent. DSOs do, however, attempt to make distributors dependent socially, ideologically, and through their sponsorship lines, financially. DSOs' quite different strategies of control flow from their distinctive social relations of work and their basis in charisma.

Although commitment mechanisms in DSOs differ from those in firms, they do resemble in important ways those used by some political groups, personal staffs, and collectivist organizations.[22] Although these groups are not necessarily based on the authority of a charismatic individual (some are), they are all, like network DSOs, mission-oriented social orders and have some measure of institutionalized charisma. Their commitment strategies are oriented toward securing the "inner justification" that flows from belief in the mission's correctness.[23] They employ "external means" that lead followers into accepting the community of believers as the arbiter of social relations.

Network DSOs pursue three strategies of control and commitment.[24] The first, *creation of a new self*, refers to an individual's development of a new social identity in terms of the organization's mission. This form of control is critical to the success of network DSOs. The second, *celebration of group membership*, refers to processes by which relationships within the organization are managed, particularly members' acceptance of the community of believers as the significant decision-making body. This strategy is also important to social control in direct selling. The final strategy, *stakeholder claims*, includes practices designed to promote organizational continuity. Although present in DSOs, stakeholder claims are not as significant as the others. In all, I identified fourteen strategies of control that are important in network direct selling and that substitute for bureaucratic management.[25]

CREATING A NEW SELF

Many organizations attempt to destroy one identity in order to put in place a new one shaped by the organization—for example, to convert a civilian to a soldier or a laywoman to a nun.[26] Fraternities "haze" pledges, and many firms put their new employees through tough training programs designed to make recruits unsure of themselves and willing to accept the firm's direction.[27] Humbling or repudiating the old self, and creating a new and "better" identity based on organizational membership, is also the ostensible purpose of a number of practices in DSOs.

Bureaucratic firms, no less than charismatic organizations, socialize their members. Firms solicit individuals' acceptance by justifying routines as efficient and effective. Charismatic orders, however, appeal as much to recruits' emotions as to any objective standard. According to Weber, charisma "may involve a subjective or internal reorientation born out of suffering, conflicts, or enthusiasm. It may then result in a radical alteration of the central system of attitudes and directions of action with a completely new orientation of all attitudes toward the different problems and structures of the world."[28] It is through enthusiasm and emotion, as much as anything else, that distributors are led to charismatic association.

Self-Transformation

Firms and "total institutions" such as convents and prisons have the opportunity to socialize participants over long uninterrupted periods, not allowing alternative interpretations of events. In DSOs distributors largely work alone and only come together voluntarily for meetings and other events. Distributors are therefore encouraged to *control themselves*.[29] In particular, they are encouraged to dispose of their old ways of thinking and acting and to adopt new ones that will ensure their success as distributors.

Every DSO I studied had distributors committed to positive thinking, a belief that if one imagines success then success will follow, and that failure is the result of poor thought habits.[30] In other words, people are what they think. An Amway distributor described this belief.

> I'm now starting to watch my thoughts. That might sound like a silly thing to do. But how many of those thoughts, if you ask yourself, are what you want? Well, most people think they don't have very much control over it. But I think you can learn how to control it.

The industry's strategy for promoting positive thinking in a solitary setting is to encourage the use of audio tapes and books about how to think one's way to success. My interviews suggest that the consumption of such materials is considerable and widely viewed by distributors as an efficacious, even critical, practice. One woman took me into her bathroom to show me the tape recorder next to her sink. Not wanting to waste time, she listened to tapes while brushing her teeth. Many distributors have a selection of tapes in their cars to use when driving. Here are two typical expressions from my interviews:

> I have a library of tapes. They are coded by "Shaklee," "Avacare," and "General Business Opportunity." If I see any good tapes at all I make them a part of my library, and people check them out. I listen to them myself and try to make them available to my people. I read a lot of motivational books. I'm reading *Think and Grow Rich* for the third time.

> My mind is sharper today because I read strictly motivational books. I listen to that type of tape. I even chose a church that doesn't have a bad attitude, a church that basically has a positive kind of attitude in its religious approach.

Some DSOs, including Amway, even have their own facilities for producing inspiring tape recordings, and they encourage, even push, their purchase.[31] At least one Amway line headed by Dexter Yager distributes its own tape recordings. Members of the Yager line are expected to buy one tape a week and a book on positive thinking every month.[32] Many are sold to the industry by independent suppliers. One manufacturer of tape recordings estimated that inspirational tapes represent $30 million in annual sales, mostly to members of DSOs.

In an industry that cannot legally sanction distributors negatively, the only generally available alternative is to use positive reinforcement and techniques such as positive thinking. This results in an extraordinarily upbeat, enthusiastic form of social relations, something I noted in all the DSOs I observed. Part of maintaining this happy atmosphere is purging negative thought patterns and avoiding persons who might question the possibility of success in direct selling. Two distributors, one from Shaklee and one from Mary Kay, described the norm against negativity, what in Amway is called "stinkin' thinkin'." The first suggests that the norm is more important when success is dependent on moving into action people who are not in a bureaucratic setting:

> Don't mingle with negative people. If you turn negative, then things aren't going to work. Previously, when I read positive thinking books it didn't mean anything. Unless you're involved with people [as in DSOs], it doesn't hold true. If you're just a carpenter or engineer, positive thinking doesn't have as much effect.

> It's discouraged—anything negative. You don't gossip. You don't say bad things about people. If they hear you doing it, or hear about you doing it, you will hear from your director. They want everyone to get along, and they don't want any negativity and problems like that.

Thinking positively and avoiding negativity help people overcome disappointments and doubts about their ability to sell or the worthiness of their work. If they think they can, they can. Conversely, if someone is not successful, blame is placed on the individual's improper attitude, not on the organization.

Confessionals

Many ideologically motivated groups encourage public self-criticism and even subject members to criticism by the group. Humbling the self in this way, especially when someone reveals thoughts or acts opposed to the group's beliefs, becomes a way of purging the impure, weak, or wrongheaded ways of a member and establishing the idea that the group cares about the individual.

A milder form of self-criticism appears to be fairly common in DSOs. Successful distributors are invited to stand up and tell what kind of person they were before they joined the group. Typically they confess to having been shy, having had low self-esteem, or having been confused and lonely, then tell how they were saved by membership in the organization.

At the Mary Kay Seminar I attended, two national sales directors, the highest-level beauty consultant, gave moving speeches before the assembly of thousands, describing their ascent from obscurity and self-doubt. They were both articulate and apparently sincere, making their claimed transformation from unsuccessful and insecure nobodies even more powerful. Indeed, the theme of the 1986 Seminar was "Starting Here, Starting Now," and the meeting featured songs and skits about a young woman looking for a new beginning.

Similarly, the president of another company reads new recruits a children's story about a caterpillar afraid to enter a cocoon. The caterpillar finds the courage through a friend and emerges a beautiful butterfly. According to the executive, "That's our challenge: to make butterflies out of all those little woolly caterpillars out there."[33]

Indeed, there is a strong feeling throughout the industry, expressed by both distributors and executives, that they are as much in the business of "transforming lives" as they are sellers of commodities.

Spiritual Differentiation

Kanter noted in studying utopian groups that many used a stratification system honoring people who best lived up to the ideals of the organization. "Members were distinguished on spiritual or moral grounds, according to how well they exemplified ideal traits of membership or how thoroughly they were committed to the community, with the more spiritual, moral, or zealous members receiving greater deference."[34]

Network DSOs all have status hierarchies, some more elaborate than others. As distributors achieve more success in the organization, they receive new titles and usually material rewards for their efforts. They are also subject to ritualized deference for their greater display of the "entrepreneurial spirit." For example, in Shaklee, where success at a certain level is rewarded with the use of a car for two years, the number of Shaklee cars a distributor has had is a measure of honor; the type of car is a further indication of status. I attended one meeting where distributors who had received their first cars were invited to stand up, be recognized, and describe their cars. Then people who had had two cars stood to be applauded, and so on. When the last person stood, a woman who had earned seven cars, she was given a standing ovation. Mary Kay unit meetings sometimes award gold beads and ribbons based on the level of weekly sales. Awards are made in reverse order, with the "lowest" given first.[35]

Meetings are also a time to display status differences. High-level distributors are sometimes invited to sit onstage with a visiting founder or to eat meals apart from other distributors. A status hierarchy, where it exists separate from a hierarchy of authority, signals that while everyone is formally equal, some have achieved higher "spiritual" levels. People who are separated are honored, and the rest are reminded of their inferior status.

Organizational status differences also provide direction for aspirations, beyond the general admonition to sell or recruit more. Distributors calculate exactly what they have to do to climb another rank.

Critical to these status ranks is that status is granted *only* in terms of the organization's ideals. One's occupational status outside the DSO, high or low, has no bearing on one's rank within. One's extraorganizational identity is irrelevant and invisible, allowing people of low status on the outside to realistically aspire to high status within the DSO. Distributors start their social climb all over when they become direct sellers. One Amway distributor spoke of his incredulity at the type of people who are given deference.

> It still gives me goose bumps just to think about how a person could come in with no experience in business or sales [and succeed]. I've listened to chicken farmers—I mean *chicken farmers*—the guys don't have any teeth. They can't speak with any etiquette at all, and they get up on the stage and they're crown direct distributors. And they say, "Ah, hell, me and Mabel, we just decided we needed some money one day." And they're multimillionaires. Really, I mean *seriously*.

Direct selling organizations differentiate not at all by intelligence, objective measures of skill, experience, or credentials, the type of traits rewarded by firms. They honor only success in the organization's terms. Whoever distributors may be in the outside world, they are "born again" in direct selling.

If self-control, confessions, and a status hierarchy of the "entrepreneurially spirited" serve to denigrate or deny one's former or extraorganizational self, then the following strategies help the distributor fashion a new identity positively associated with the DSO.

Institutionalized Ideology

Charismatic orders aid the individual in identifying with something higher than self, a larger vision that gives meaning and direction to life. In DSOs this vision is embodied in part in the organization's mission or ideology. As I discussed in chapter 5, the ideology of the "American ethic" is consonant with the values and predispositions of people in this country and serves as an important attraction for recruits. Ideology, though, is also a mechanism for creating a new communitarian persona: the ideology of the leader becomes diffused throughout the group of distributors:

> Merely by virtue of their participation in the system, members could partake of its special fund of qualities. In a sense, this is a charisma of belonging, for all members gained a measure of charisma just by being members, and the degree of awe surrounding the system was correspondingly enhanced by virtue of the fact that only a great and powerful system could distribute some of its magic to ordinary members.[36]

Many distributors express pleasure in being associated with what they perceive as an important moral enterprise, not just a profit-making business. This association helps them create a "better" self, someone identified with an elevated purpose. Membership is a way of declaring not only what they believe, but who they are.

Leadership

While ideology may be diffused thoughout a charismatic membership, the presence of a leader creates an ideological focus. DSO leaders such as Mary Kay Ash, Art Williams, Rich DeVos, and Jay Van Andel concentrate the charismatic impulse in their persons. This serves at least three functions in network DSOs.

First, by their (to members) special qualities, leaders justify the commitment asked of distributors. The expressions of awe and reverence that these and other DSO leaders elicit are, to an outsider, extraordinary. It is hard to imagine that there are many other business leaders, including "charismatic" individuals such as Lee Iacocca, who inspire such devotion.[37] For example:

> Art Williams is my hero. I haven't told you that yet, but he's absolutely my hero. Never lied, never been out of integrity with me, and he sets the example. He just keeps setting it, and so there's no question I look up to him in every area of life.

> When I got into the business and people would talk about [Amway founder] Rich DeVos I would go, "Oh, my God, they talk about him like he's God or something."

> [Shaklee was] a remarkable man. He was far ahead of his time. He developed Vita-Lite minerals, the first product, a year before the word "vitamin" was even coined. He's [had] a special place in my heart.

> Meeting Mary Kay was quite an experience. You could just feel the power. It was a very unusual experience. You can feel the powerful vibes and charisma.

Some expressions even suggested the leader's "miraculous" powers.

> [Shaklee] demonstrated [belief] when he got X-ray burns and they were going to amputate his hip and his arm and he said, "No, I'd rather die a whole man." And it took him three years, but he recovered. Well, you've got to believe then.

Second, not only are these special leaders worthy of devotion because of their extraordinary qualities, they provide a "center" to far-flung organizations, a place for the community to anchor its emotions. Distributors frequently express affection for their leaders, even if they know them only from afar.

> Mary Kay is just fabulous. She is so much fun. As soon as you're around her you just feel charged up. She makes you feel fabulous. She's real kind and warm and always gives you so much encouragement. I've gotten up real close to her and talked to her.

> Even watching [Mary Kay] on TV is real hard for me. I just get this knot in my stomach whenever I see her or listen to her talk or anything.

For her part, Mary Kay Ash acts in a caring and nurturing way toward the women in her organization, treating them as people worthy of her attentions. She sends them cards on their birthdays and on their anniversaries in the organization. She replies personally to letters from any of the more than 150,000 beauty consultants. Whenever she hears of illness or personal suffering, she expresses concern, according to the beauty consultants. At the 1986 Seminar she told the assembly she was worried about their health and asked every woman present, as a favor to her, to learn how to do a breast self-examination to fight cancer, their common enemy. An instructional film on the technique ran continuously during the convention. Such practices create the sensation of a direct and personal relationship between leader and follower.

Perhaps the most important function of a leader in DSOs, however, is as an exemplar. All the early founders started as "ordinary" people who achieved great success by following an entrepreneurial ideology.[38] Each is "proof" that direct selling can propel an average person to great financial and moral heights. The biographies of these leaders are rags-to-riches stories about how they, through proper outlook and hard work, became successful.

Top distributors serve as exemplars too—what Weber called "virtuosi."[39] By their great success in following the leader's vision, they are living proof of the mission's value. These top exemplars are also bearers of charismatic authority. As one of Mary Kay's national sales directors put it, "To them I am Mary Kay. I would do anything she would do."

Network DSOs face the problem of all organizations that are founded on the person of a leader: the problem of succession on death or retirement. Many charismatic organizations do not survive the loss of their leaders; those that hope to must lay plans for the routinization of charisma.

Because most large network DSOs were founded in the 1950s and 1960s, a generation of founders is passing on, pressing the industry to consider succession strategies.

For example, Mary Crowley and Forrest Shaklee died in the mid-1980s, and Mary Kay Ash speaks publicly of her eventual death.

Two strategies, both described by Weber, seem to be emerging in network DSOs.[40] The first is the leader's designation of a successor. In Mary Kay Cosmetics the national sales directors are assuming the role. An executive in the company described the process.

> She has prepared the organization for her not being here forever. She has developed the national sales directors and tried to develop in them philosophies that parallel her own. There are fifty-nine of these ladies who are remarkable human beings that I think, by and large, reflect all that is good about Mary Kay Ash. So should she elect no longer to have an active part in the company, I don't think the company at that point suffers. It might have years ago when it was a fledgling company and it took so much of her own personal presence and energy to get it going.

In fact, my interviews suggest that the strategy is proving acceptable to the sales force. For example:

> At first I was worried about [when Mary Kay's gone], thinking the company's all going to fall apart when she dies. But it never, never will. Because when you go to Seminar you can see what a great role the national sales directors play in the company. So you know that it will go on. [Mary Kay told us], "Now when I go, you all don't sit down and weep. You go out and hold a ten-show week."

The second strategy of charismatic routinization is heredity, to invest the mission in one's children. This is a strategy that has been pursued, at least in part, by Shaklee Corporation and Amway.[41] Both companies have invited the founders' children to play visible roles. Mary Kay Ash's son Richard Rogers, who founded the company with her but originally served in an "inside" administrative position, is, some members say, being groomed to assume some of the emotional functions of leadership. As one woman put it, "Her son has become kind of an endearing—or endeared—figure. She may be doing that on purpose. I assume so."

The children of both Amway founders have taken active roles in the company, but Amway is also pursuing a "depersonalization" strategy. Executives are modifying some of the original ideological zeal and repositioning the company as a powerful distribution network. This transformation, however, is being pursued neither wholeheartedly nor uniformly, according to one observer.

Although Shaklee's two sons have been active in the corporation, serving on the board of directors and making public appearances, neither ever ran the company. When Shaklee retired a series of professional managers assumed control. Gary Shansby took over in the mid-1970s, first as a consultant, then as chief executive officer. He was the first CEO to attempt to shape the company in important ways, and as one person put it, Shansby displayed "an ego as big as the world." The distributors watched him carefully to see if so self-assured a man would subordinate himself to Forrest Shaklee's philosophy.

Shansby instituted a number of "rational" product and marketing changes, such as reformulating products and introducing nonnutritional items like cosmetics. Some changes infuriated distributors who believed that Shansby, an outsider, was violating Shaklee's principles. One distributor told me that when several of them were having their picture taken with the newly appointed Shansby and his new management team, they asked the managers to stand at the ends of the group. If Shansby did not learn to embrace Shaklee's principles, the distributors planned to cut him and his aides off the ends of the photograph.

Ironically, some of the changes Shansby initiated made the products more natural. Product labeling requirements became more stringent in the 1970s, and Shansby ordered the removal of mineral oil and chemical preservatives from some of the founder's original formulations. The changes reduced the shelf life and altered the consistency of some products, causing outrage among the distributors. They blamed the upstart for "ruining" Shaklee's creations. The company was faced with the unhappy choice of revealing that the founder was not the purist the sales force believed or restoring the nonnatural ingredients.

The company sent a public relations official out into the

field for "probably six or seven months straight to try to calm people down," according to one observer. The company "did some waffling" and explained that the formulations had changed over the years. The new products were the *true* expression of the original ideology, not the ones they had been selling. The incident made Shansby realize that he had to subordinate himself and his ideas to the founder's vision, not follow some abstract notion of what was rational.

Is having a charismatic leader critical to running a network DSO? It appears to be an important but not essential ingredient in ensuring success. Tupperware, for instance, is a large and prosperous network DSO that grew without the presence of a sales force leader. Earl Tupper developed the plastic Tupperware is made of and the special seal. After attempting to sell the products through retail outlets, Tupper decided that the containers benefited from personal demonstration. In the early 1950s he invited Brownie Wise, like Mary Kay Ash and Mary Crowley a successful and dynamic Stanley Home Products distributor, to head a direct sales company. Wise was reportedly very successful but developed, as one observer said, "a big head." She clashed with Tupper, who fired her. Wise attempted to regain personal control of "her" organization by establishing a rival DSO. Because distributors were legally independent but emotionally tied to her, this was a feasible strategy.[42]

The confrontation came during the annual Jubilee when the distributors were assembled en masse. Wise took out a full-page advertisement in the local paper inviting the Tupperware dealers to join her in a new organization. The president of Tupperware bought a thousand copies of the paper and placed one on each chair in the auditorium. When the distributors arrived that day for Jubilee, he asked them to turn to Wise's advertisement.

According to a former Tupperware executive, "He said, 'Anyone who wants to join Brownie can leave right now.' Not a soul moved. What happened there was the birth of the unity of that company as an organization. [Adversity] in Tupperware coalesced the company, and it never looked back."

This emotional moment, a mass declaration of loyalty to the company, may in fact have served as an important unifying force during Tupperware's early period of growth, and it may have substituted for a leadership figure. But Tupperware is qualitatively different from the other network DSOs I examined. It is more concerned with relationships at the local level, and none of the distributors I interviewed knew anything about Earl Tupper. It also has more "legalistic" relations than any of the other organizations I became familiar with.[43]

While a charismatic leader may not be an essential ingredient in network DSOs, it may be a "natural" outcome of this form of organization—or as Weber scholars often put it, there may be an "affinity" for such a leader. For example, I asked the president of one fast-growing company that sells children's products if she felt the need to play the same role Mary Kay Ash plays. She denied that she chose to be a charismatic figure but claimed that her distributors "have pushed me into it."

Moreover, with time and experience, knowledgeable industry observers have realized how important a leader can be in creating commitment and social order. The vice-president of a newly established cosmetics company said she and her fellow executives discussed whether to have such a leader. "Charisma" became, in this company, a business decision. (They decided that, because they had no obvious candidate, they would forgo the attempt.)

Guidance

A charismatic group may help a new recruit learn appropriate behavioral norms by giving directions for even the most insignificant actions. Guidance "reinforces the role of the organization as an order-creating power," Kanter says, and limits the decision-making autonomy of the individual.[44] In DSOs, for example, new recruits are often urged to do a certain number of parties or demonstrations of the business opportunity in a limited period because that's what "winners" do. Although these urgings are not orders, they are backed with peer pressure.

There is also a strong norm to follow to the word the companies' suggested sales talks, which are given in detail in training manuals. Again, because distributors are "independent" the suggestion has no legal force, but the social pressure is strong. One distributor described her experience.

> If you're around successful people I think it rubs off on you. The way they act, the way they dress, things like that. In a lot of the training they actually give you the words to say. They say, "If you don't feel comfortable doing this, stand in front of a mirror and do it until it feels comfortable, because we've found that this works."

Conformity serves the organization in two ways. First, sales talks learned by rote probably ensure some minimum of competence in selling products. Second, such conformity creates uniformity and order in a sales force removed from bureaucratic direction.

The upline plays an important role in "guiding" distributors. Sponsors and high-status distributors direct by example, and in some instances they demand obedience "on faith." Steven Butterfield, a disaffected Amway distributor, described his experience with guidance:

> Even if new people that I worked hard to bring in start quitting after they get visits and phone calls from zealous leaders, I should not question or disagree with what they do, but have complete confidence in my upline's judgment. Those who quit because they get too much pressure to buy tapes or attend functions would have quit anyway, and I am better off without them. Some actions of my Direct [a status level] may puzzle me at first, but I must believe that he would never do anything harmful to my business. . . . He must know what he is doing; he is the expert and I am the novice. Whenever I have doubts, I should plug in a tape and listen to it before I go to bed. . . . Dexter [Yager] is the final authority, not only for how to build "my" business, but for all the major decisions in my life.[45]

Butterfield's reported experience was more extreme than any my informants described, but the importance of unreasoned faith in the upline was not uncommonly expressed. The upline's success, their being filled with the "spirit," gave them charismatic authority.[46]

In some DSOs, including Amway and Shaklee, the upline is also the source of bonus money. Each level in the line pays each level below it. This creates a regular opportunity for the upline to make contact with downline distributors and praise or encourage. This form of payment and control is reminiscent

of internal subcontracting and other forms of worker coman-
agement practiced by factory owners in nineteenth-century
England and America. The upline's payment of money recalls
Stephen Hill's description of the "skilled men [who] hired their
own helpers and paid them out of their own wages."[47]

CELEBRATION OF GROUP MEMBERSHIP

Charismatic orders often attempt to control members' relationships outside the group, eliminating or limiting those that
compete with group cohesion. In extreme cases all contact
with the outside world is renounced. For example, utopian
communities often prohibited contact with noncommunitari-
ans. Even today, in the midst of individualist and romantic
American culture, devout religious groups have strong norms
against marrying outsiders who may threaten devotion to the
group's way of life. Similarly, priestly orders often require celi-
bacy of their members, claiming that family and sexual ties
interfere with serving the religious mission. Renunciation,
when it occurs in network DSOs, is not nearly so stringent, for
economic as well as organizational reasons. Far more important is the creation of community, a substitute for extraorganizational social relations.

Institutional Completeness
There are several ways to limit contact with people outside a
social group. Physical boundaries such as high walls, geographic isolation, and social distance caused by, for example
racial differences are examples.[48] None of these are employed
by DSOs, for good reason: it is critical to the economic success
of the mission that distributors mingle with the public, because that is the source of sales and recruits.

At the same time, some DSOs practice a form of what
Arthur Stinchcombe calls "institutional completeness"—providing for all the needs of members, making outside contacts
unnecessary.[49] In direct selling, institutional completeness ex-
tends only to social relationships, but for committed members
it is clear that their emotional and social lives are lived with
other distributors. They meet with each other regularly, may
vacation together at DSO-owned resorts, and in other ways

function as a community. An Amway distributor spoke about how intraorganizational ties develop:

> While you're moving up [the status hierarchy] it's just fantastic. After you're there you really start to feel good because people care about each other. A circle just sort of grows, and you begin to do things with the people that are involved in it.

The frequent use of positive reinforcement to motivate action is especially powerful for people who may hear little appreciation outside DSOs, whether at work in a firm or from their families. Enthusiastic acceptance and praise draw the individual closer to the community.

> People that are actively doing the business are involved and they are involved with a lot of people. They attend a lot of meetings. They go to a lot of seminars. And they're constantly getting "good" forced on them, presented boom, boom, boom, positive, positive, positive.

An important source of institutional completeness in DSOs is the integration into the group of distributors' families, even in organizations where only the women sell, as I discussed in chapter 4.

Compartmentalization

While at one level distributors are urged to see themselves as part of a larger enterprise, their relationships in the organization may in fact be channeled or compartmentalized. As Kanter noted, "Seeking renunciation, a community discourages relationships both outside the group and with internal subunits, in order to provide maximum strength to the entire system."[50] Keeping intimate contact within units or lines ensures that the distributor has the opportunity to develop intense ties.[51] For example, the four Seminars held by Mary Kay Cosmetics are organized by units, not by the geographic residence of beauty consultants. Women can see "their" directors receive awards and travel with women who are organizationally related in the larger sisterhood.

Also, in some Amway lines there is a prohibition against "crosslining." Crosslines are people who are on different "legs" or branches of a genealogy. Although they all descend from the same upline, they are "cousins" rather than "siblings." Cross-slining refers to associations across legs, discouraged in Amway lines that press distributors to look only to their own upline for guidance. It may also limit the spread of "negativity" if it infects one leg of distributors, who begin to fall away.

Institutional completeness and compartmentalization work to limit and channel the social relations of distributors. The following strategies help the individual find a sense of unity or "groupness" within the community of distributors.

Homogeneity

Homogeneity works to ensure that there is a basis for relations within the organization, that people associate with others like themselves. Although the composition of direct selling organizations is racially, educationally, and in other ways mixed and headquarters officials are often social worlds apart from the sales force, distributors' lines or units reflect their social networks: distributors recruit their friends, relatives, and others with whom they come in social contact.

Homogeneity in the social composition of lines is a basis for community over which the headquarters staff does not exercise control. It merely happens as a consequence of recruitment within social networks. For example, the president of one DSO, a white businessman working from a New York City office, found to his surprise that within a few years many of his distributors were black women in California.[52]

Common Efforts

Shared work creates a sense of involvement with the group and a stake in its well-being. Some DSOs reward unit or line efforts as well as individual selling and recruiting. Team awards are both a way of increasing productivity, like all awards, and a way of developing commitment to the group. As one woman put it, "When you're trying to help the rest of your team, you have a tendency to work harder than if it's just for yourself."

Mary Kay's pink Cadillacs and pink Buick Regals are awards given to directors whose units achieve high productivity levels; they can be won only through group efforts. Although only the director gets possession of the car, beauty consultants consider it a mark of prestige to be in a "pink car unit" and work hard to help the director earn one.

Regularized Group Contact

Every time a distributor meets with members of the organization it is a reminder of membership, an opportunity to share common problems as well as to receive praise for successes. A common expression is, "If you had a bad week, you need us; if you had a good week, we need you."

Because DSOs have no fixed place of work where face-to-face relations occur in the course of doing business, regular meetings in homes and public meeting rooms are critical to sustaining a sense of community. Active distributors usually attend at least one meeting a week with close members of their line and one larger regional meeting a month. The pressure to attend meetings is great, and attendance is generally viewed as a sign of commitment and proper outlook. Conversely, failure to attend causes concern within the group. One person told me that if a distributor misses one meeting "she's sick; if she misses two, she's dying; if she misses three, she's dead" and written off by the group.

Meetings are typically occasions for sharing information on new products, giving recognition for weekly sales performance, and introducing guests to the organization. In some organizations, including Tupperware and Mary Kay, they provide an opportunity to sing company songs such as "I've Got That Mary Kay Enthusiasm" and otherwise celebrate unity.

Although distributors admitted there was great pressure to attend meetings, most expressed pleasure at going. One Tupperware dealer, for example, said, "Rally is every Monday morning. I wouldn't miss it. I'd kill to go to Rally." Meetings become an important social occasion as well as a business function for many. Some women said meetings were precious personal time away from family and household responsibilities. Organizationally, Kanter notes, routine meetings "bring together the entire collectivity and reinforce its existence and meaning, regardless of the purpose of the gathering."[53]

Ritual

Perhaps the most publicly distinctive feature of network DSOs as compared with firms is the frequency and importance of ritual. Rituals are social occasions noted primarily for their symbolic, rather than utilitarian, purposes. They are a way of affirming the beliefs of the group and, when they become regularized, of attesting the continuity of the group's way of life and ideological commitment. Firms have ritual observances, such as retirement dinners, but they generally do not have the frequency or importance of ritual practice in direct selling.

DSOs have rites of passage when distributors achieve new status ranks. For example, Mary Kay Ash invests new directors by administering a public oath. New Amway direct distributors are flown to headquarters to meet the founders and be recognized by the staff. A Tupperware dealer described their ceremony for investing a new manager:

> When a person becomes a manager they have this ceremony. It's the neatest thing—I'm about ready to cry during the whole thing—because these people stand up on the stage, the managers. And each manager has a flower for the new manager. Then they go along and hug her into the distributorship. So she ends up with a big bouquet. That's when she gets her car and they hand her the keys.

Distributors have noted the difference between status mobility in a firm, where it rarely brings so much as a handshake, and in direct selling, where it is subject to community recognition.

Recognition ceremonies are frequent and important in direct selling. Anytime distributors achieve a productivity goal of any importance they are publicly praised and awarded gifts of both monetary and symbolic value. Amway, for instance, has an "Inner Circle" award for sponsoring recruits early in one's affiliation with the company. It is a public sign of having a winning attitude, of being someone to watch. Mary Kay has a coveted Bumble Bee award. Company lore says that according to the laws of aerodynamics the bumblebee should not be able to fly: its body is too big for its wings. In fact, it does fly. The award symbolizes the possibility of achievement in the face of great odds. Tupperware gives awards of gifts for the home, consonant with its philosophy of caring for the family.

That awards are given frequently and for even small achievements does not seem to dampen distributors' enthusiasm for receiving them.

I brought the most guests to a meeting in one month. I got the bracelet for that. I won a ring for doing an order. It's a replica of Princess Di's engagement ring. It's nice even if it's not something big. It gives you a good feeling because you're getting rewarded for something you did, and most companies don't do that. They just say, "Oh?" and don't even recognize what you do sometimes.

Although some awards are materially valuable, distributors spoke of what they represented as being even more important. Some are so proud of their achievements that they wear dozens of jewelry awards on banners, like scouting badges or military decorations. To an outsider they seem like excessive displays, but not to a member of the community.

When we women get excited over getting a star, it's not what you get, it's the idea of accomplishment. You get to wear as many of your decorations of honor [as you like. It's as though] you were in the war and everybody knows what you've achieved.

Executives in the industry are sophisticated about the symbolic value of recognition awards. They give items of jewelry and other merchandise, rather than cash, because the items continually remind the distributor of the company. Cash awards are invisible and can be spent by spouses.

Annual meetings such as Seminar, Jubilee, and Shaklee's International Convention are important occasions for ritual observance. The founder, the organizational philosophy, and the community itself are held up for devoted expressions. They are also powerful occasions of mass emotional release.[54]

STAKEHOLDER CLAIMS

While communitarian mechanisms channel individuals into finding satisfaction within the group, stakeholder strategies work to ensure continued commitment.

Sacrifice

In some charismatic orders individuals are asked to give up property to the community, to work without remuneration, or in some other way to commit personal resources to the group. Such sacrifices make membership more valuable because it "costs" more, and people who have "paid a price" are less willing to abandon the group. It is also a sign of trust in the community.[55]

In direct selling the financial investment is purposely kept modest to encourage as many people as possible to join. There is a widespread ethic of sacrifice of oneself to others, however. Distributors are expected to aid other people in their climb to success without regard for their own financial reward. For example, they are expected to lend each other products and to assist each other in improving selling and recruiting techniques. Although sponsors and uplines may be financially rewarded for assistance to the downline, the ethic is in force even when there is no possibility of financial gain, although this varies by organization and by line. In Mary Kay, where the ethic is strong, there is even an award for selfless work on behalf of others, the prestigious Miss Go-Give award. It is typically won by a woman who assists beauty consultants who have moved to her area but are in other directors' units and who therefore receives no remuneration for her work.

Investment

Like sacrifice, investment speaks to committing resources to the community, resources that would be lost if membership were discontinued. After someone achieves a modest level of success, investment becomes a critical factor in sustaining commitment in network DSOs. A distributor who drops out loses all future financial rewards from downline members. When someone leaves the line "shortens," and the financial rewards go to the new, closer upline relations. Customers who have been courted and recruits who have been sponsored are "sunk costs" of past efforts.

There are social costs of leaving, too. Although most people are attracted to network DSOs as a money-making opportunity, for many the social and communal benefits become even more important with time. Network DSOs, if they are successful, create an emotional life: a commitment to ideology, a new self, and new friends. Leaving selling, to a devotee, means more than leaving a job.[56] The threat of losing one's emotional set can help sustain one's flagging commitment to selling. Perhaps more important, one's status level in direct selling is recognized only within the DSO, not even across DSOs. A physician may leave a medical practice to join another with status intact, but a distributor who quits leaves behind the status rewards of a mobility climb.

DO THE CONTROLS WORK?

Control strategies in direct selling have two obvious advantages. First, to distributors they hardly seem like controls. What a sociologist sees as "controlling" is to a distributor an expression of belief and enthusiasm. While working toward fostering entrepreneurial community, these controls seem to spring from genuine caring and joy in pursuing a joint undertaking. In fact, I have no doubt that most distributors do not experience these commitment mechanisms as manipulative.[57] Indeed, many distributors compared what they saw as oppressive bureaucratic settings with the relative freedom they find in direct selling. Some DSOs, including Amway and United Sciences of America, make this an explicit point in recruitment.

The second advantage of these controls is their low cost to management. For the most part, distributors control themselves and each other. As one executive told me:

> The field should manage itself, it really should. We never get involved in recruiting; the sales force recruits its own. It has a large part in training its own, and it tends to pretty much operate as a totally separate field. If it were not for [annual meetings], a great many of these people [in the corporate offices] would never see anyone from the field. They don't even come to these offices to get products.

The tiny, in comparison with those of firms, headquarters staffs are possible when managers have only modest supervision tasks to perform.

The trade-off, however, is the lesser effectiveness of DSO controls. In particular, the motivation of a salary is absent in direct selling and is an important factor in high turnover levels, which probably average no less than 100% a year.[58] With some exceptions, the industry has done well in recessions and less well during economic recoveries. Although many people may enjoy working under the conditions offered by DSOs, they apparently also enjoy the security of salaried and wage labor when given a choice.[59]

Moreover, many direct selling controls solicit commitment to the sponsorship line, not only to the headquarters and the founders. Powerful and independent upline sponsors can challenge the control of a founder. Amway reportedly has faced this difficulty with lines that represent hundreds of millions of dollars in annual sales. Distributors said that at some "family reunions" the logo of an upline "jewel" is displayed and mention of Amway is secondary or even absent.

Network DSOs have responded in at least three ways to the challenge of bolstering controls. First, some direct selling organizations are attacking the notion that employed labor is secure. They have been aided by widespread reports of layoffs in core industries and in middle management. Several women told me they felt more secure working for themselves, where they cannot be fired or laid off. The industry is just beginning to emphasize the "insurance policy" of having at least one spouse start a direct selling business "just in case" the primary wage earner is laid off or fired.

Second, at least one DSO is instituting "voluntary controls." In effect, it invites distributors to *submit themselves* to the type of bureaucratic controls used by firm sales forces. The president of this company spoke about his effort:

> They're independent, so how do you control? We ask them to volunteer to be controlled. Think about that. We have a program we call a task force program. To be on it, they must volunteer, and what they're volunteering to do is be controlled. They're volunteering to put on so many shows, they're volunteering to sponsor so many new people. For that they get extra money and they can earn an extra $100 to $1000 a month by being on this voluntary control program.[60]

The third strategy being pursued by the industry is to make direct selling more explicitly career oriented. For example, Mary Kay has started a "VIP" program that rewards steady midlevel production. An executive described the company's strategy:

The VIP program awards the use of [a beige] car, and probably the individual can comfortably make $15,000 a year. That is an opportunity tailored to an upscale woman who perhaps has some other kind of career, maybe she is a teacher or nurse. . . . [If she succeeds at that level she can] go on and run a directorship of her own. She can make that next jump to $30,000 to $50,000 range, but we need a lot of women in that midrange group who see that this is a career opportunity. They are getting not only the financial rewards but the other psychological rewards [of direct selling].

Making distributors more "professional"—by giving them sophisticated sales training directed by the headquarters and by emphasizing a steady income for fewer people as opposed to pin money for many—poses a threat as well as offering a promise: companies risk alienating their usual source of recruits. This same executive described the dilemma:

You make them more professional. You make them more oriented to career as opposed to our more traditional hoopla. This is where I have run into conflict with myself, you see, because I am very comfortable with rewarding people with pink Cadillacs, with our meetings, with all the stuff that goes on. I see that that works, and it is going to take a lot for me to change much of that. . . . The hoopla, I honestly believe that some of that must change, but I can't bring myself to figure out what that is just yet.

The industry faces the choice of becoming more like firms—recruiting for expertise, instituting more controls at the top, having more sedate and businesslike gatherings—and perhaps gaining a measure of stability. In becoming more like other business organizations, though, network DSOs risk losing the appeal that makes them an attractive alternative to employment for many—the emotional and missionary character that is distinctive to direct selling.

CHARISMA AND ECONOMY

Modern business management is based on rationally calculating risk and organizing in a methodical manner to achieve profit. Indeed, it is the systematic and impersonal orientation to economic matters that distinguishes modern capitalism from earlier economic forms. It was the historical emergence of a routine approach to gaining a livelihood, an approach that we take for granted today, that fascinated Weber and provided the basis for much of his scholarship.

Economic rationalism, while predominant now, is not the only form of economic action even today. Weber briefly discussed "irrational" forms of economizing that involve great risk, both financial and personal, in the pursuit of gain. (By "irrational" he meant not subject to methodical pursuit or calculus.) For example, Weber associated "booty" or "adventure" capitalism with charisma, as Bendix reminds us: "Colonial exploitation, risky financial transactions, private financing of military ventures, and slave trade or piracy are all forms of 'booty capitalism,' in which the stakes are enormous and success frequently depends upon the spellbinding leadership of some individual."[61] This type of capitalism differs from bourgeois capitalism in the amount of risk involved (which may include life and limb), the futility of applying rational analytic techniques to highly uncertain settings, and the repudiation of a systematic, mundane approach to life. Nor does adventure capitalism require the individual to "subordinate personal desires and happiness to the demands of routine." Rather, "it is a form of action that gives full rein to one's personal ambitions."[62] Although direct selling does not entail much risk, it certainly gives full rein to ambition, and people are often driven by dreams of riches. It also lifts economic pursuit from the mundane into the moral and emotional realms.

Although an unemotional economic rationalism dominates the American economy, it does so in tension with other important strains of American culture. American workers, like those in other industrialized societies, subjugate personal impulse to corporate necessity. They do so, however, in a society that highly values individual success. Direct selling is a way for many Americans to resolve the tension between a routinized work life and the desire to pursue economic individualism.[63]

CHAPTER SEVEN
Economic Uses
of Social Relations

In the 1930s the direct selling industry faced a critical dilemma: they could be relieved of the burdens of a costly employment relation and lose supervisory control over their work force, or they could maintain a controlling employment relation and assume the financial obligations that were attaching to employers. The far-flung nature of the DSO work force, and the part-time and inefficient character of direct selling, gave industry leaders little choice. Eventually all but one of the DSOs decided to treat their workers as independent contractors. DSOs were no longer employers able to supervise the selling activities of the people on whom their profits rested. They could suggest, inspire, and solicit work, but they could not require it.

How could they get people to work with neither the carrot of a salary nor the stick of supervision? Barred from the bureaucratic and directive practices of the developing discipline of sales force management, the industry was forced to introduce new, legal strategies of control or face oblivion. Companies that survived the control crisis—network DSOs and to a lesser extent other forms of direct selling—responded to the challenge by becoming social engineers and pursuing two types of social control.[1] First, they created a new type of economic actor, an "independent entrepreneur" committed to selling their products. Second, they manipulated the social bonds of distributors to favor commercial ends. They appropriated existing social networks in support of selling and created conditions that favored the formation of new social networks among distributors. These social engineering strategies substituted for bureaucratic management. The strategies were successful because industry executives came to under-

160

stand the economic utility of manipulating Americans' social relations and aspirations at a historically propitious moment.

In this chapter I make three points about the relation of social structure to economic action in direct selling. First, I argue that although "self-control" and "network controls" are economically rational strategies for pursuing profit, they work *through* social conditions and institutions, not in spite of them. The effectiveness of self-controls rests, at least in part, on the cultural value Americans place on entrepreneurialism. Social network controls are effective because of people's perceived and experienced conditions of work. Distributors are willing to submit to network controls because they are more acceptable than rational-bureaucratic alternatives. Institutionalized beliefs and relations are critical supports of direct selling organizations.

Second, I argue that though these forms of "soft control" have been raised by necessity to a managerial art in direct selling, there is evidence that the personalistic strategies of self-control and social network control are being pursued in firms as well. The experience of the direct selling industry suggests that less rational forms of control may in fact be more economically rational for some types of work and for some types of workers.

Third, I consider the necessary institutional bases for the direct selling form of organization. Brief evidence from other market economies suggests that social structural conditions are critical factors in the success of the DSO. I consider why DSOs are doing poorly in Europe but are spreading rapidly in Asia.

THE SOCIAL BASES
OF CONTROL IN DSOs

When Frederick Winslow Taylor established the first systematic strategy for controlling workers at the turn of the century, he began with two assumptions: that workers were motivated only by money, and that workers should be dealt with as individuals.[2] The right pay formula and a job suited to an individual's abilities were the critical elements for productive work. Although Taylor's ideas are still very much with us and are represented in the academic discipline of economics, his formula has been modified in practice in the decades since. Most notably, industrial psychologists have argued that people have social as well as economic needs and that employers would do well to acknowledge the influence, for example, of the work group on productivity. Social psychologists have pointed out that groups of employees develop solidarity that can help or hinder performance.[3]

Although recognizing the importance of noneconomic social factors, industrial psychology has largely proceeded from the point of view of the individual: What motivates a person to work? How does a worker's need for achievement influence behavior on the job? What attributes make a good work-group leader? How can we structure a job to satisfy a person's needs?[4]

Unknown to themselves, direct selling executives developed a control strategy based on neither an economic nor a psychological model. They pursued a *sociological* strategy, one that assumed economic actors are not born but *made* by the social structure in which they are placed, and one that recognized the power of even social relations outside the workplace to motivate economic action.[5]

The Social Construction
of an Economic Actor

DSOs recruit people who want to make money, but they must compete with salary-paying employers in satisfying workers' financial needs. Unable to give a paycheck, DSOs offer distributors something employers cannot give: a socially valued, independent status. They turn housewives and truck drivers into "entrepreneurs." They make teachers and secretaries "businesspeople." This transformation yields two things: a new persona dependent on the organization for its maintenance, and a self-managing worker driven to achieve entrepreneurial success.

The industry could pursue this strategy only because being an entrepreneur is widely valued in American culture. Direct selling organizations hold up the "entrepreneur" as an esteemed social role to which they give access. They awaken the desire for entrepreneurial status, guide its formation, and sustain its existence.

What is an entrepreneur? Why have so many men and women worked to become one by selling soap and cosmetics to their neighbors and friends? Definitions differ, but many economists accept that entrepreneurs have two characteristics.[6] Most, following Schumpeter, see innovation as essential.[7] Entrepreneurs do something *different* that has economic consequences: they invent a product, refine a production process, develop a new marketing scheme. Some others believe that risk bearing is critical to entrepreneurship. An entrepreneur puts money on the line.[8]

By even a generous interpretation of economists' definitions, distributors are not entrepreneurs.[9] They perform highly routinized selling and recruiting behaviors. Innovation is neither necessary nor welcome. Financial risk is purposely kept low by DSOs who hope to appeal to a large number of recruits. Distributors risk only the absence of a paycheck, and while that may be personally risky, it is not of the same order as putting one's savings at risk. What distributors do is not entrepreneurial to any economically significant extent.

Entrepreneurship, however, is more than a type of economic action. It is a powerful social ideal that came about with the emergence of capitalism. As historians who have studied ideologies of success suggest, the popular ideal of the entrepreneur has supported the needs of the capitalist economic system.[10] Cultural ideals—the type of person one *ought* to be—are socially influential because they orient individuals toward their pursuit.[11] The entrepreneurial ideal in this country has been a flexible one, evolving with the changing needs of a capitalist economy. The Protestant ethic, with its ascetic individualism, was eventually transformed into more secular and consumption-promoting versions with the changing needs of the marketplace.[12] In DSOs the ideal has changed once again, molded by powerful economic actors to the needs of an industry.

Direct selling organizations emphasize less what distributors do than *who they are* as being entrepreneurial. The industry taps into the historically developed cultural understandings and ideals of this country and shapes them to suit its business ends. DSOs, like many Americans, associate entrepreneurialism with ambition, self-direction, and autonomy. The industry makes ambiguous character traits the foundation for specific selling activities. For example, they remind distributors that real entrepreneurs persevere even in the face of difficulty, and that booking more parties during a slump is a sign of the entrepreneurial spirit.

More than anything, though, within the industry entrepreneurialism represents the strength of character to avoid the security of wage or salaried labor. DSOs take their single most significant liability—the absence of a paycheck—and interpret it as an advantage. Direct selling entrepreneurs are willing to risk their financial security on their own ability to sell the DSOs' products.

In women's DSOs especially, the entrepreneurial ideal is "softened" and even repudiates competitiveness and ambition that do not incorporate a moral dimension. Women should be ambitious, but only in the service of their families or their personal security. Encouragement toward entrepreneurial action is modified to appeal to women in their roles as wives, mothers, and homemakers. As Mary Crowley of Home Interiors and Gifts put it, "Success is like housework—it is so daily. You have to do it all over again every morning."[13]

Entrepreneurialism represents an amalgam of traits highly valued in a meritocratic society. The industry tries to get recruits to see themselves as entrepreneurs and shapes that understanding toward DSO profit making. To the extent that the entrepreneurial image is appealing, and to many American men and women it is, distributors are led to embrace the model proffered by DSOs. Because of their class and gender, for most the only realistic access to "entrepreneur" status is through direct selling. The economic actor that the industry cultivates is led toward an inner compulsion to sustained selling and recruiting activity.

Entrepreneurial self-control was a direct selling management strategy dictated by the regulatory environment as it developed historically in the United States and by the industry's loss of the employment relation. However, it is a strategy that, quite apart from historical necessity, has important advantages. Self-control does not *feel* controlling. If an individual accepts the standards that attach to the social ideal—and this is a critical hurdle—then there is a perception of self-determination. There is an experience of autonomous competence.

In teaching distributors strategies for self-control—self observation, self-goal-setting, self-criticism—the organization is
perceived as helping individuals achieve their own goals, not
as manipulating workers to an alien end established by management. The organization is a benevolent "helper," not a
profit-seeking "controller."

Creating a new economic actor oriented to direct sales
entails more than teaching job-related skills. It is more than
training a beauty consultant to apply cosmetics or close a sale.
It is a socialization strategy that establishes a diffuse standard
for behavior. It incorporates, certainly, specific activities, but
just as important, it aims to create a self-perception, an emotional orientation, and even a political view. Once embraced,
the entrepreneurial persona is far more difficult to disengage.
Its loss represents no less than the forfeiture of a significant
portion of one's "self." Many fall by the wayside in so demanding a socialization process, but for a committed core the transformation is truly a "born again" experience. As a Mary Kay
consultant put it, "This is not a business, this is a way of life."

The "entrepreneur" is a useful cultural model that many
members of the industry have astutely appropriated to their
own ends (or at least were lucky to adopt). The strategy of
creating "entrepreneurs" is clearly profit seeking and economically rational. It is a strategy that works not outside social
conditions, but by *utilizing* a keen knowledge of Americans'
desires, frustrations, and social ideals.[14]

The Commercialization of Social Relations

It is an exquisite irony that the direct selling industry works
so hard to create an organization that rests on family bonds
and even emulates a family in its organizational relations.
Early capitalists were faced with precisely the opposite problem: how to *destroy* the personalistic and traditional ties of
family and community. As Karl Polanyi put it, "The noncon-
tractual organizations of kinship, neighborhood, profession
and creed were to be liquidated since they claimed the allegiance of the individual and thus restrained his freedom."[15]
Workers had to be "free" to labor conscientiously for someone
else and needed the "freedom" from traditional obligations and
benefits to follow the dictates of hunger. As Charles Perrow

wrote, "Modern bureaucracy depends on a particular social structure: a citizen must not be able to survive on his or her own but has to work for someone else."[16]

The development of capitalist enterprise required that industrialists pursue strategies for, on the one hand, liberating workers from their social relations and, on the other, binding them to the work process. Richard Edwards's historical study demonstrates the forms of organizational control that were developed to those ends in firms since the 1800s.[17] Early managers used the simple controls of direct supervision of the labor process. Later, technical controls, such as machine-paced assembly lines, were built into the physical structure of the labor process. Most recently, managers have discovered the utility of rules, regulations, and other bureaucratic controls that can be embedded more invisibly in the organization of work. All three forms of control are strategies for creating individual discipline and rewards and for isolating the worker from solidarity with others. Importantly, all three are impersonal controls that subordinate the individual to the interests of the organization. Even the supervisor acts not as a person, but as an impersonal agent of the owners.

Weber, like Polanyi, expressed fears about the consequences of overrationalized relations, where people's social needs were subordinated to production and moral considerations were secondary to profit making. He saw, correctly, that the economically superior organization of the firm and its bureaucratized relations were becoming the dominant social institution of capitalism. He described bureaucracy as an "iron cage" that would imprison modern individuals by destroying connections between them and by neglecting higher ideals.[18]

Weber's prediction has largely been realized. The bureaucratic firm and the bureaucratic public agency are the central institutions of an advanced industrial society. Contractual and rule-regulated relations dominate social ties, particularly, but not exclusively, in the marketplace.[19]

Why, then, should DSOs, a *less* rational form of enterprise, emerge? Why should a form of business that *builds on and maintains* social bonds be successful after years of bureaucratization? My interviews with distributors suggest that bureaucracy has spawned its antithesis in direct selling, that the very fact of impersonality has made people receptive to an industry that provides a community of relations. The modern distributor finds appeal in personalized work relations where the controllers are people who care about each other, or at least appear to. Distributors are not concerned that this caring may be entwined with the self-interest of sponsors when the alternative is a bureaucratic boss (whose own careerist ambitions may be involved in supervision).

The changing characteristics of workers no doubt also contribute to the effectiveness and appeal of personalistic controls. Women find the nurturing, noncompetitive nature of network relations comfortable both to give and to receive. Younger distributors, like many youthful workers, are demanding more than money for their labor. They want meaning and a measure of autonomy. The presence of both entrepreneurial community and entrepreneurial individualism in direct selling gives them at least an attenuated form of both.

Moreover, executives in the direct selling industry understand, just as do the leaders of many social movements, the power of preexisting social relations and networks in recruiting distributors and channeling their actions.[20] Executives have always brought work home and used social ties to advance their careers, but DSOs have penetrated the social bonds of "ordinary" Americans of the middle and working classes. The kinship networks of working-class people, especially, are deep, dense, and geographically close. They are ideally suited for economic exploitation. In direct selling social bonds are not an encumbrance but an *instrument* for soliciting and controlling a sales force and for appealing to customers.

IS LESS RATIONAL MORE RATIONAL?

Direct selling's choice of personalistic controls was constrained by the character of its work process and its renunciation of the employment relation: the industry was faced with a work force that was out of reach geographically and legally. Firms that organize employees in a workplace have no such constraints, of course, yet there is evidence that personalistic, "less rational" forms of control are emerging within firms.

Self-control and network controls, essential to sustaining commitment in DSOs, are becoming increasingly useful in bureaucratic settings as well. Young managers are encouraged to be "self-starters" and to "take a project and run with it." Organizations that were once rigidly hierarchical are tolerating, and even encouraging, self-governed behavior. A popular book in the 1980s coined a word for it, "intrapreneuring"—demonstrating the social characteristics of entrepreneurship within a bureaucratic setting.[21]

Social network controls are also increasingly in evidence in firms. Quality circles, matrix structures, autonomous work teams, group bonuses, and other organizational practices that break down hierarchical barriers and throw people together are the current managerial rage in a number of industries. Even labor and management at General Motors—historical antagonists—are going to "jointness" school together in an effort to create social bonds that bridge a status and authority gap. One GM division, reminiscent of DSOs, holds a week-long "family awareness workshop" so that workers and supervisors can practice making decisions together.[22]

An army of "corporate culture" consultants is leading a tranformation of both the ideological and the structural underpinnings of firms to bring them a sense of community.[23] In multiple ways, workers are being encouraged to see their fates as entwined and to experience themselves as part of a corporate whole tied together by common ideals. The independently efficient worker motivated only by money, the vision of Frederick Taylor, is no longer the vision of many corporations.

Firms are no doubt finding that promoting "less rational" controls is an effective means for maintaining worker commitment for some of the same reasons that DSOs find personalistic controls effective. The "intrapreneurial" status, being seen as a go-getter rather than an obedient official, has as much appeal to employed workers as "entrepreneurship" does to distributors in this country. In fact, that socially valued attribution is perhaps even *more* tempting to employed workers, precisely because they are employed in a society that reveres the independent businessperson. Intrapreneurship allows workers to maintain the facade, and perhaps the reality, of semiautonomy in a structure where they are legally and financially subordinate.

The demography of firms has also changed, and like DSOs, firms find that increasing numbers of workers are women. There is no reason to expect that the gender-related appeal of "soft controls" is any less in firms employing women than in women-dominated DSOs.

I conjecture, though, that personalistic controls are becoming commonplace in firms for reasons that have no counterpart in DSOs. Firms, I believe, have begun to reach the limits of rationality as a strategy for controlling workers.[24] Social scientists have for years documented the problems caused by overrationalized work relations. Workers who feel like cogs, just one more piece in the corporate machinery, display predictable pathologies: alienation, burnout, rule ritualism, absenteeism, low productivity, even sabotage. Several distributors spoke about the character of their lives under the rationalized conditions of firms, giving evidence of firms' inability to engage them in any profound way:

> We have a thing called the "believer's pin" for the sale of the first $100 worth of products. I have seen grown men, people that are bankers, real staid, conservative bankers [break down]. You know, they never have been acknowledged [before].

> I knew my boss and his wife, and we were all real close. We were almost like a family, and I was real loyal to him as an employee. But I could count on one hand how many times I was given a compliment in those years I was with Harry. It's not his fault. He was busy. He had a big business to run. But I was never told, "You did a good job on that sale." Or "I'm glad you're here today." Or anything like that. I started Tupperware, and in the first month I had recognition onstage. I was given gifts. I was told, "You're doing a terrific job." Right from the start the strokes were there.

> I believe you've got to recognize people, and that's one of the downfalls of corporate America today. The boss gets all the credit, and the employees take all the crap. In our team, when they accomplish things we pass out pins and T-shirts and plaques. And, doggone, that changes their lives around to know that somebody cares about them, somebody believes in them. People will do whatever it takes to win if they know somebody cares about them. That's what this business is all about, and I love being part of that.

Young and educated workers with higher expectations than their parents are even more susceptible to the costly social diseases that come from depersonalized, routinized, underrecognized work. The much-publicized success of participatory industrial systems in Scandinavia and Japan has, I believe, inspired alternatives to traditional rational-management responses in this country.

It is also clear from decades of experience that some types of work are poorly served by bureaucratic arrangements.[25] Interdependent work that relies on solidarity, respect, or mutual trust is poorly served by bureaucratic structures that create authority differences. Productive teamwork, whether among engineers in a high-tech company or among coal miners in a dangerous mine shaft, depends on the strength and character of relatively egalitarian social bonds in the workplace.[26]

Professional workers, increasingly employees rather than independent practitioners, are also ill suited to some types of bureaucratic control. They possess knowledge that nonprofessional managers do not have, and they have been socialized to work independently according to their own judgment.

Nor can much service work, as Arlie Hochschild observed, be mandated by a supervisor.[27] Some services depend on the creation of a social relationship between a worker and a customer, which cannot be produced at the turn of a switch. An airline cabin attendant, for instance, must create a believable performance of friendliness toward passengers to effectively sell the company's product. The more management can do to get the employee to genuinely embrace the appropriate emotional posture, the better the performance, and the more business interests are served.

The emotional orientation of much service work, the dedication to standards required of professionals, and the commitment to a fellow employee's success or safety cannot be managed effectively from without. Only the wholehearted complicity of the *person* of the worker produces quality work. Physical labor can be exacted through supervision, but intellectual, emotional, and morally committed labor is more elusive. It requires commitment to ideals as well as routines and to people as well as positions.

When the dominant metaphor of the workplace is transformed from a pyramid of pigeonholes to a community of fellows, social bonds take on new meaning. They become not an unwelcome disruption of hierarchical order, but the means through which the community achieves its purposes, however elevated or mundane they may be. Socially constructed selves and manipulated social relations are the new management technology of many modern workplaces.

When it occurs, accommodating and even utilizing workers' social needs and skills modifies the ambience of bureaucracy, softening the paramilitary character of the ideal type Weber described. But an overlay of emotion, of permitted confraternity, in no way challenges the premises of bureaucratic organization in the absence of a more profound transformation. Workers are still separated from ownership in most firms; they sell their labor, and perhaps even their selves and social relations, to someone who profits from their management. Control is still authoritarian; the boss may be more likeable after sensitivity training but is still the boss. Work schedules are becoming more flexible in some companies, but for most employees work and family still do not mix.

Social bonds that connected workers to each other and to loved ones outside the plant door were once the object of a concerted managerial purge in the pursuit of profit. That millions of people have flocked to the direct selling industry in search of an alternative way to work suggests that social bonds can be a powerful motivator of committed and profitable economic action, not necessarily an impediment.

INSTITUTIONAL FOUNDATIONS OF ECONOMIC ORGANIZATION

Organizational forms develop and are successful for reasons beyond objective economic measures.[28] Clearly, favorable market conditions are necessary to the success of economic organizations. For example, organized direct selling found a niche after the Civil War because of the advantages of personal selling in an era of mass marketing. It grew in the years after World War I because an oversupply of labor and excess production capacity favored recruiting and stimulated consumption.

It grew in the 1970s in part because people were looking for new sources of income in an era of economic stress. Favorable economic conditions have been a necessary but not, I would argue, sufficient explanation of the growth of DSOs.

Economic organizations, if they are to prosper, must fit into a conducive social and political environment. Direct selling has worked well in the United States because of market conditions, but also because of the character of state/business relations. The United States government, for example, supports a particular type of employment relation: costly enough to make independent contractors an attractive labor supply, but with unemployment benefits insufficient to discourage recruiting those who are out of work. Although Green River laws impede access to homes in some communities, for the most part direct selling in the United States thrives in a political setting that supports independent commercial activity.

Direct selling also works in the United States, I have argued, because of its ideological compatibility with individualist American culture and the work experience provided by many United States firms. Certainly network DSOs succeed in part because of the relatively open character of social ties between people in this country.

Although objective economic conditions suggested to some American direct selling executives that Europe would be a fertile market for their products and recruiting efforts, they found this was not uniformly so. Northern Europeans did not greet direct selling with the enthusiasm of Americans. Laws restrict market entry and access to homes far more there than in this country. The ideological climate is hostile too, according to one industry executive:

> In Europe the [DSOs] are in bad shape because Europe is much more socialistic, and the free enterprise spirit . . . it's not there. It's definitely a matter of spirit in this business, and that's lacking. Plus they have a retailer antipathy [against tradespeople] that we have overcome here for the most part. It [remains] very strong there. I would say sales are flat to poor there.

A historical legacy of distaste for commerce, generous employment benefits in social democratic countries, and perhaps in some nations a more participative bureaucratic firm pose obstacles to direct selling organizations.

This same executive noted, however, that Italy and Spain were good arenas for direct selling. These countries have fewer worker protections and social welfare benefits. They also have growing informal sectors where petty businesses flourish, suggesting that the "entrepreneurial spirit" is alive in southern Europe.

Though the outlook for much of Europe is bleak, the nations of the western Pacific rim are absorbing DSOs at a rapid rate. The diffusion of this type of organization is only beginning, but success is promising, according to several executives. In 1985 Japan's one million distributors sold $11 billion worth of products.[29] If automobile sales are included the number jumps substantially: in Japan 75% of new cars are sold by door-to-door salespeople, more than $25 billion worth in recent years.[30] Direct selling is growing in Malaysia, Singapore, and Hong Kong.[31] The prospects are so good in Asia that Amway has shifted its international focus from Europe to the Pacific basin, which now represents 75% of its international revenues.

Why is direct selling successful in Asia? Three reasons are now common wisdom in the industry, each having to do with the cultural and social characteristics of Eastern civilization. First, as an Amway executive put it, these are all "very structured societies." Asians recognize status gradations in their everyday social interactions and have multiple social institutions, from the family to the firm, built on the notion of a status hierarchy. The status hierarchy of companies like Amway fits Asians' preconceptions about the proper ordering of social relations. Second, direct selling executives find the entrepreneurial spirit strong within the region. In essence, they see the Confucian ethic serving as an ideological support for economic activity much as the Protestant ethic did here. As one member of the industry put it, "The Chinese have been peddlers since day one." Finally, direct selling companies are discovering that all these nations have extended family networks that make recruiting and selling particularly easy.[32]

The conditions that apparently make direct selling work in Asia are certainly not the conditions that make it work here.

In both instances, however, this form of organization takes root because of the character of the political and social, as well as economic, structures of society.[33] To use Mark Granovetter's conceptualization, direct selling, like all forms of organization, must be "embedded" in social relations and institutionally sustained.[34]

The conditions that supported the growth of direct selling in this country are to some degree transitory, of course. Economies shift, states change their policies, and ideologies evolve. Direct selling's phenomenal growth at a particular moment attests that it has been an apt solution to the historically particular problems of workers and owners. The industry is aware, however, that at least in this country it survives in part because of the unequal, rationalized, and uncertain conditions of bureaucratic employment. DSOs are attractive because so few employers accommodate the social preferences and family realities of women workers. Ironically, direct selling organizations have a stake in the persistence of impersonal workplaces and meaningless work.

APPENDIX
A Note on Methods

I began this study because the publicized practices of some DSOs piqued my interest. The effusive rituals they celebrated seemed like an interesting counterpoint to the more routine life of most businesses, and I decided direct selling was worth a closer look. Summary statistics that I requested of the Direct Selling Association staggered me: millions of Americans were participating in this flamboyant industry. Just as surprising, there had been almost no social-scientific study of this subject. I was on my own.

I thus began my inquiry with very fundamental questions: Do DSOs represent a distinctive form of economic organization or merely a bureaucratic variation? Are they a socially cohesive approach to organizing economic activity or simply federations of independent entrepreneurs? To answer these questions I believed it was important to study successful and established DSOs—archetypes, if you will, of the direct selling form. I was interested in understanding what appeared to be *typical* characteristics of direct selling organization, not the characteristics of marginal examples or a hypothetical "average."

In this regard I was following the logic of typological analysis, a methodological approach made famous by Max Weber's creation of ideal types of bureaucratic, charismatic, and traditional forms of organization and his typologies of forms of social action. An ideal type is a generalization that summarizes the features of a social formation or pattern and posits a relation between the features or variables. It is a kind of model logically similar to those used in quantitative analysis, although the elements are not assigned numerical values. Unlike most economic models, which are often logical constructs created in the minds of researchers, ideal types are based on empirical observation.[1] They are sociohistorical abstractions of real instances of a phenomenon.

Like all models, ideal types can be very useful. They organize our thinking about discrete cases that seem to be related in some way. While an ideal type is not in itself a hypothesis, it can assist us in hypothesis formation. In fact, each element of an ideal type can be expressed as a hypothesis. Perhaps most important, ideal types are an aid in comparison. Their utility, Guenther Roth says, "lies in serving as base lines for identifying the distinctiveness of a case."[2] We can compare a case with the model and can use the model as the basis for comparing a number of instances. An ideal type gives us a baseline for identifying and expressing variation. These qualities make ideal types especially useful in trying to organize our thinking about something that has not been studied before and in comparing a limited number of cases.[3]

Ideal types have important limits, though. As abstractions, they can never be proved "true" or "false." They are merely constructs. The proper test of an ideal type is how well it serves its intended purpose: Is it useful? In addition, by itself a model cannot speak to causation. *Why* a particular configuration seems to have emerged is beyond the scope of typological analysis. In Weberian sociology causal explanations are the aims of "secular theories" of historical development and "situational analysis" of the influence of particular events in a given setting.[4]

In trying to create an ideal type of the direct selling form of organization, I did not seek a random sample. Rather, I chose to study several large and prominent DSOs that I expected would show variation. I wanted to know what elements seemed "necessary" to the logic of direct selling and how far and in what ways individual cases might vary from the model. Mary Kay Cosmetics uses women distributors and sells cosmetics through parties called "beauty shows," held in consumers' homes. Shaklee Corporation uses both men and women distributors, though women predominate, and sells primarily health-care items both through parties and person to person. Amway sells through both men and women, but it encourages married couples and sells a variety of goods person to person.

These companies have some variation in gender-related appeal, in product, and in selling approach. All, however, are among the top ten DSOs in the United States.[5]

I supplemented these "core" cases with analyses of two other DSOs that differed in some ways I thought might show important variations in direct selling organization and social relations. A. L. Williams, unlike many network DSOs, relies mostly on men distributors. Tupperware, unlike many DSOs founded since the 1940s, does not rely on a charismatic leader to provide an emotional center and a personalized basis of commitment. These five cases show important variations in direct selling practices. Just as firms are more or less bureaucratic, real DSOs are more or less like a "model" DSO. Some DSOs, in fact, incorporate bureaucratic elements, and all the larger ones are managed by a bureaucratically organized headquarters.

I used several types of data in developing the model shown in table 4. My primary source was ninety-five interviews with industry participants, including distributors, executives, and trade association officials. My interviews were semistructured and organized to yield data about such features as social relations, organizational arrangements, and comparisons with other types of work. All the interviews were transcribed and coded by topic. I developed files on each topic so that I could compare individual responses to a particular question by company and could compare responses between companies.

I supplemented these interview data with materials I gathered on forty-two other DSOs that responded to a survey. Many DSOs gave me training materials, data on their structural arrangements, and information on organizational practices of various sorts.

In addition, I attended numerous industry activities as an observer and sometimes as a participant. This fieldwork took me to recruitment meetings in motels, to regional and national conventions, to sales parties, and to meetings of industry executives over a period of about four years. My participation in these events helped me to enter, at some level, the world of my informants and to understand not only what they did but why they did it and the meanings their actions held for them. Although this book does not represent the culmination of an ethnographic method, my observational activities were intended to supplement my structural analysis with an interpretive analysis. As Weber put it, sociology is "a science concerning itself with the interpretive understanding of social action and thereby with a causal explanation of its course and consequences."[6]

In addition to developing a model of the direct selling organization, I tried to uncover some of the historical forces that led to its formation. I was aided enormously in this task by finding a set of archival materials. Prompted by my requests to look through old trade association files, the Direct Selling Association gave me a box of yellowing papers that had been stored away for years. To my great good fortune, the box contained verbatim transcriptions of trade association meetings held between 1924 and 1938. As I describe in chapter 2, this period between the two world wars was critical for the development of the direct selling form. I felt like an eavesdropper as I read the words of men who were grappling with the effects of the depression, with goverment regulators, and with their competitors in the retail industry. This archival material was supplemented by the work of economic historians and more recent examinations of labor force changes.

Notes

CHAPTER ONE

1. Ed Bean, "Arthur Williams Sells a Lot of Insurance, Riles His Competitors," *Wall Street Journal*, 4 March 1987, p. 1, and Thomas C. Hayes, "Crusading for Term Life Insurance," *New York Times*, 11 May 1986.

2. Direct Selling Association, *A Statistical Study of the Direct Selling Industry in the United States: 1980–1984* (Washington, D.C.: Direct Selling Association, 1985). Figures include direct sales by all forms of DSOs but exclude direct selling insurance companies such as A. L. Williams and Prepaid Legal Services that are not members of the Direct Selling Association.

3. Michael Korda, *Power! How to Get It, How to Use It* (New York: Random House, 1975).

4. Michael Maccoby, *The Gamesman* (New York: Simon and Schuster, 1976).

5. Rosabeth Moss Kanter, *The Change Masters* (New York: Simon and Schuster, 1983).

6. William H. Whyte, *The Organization Man* (New York: Simon and Schuster, 1956).

7. Ibid., p. 153.

8. "Charisma" and "charismatic" in everyday usage refer to a winning personality. Sociologists use the term to refer to a special bond between a leader and followers, and I use it in that technical way in writing about some DSO founders and their distributors. See chapter 5.

9. Cf. Mary Kay Ash, *Mary Kay* (New York: Harper and Row, 1981); Mary C. Crowley, *Women Who Win* (Old Tappan, N.J.: Fleming H. Revell, 1979); Richard M. DeVos, *Believe!* (New York: Pocket Books, 1975); Forrest C. Shaklee, *Reflections on a Philosophy* (New York: Harper and Row, 1973).

10. Mary C. Crowley, *Be Somebody . . . God Doesn't Take Time to Make a Nobody* (Dallas: Crescendo, 1974).

11. Early organization theorists grappled with trying to define "organization" but conceded that organizations come in too many varieties for a single definition to be both useful and encompassing. Population ecologists—organization theorists who study large groups of organizations over time—have contributed the notion of "form." A form is a class of organizations that share many of the same attributes, although they are not necessarily identical. See Bill McKelvey and Howard Aldrich, "Populations, Natural Selection, and Applied Organizational Science," *Administrative Science Quarterly* 28, no. 1 (1983): 101–28.

12. Max Weber's typology of bureaucracy, described in *Economy and Society*, ed. Guenther Roth and Claus Wittich (Berkeley: University of California Press, 1978), is the standard used by organization theorists today.

13. Bureaucratic organization and the employment relationship are two analytically separate but historically linked developments of modern industrial capitalism. See Sanford M. Jacoby, *Employing Bureaucracy: Managers, Unions, and the Transformation of Work in American Industry, 1900–1945* (New York: Columbia University Press, 1985).

14. Weber and Marx wrote at a time when factories were the new means for producing goods and factory organization was revolutionizing social relations. Direct selling distributors do not "produce," in the sense that they do not manufacture. However, like many contemporary workers in, for example, the transportation and financial industries, their work is "service producing."

15. Ownership and management are often separated in industrial enterprise, especially in publicly traded companies. In their famous book, Adolph Berle and G. C. Means questioned whether managers would control the corporation in the interests of absentee owners. However one chooses to answer this question, it is clear that workers lose control in the firm. See *The Modern Corporation and Private Political Economy* (New York: Macmillan, 1932).

16. For a discussion of Weber's and Marx's views on these issues, see Stephen Hill, *Competition and Control at Work: The New Industrial Sociology* (Cambridge: MIT Press, 1981), chaps. 1 and 2.

17. Daniel Nelson discusses strategies for managing the family in this country in *Managers and Workers: Origins of the New Factory System in the United States, 1880–1920* (Madison: University of Wisconsin Press, 1975).

18. Mark Granovetter, "Economic Action and Social Structure: The Problem of Embeddedness," *American Journal of Sociology* 91, no. 3(1985): 482.

19. Reinhard Bendix has succinctly summarized Weber's contention "[that] men in society act with and against each other on the basis of their material and ideal interest and that they stand in a relation of authority and obedience on the basis of shared understandings." *Max Weber: An Intellectual Portrait* (New York: Anchor, 1962), p. 286.

20. DSO-type organizations may be used for noneconomic functions, though. The antiwar organization Beyond War has a network-like technique for disseminating its ideological message. Women in Argentina have been using their understanding of the Avon and Mary Kay Cosmetics organizations to build a grass-roots political movement to implement democratic changes. See Shirley Christian, "Democracy Calling: It's Women's New Selling Job," *New York Times*, 20 November 1986, p. 4.

21. Transcriptions have been edited lightly to make the spoken word clear in writing.

22. The products sold via direct selling range from pet food to encyclopedias, but cosmetics, fragrances, and skin care preparations represent the largest category of sales (28%). Other important categories include decorative accessories (15.5%), nutritional products, beverages, and food (11%), home appliances (7.5%), and housewares and kitchenware (7%). Direct Selling Association, *A Statistical Study of the Direct Selling Industry in the United States, 1980–84* (Washington, D.C.: Direct Selling Association, 1985), p. 8.

23. Income figures for distributors are difficult to confirm and, even where averages are available, difficult to interpret because distributors work variable schedules. Low average hourly income reported to me was about $7, with a high figure of about $25 for personal sales. People who had developed sizable, active downlines could make considerably more. Annual averages appear to be modest, according to information given me by DSOs, typically $2,000 to $8,000 for part-time work of less than twenty hours a week. Active distributors working more than twenty hours a week reportedly earn $10,000 to $20,000, but "very successful" distributors (a tiny percentage) can make $75,000 or more annually.

24. Arthur Stinchcombe has argued that organizations that develop at about the same period will have similar properties and that these will endure even with changes in the organizations' environments. DSOs developed before 1940 are likely not to have networks, whereas those developed after then generally do. See chapter 2 for further discussion. Arthur Stinchcombe, "Social Structure and Organizations," in *Handbook of Organizations*, ed. James G. March (Chicago: Rand McNally, 1965), pp. 155–65.

CHAPTER TWO

1. For a history of salesmen in the United States to the turn of the century, see Charles Bennet, *Scientific Salesmanship* (Saint Louis: American Efficiency Bureau, 1933), chap. 6.

2. Thomas D. Clark, *Pills, Petticoats and Plows: The Southern Country Store* (Indianapolis: Bobbs-Merrill, 1944).

3. Alfred D. Chandler, *The Visible Hand* (Cambridge: Harvard University Press, 1977), p. 217.

4. That quintessentially American male role, the traveling salesman, was filled by men who worked for jobbers or wholesalers, and later for manufacturers. Their work was to show samples of their employers' wares to storekeepers, not to sell at retail. They were not independent in the way Yankee peddlers were but "were monitored, evaluated and directed by a general sales manager and his staff." Chandler, *Visible Hand*, p. 219.

5. An interesting social history of the department store in the United States at this time is Susan Porter Benson, *Counter Cultures: Saleswomen, Managers, and Customers in American Department Stores, 1890–1940* (Urbana: University of Illinois Press, 1986).

6. For example, Earl Tupper found that the distinctive seals on Tupperware were frustrating to people who had not been schooled in their use. Alcas Cutlery, maker of Cutco knives, uses dramatic demonstrations to show the superiority of their products, which look like their less-expensive competition.

7. *Report and Minutes of 1926 Annual Convention* (Winona, Minn.: National Association of Agency Companies, 1926), p. 13.

8. In 1920 the trade association listed members in the following business categories: automobile accessories, beads, corsets, clothing, cutlery, dress goods and laces, extracts and food, hosiery and underwear, medical preparations, novelties, nurseries, oils and greases, poultices, poultry, raincoats, sadirons, seeds, and soaps.

9. Thomas G. Marx, "The Development of the Franchise Distribution System in the U.S. Automobile Industry," *Business History Review* 59(1985): 465–74. Even today, direct selling is the primary way cars are sold in Japan, with more than 80% of Toyotas sold by direct distribution.

10. The appeal of the city was mixed with fear and antipathy. The city was seen as a site of corruption and the commercialization of relationships. The Populist movement was in part a response to the perceived social disorder nurtured by urban society. See Richard Hofstadter, *The Age of Reform* (New York: Knopf, 1955).

11. Raymond Edward Reis, "The American Salesman: A Study of a Direct Sales Organization," Ph.D. diss., University of Illinois,

1958, p. 22. This work studies the operation of a branch office company.

12. The lore on peddlers and commercial travelers is extensive, much of it stressing their glamor for rural people, especially boys. For example, Gerald Carson writes that "he brought with him the very taste, the acrid, exciting smell of the city and seemed a shining figure, a modern, commercial knight-errant, scouring down the pike in his buggy, his lance a Westfield whip, his helmet a derby hat, his buckler a tin sample case." *The Country Store* (New York: Oxford University Press, 1945), p. 158.

13. *President's Report of the 1924 Annual Convention* (Winona, Minn.: National Association of Agency Companies, 1924), p. 8.

14. Ibid.

15. *Rawleigh News*, 1913, reprinted by the W. T. Rawleigh Company.

16. Alfred C. Fuller, *A Foot in the Door* (New York: McGraw-Hill, 1960), p. 112.

17. Ibid., p. 113.

18. Julie A. Matthaei, *An Economic History of Women in America* (New York: Schocken Books, 1982), p. 160.

19. Fuller, *Foot in the Door*, p. 133.

20. *Report and Minutes of the 1925 Annual Convention* (Winona, Minn.: National Association of Agency Companies, 1925), p. 8.

21. Ibid.

22. J. C. Aspley, *Intensive Sales Management* (Chicago and New York: Dartnell Corporation, 1929), p. 13.

23. Roland Marchand chronicles the rise of advertising in the 1920s in *Advertising the American Dream: Making Way for Modernity, 1920–1940* (Berkeley: University of California Press, 1985). A number of the advertisers he writes about, including the Hoover Vacuum Cleaner Company and Realsilk Hosiery, sold door to door.

24. There are no figures showing the number of women in direct sales in this era, but some advertisements solicited both men and women, particularly for the sale of women's clothing. A self-report survey published in a direct selling publication yielded over six hundred responses in 1926. Asked the percentage of women respondents, the surveyer replied, "Comparatively few. I cannot give you the exact percentage, because that did not fit into our ideas." *Report and Minutes, 1926*, p. 15.

25. "President's Report," in *Report and Minutes of the 1925 Annual Convention* (Winona, Minn.: National Association of Agency Companies, 1925), p. 8.

26. Ibid.

27. *Report and Minutes of the 1927 Annual Convention*

(Winona, Minn.: National Association of Direct Selling Companies, 1927), p. 4.

28. In 1984 Green River ordinances were legal in twenty states and unconstitutional in twenty others; the DSA was lobbying against them in the remaining ten state capitols.

29. "Direct Selling Takes a New Direction: NADSC—1910 and After," unpublished manuscript in DSA archives.

30. *Minutes of 1932 Annual Meeting* (Winona, Minn.: National Association of Direct Selling Companies, 1932).

31. *Proceedings of Annual Meeting. 1930* (Winona, Minn.: National Association of Direct Selling Companies, 1930), p. 171.

32. NADSC, *Minutes, 1932*, p. 8. This observation, if correct, suggests that direct selling was pursued even by the elderly unemployed during an era without social welfare benefits. A nineteen-year-old veteran of the Civil War, which ended in 1865, would have been seventy-one in 1927.

33. Fuller, *Foot in the Door*, p. 177.

34. Herman Kogan, *The Great EB: The Story of the "Encyclopaedia Britannica"* (Chicago: University of Chicago Press, 1958).

35. A general discussion of the effect of the Great Depression and subsequent state intervention in employment matters can be found in Sanford M. Jacoby, *Employing Bureaucracy: Managers, Unions, and the Transformation of Work in American Industry, 1900–1945* (New York: Columbia University Press, 1985), chaps. 7 and 8.

36. Joseph Schumpeter recognized that this "type of state-supervised industrial self-government the gist of which, stripped of phraseological mimicry and apart from the provisions about labor, was legal recognition and official encouragement, amounting to compulsion, of a modified form of the German cartel which, quite independently of this legislation, tended to grow out of the activities of trade associations." *Business Cycles* (New York: McGraw-Hill, 1939), p. 992.

37. See Alfred D. Chandler, *America's Greatest Depression, 1929–1941* (New York: Harper and Row, 1970), pp. 223–39.

38. *Proceedings of the 1928 Convention* (Winona, Minn.: National Association of Direct Selling Companies, 1928), pp. 13–14. Some DSOs pay workmen's compensation today. According to Neil Offen, president of the Direct Selling Association, "These people are not employees and therefore worker's compensation claims are really not technically valid, but the reality of that type of situation is that often a compromise is made—a payment is made with a disclaimer saying, this doesn't indicate any admission that these people are em-

ployees but rather it's just the cheaper way to go." Remarks made at Direct Selling Education Foundation Academic Seminar, Boston, 1–2 November 1984.

39. NADSC, *Proceedings, 1928.*

40. The industry's record in this regard was spotty until the successful consumer movement of the mid-1960s threatened to produce legislation restricting direct selling. Since then the DSA has been exemplary in promoting consumer-protection legislation and public discussion of consumer issues. For example, the DSA worked with consumer advocate Ralph Nader to support "cooling off laws" that give the purchaser of a product worth $25 or more three days to cancel the sale for a full refund, a protection against high-pressure sales.

41. *Annual Convention Report, 1936* (Winona, Minn.: National Association of Direct Selling Companies, 1936), p. 2.

42. Some companies voluntarily paid workmen's compensation and employers' liability insurance. However, some DSOs doing business in more than one state claimed in the 1920s and 1930s that states could not impose a tax, including workmen's compensation payments, on interstate commerce. See NAAC, *Report and Minutes, 1925*, p. 7.

43. *Proceedings of the Annual Convention, 1935* (Winona, Minn.: National Association of Direct Selling Companies, 1935), p. 32.

44. *Annual Convention Report, 1934* (Winona, Minn.: National Association of Direct Selling Companies, 1934), p. 12.

45. Ibid., p. 19.

46. Ibid., p. 30.

47. Gordon Hylton, "The Great Depression: Causes and Impact," in *The Coming of Managerial Capitalism*, ed. Alfred D. Chandler and Richard S. Tedlow (Homewood, Ill.: Richard D. Irwin), p. 593.

48. NADSC, *Proceedings,1935*, p. 19.

49. Federal attempts to challenge the employment status of distributors were modest during the 1940s; the only DSO that agreed to treat distributors as employees was Electrolux, still the only DSO with an employee sales force. Enforcement of "status laws" was also lax in the expansionary 1950s, but in 1968 the Internal Revenue Service began a vigorous campaign to have direct distributors declared employees. The campaign lasted ten years—five at the administrative level, five in litigation. When the IRS lost in court it argued before Congress for a statutory change, but the Tax Equity and Fiscal Responsibility Act of 1982 specifically declares direct sellers and real-

tors independent contractors for federal tax purposes. This not only exempted DSOs from paying FICA, it preserved the recruiting attraction of having tax-deductible business expenses that the IRS opposed.

50. For a discussion of post-World War II trends in the industry, see Victor P. Buell, "Door-to-Door Selling," *Harvard Business Review*, May-June 1954, pp. 113–23.

51. For example, executives of branch office companies were invited to address the membership about their personalized recruiting practices, novel to home office companies that relied on direct mail and advertising to generate prospective salesmen.

52. NADSC, *Minutes, 1932*.

53. Today most home office operations are a variant of direct mail marketing where a distributor takes orders from a catalog.

54. While most attribute the "discovery" of the party plan to Beveridge, some credit West Bend, a manufacturer of aluminum pots, with the innovation. Both were early users of this technique.

55. There were a number of DSOs that employed women from the turn of the century. In 1932 the Charis Corporation had 6,000 "corsetiers" who sold tailor-made corsets and undergarments fitted in consumers' homes, and in 1936 the Spirella Company of Niagara Falls, New York, had 4,000 corsetiers. Avon Corporation, no doubt the largest DSO using women distributors at the time (as it is today), had 26,000 salespeople in 1936. Such figures suggest that by the 1930s no fewer than 10% of distributors were women. See NADSC, *Annual Convention, 1936*, pp.7, 17, and NADSC, *Minutes, 1932*, p. 2.

56. One study explores the economic consequences of using social networks as an entry to consumer markets via home parties. The researchers found, contrary to economic models that see effective price as the primary determinant of demand, that social obligation can influence purchase behavior. See Harry L. Davis and Jonathan K. Frenzen, "Neighborhoods, Social Networks, and Market Access," working paper, Graduate School of Business, University of Chicago, 1986.

57. For an analysis of party plan selling, see Dorothy E. Peven, "The Use of Religious Revival Techniques to Indoctrinate Personnel: The Home Party Sales Organization," *Sociological Quarterly* 9 (1968): 97–106.

58. C. Wright Mills, *White Collar* (New York: Oxford University Press, 1953), pp. 161–62.

59. Ibid., p. 161.

60. Direct Selling Association, *A Statistical Study of the Direct Selling Industry in the United States, 1980–84* (Washington, D.C.: Direct Selling Association, 1985), p. 8.

61. "Tracing Our Roots," *Multilevel Marketing News*, January 1984, pp. 20–23.

62. For a popularized history of Amway, see Charles Paul Conn, *The Possible Dream* (Old Tappan, N.J.: Fleming H. Revell, 1977).

63. *Proceedings of the 1929 Annual Convention* (Winona, Minn.: National Association of Direct Selling Companies, 1929), pp. 32–33.

64. "Ponzi Dies in Rio in Charity Ward," *New York Times*, 19 January 1949, p. 56.

65. Some pyramids in recent years have tried to take on the trappings of legal network DSOs by imposing, for example, large start-up fees and recruiting mostly on the basis of the opportunities for sponsoring others, not product sales.

66. Brownie Wise, a successful Stanley distributor, was recruited by Tupperware to create a home party sales organization to sell the products developed by inventor Earl Tupper.

67. Louis Harris and Associates, *The Public Looks at Direct Selling* (Washington, D.C.: Direct Selling Association, 1976), p. 65.

CHAPTER THREE

1. The environment is not only outside the organization, of course, because people bring new ideas and technologies within organizational boundaries. W. Richard Scott describes organizations' boundaries as "sieves, not shells, admitting the desirable flows and excluding the inappropriate or deleterious elements." *Organizations: Rational, Natural, and Open Systems* (Englewood Cliffs, N.J.: Prentice-Hall, 1981), p. 180.

2. In recent years scholars have recognized that the social and historical contexts of organizations are critical to understanding their birth, growth, and decline. Organizations, in this view, are not isolates but are embedded in a given moment of history and are a response to a set of social and economic conditions. The environmental view of organizations is an important corrective to the earlier practice of looking at organizations one at a time, apart from any consideration of their contexts. Important discussions of the ecological view of organizational environments include Michael T. Hannan and John Freeman, "The Population Ecology of Organizations," *American Journal of Sociology* 82, no. 5(1977): 929–66 and Howard E. Aldrich, *Organizations and Environments* (Englewood Cliffs, N.J.: Prentice-Hall, 1979). What has come to be known as the "institutional school" of organizational analysis argues that the ideational and symbolic environment of organizations has an effect on organizational form and

practice. See John W. Meyer and W. Richard Scott, *Organizational Environments: Ritual and Rationality* (Beverly Hills, Calif.: Sage, 1983), for a discussion of this view of the environment.

3. I have written about the effect of structural conditions on interaction before. See Nicole Woolsey Biggart and Gary G. Hamilton, "The Power of Obedience," *Administrative Science Quarterly* 29, no.4(1984): 540–49, and Gary G. Hamilton and Nicole Woolsey Biggart, "Why People Obey: Theoretical Observations on Power and Obedience in Complex Organizations," *Sociological Perspectives* 28, no.1(1985): 3–28.

4. The institutional school of organizational analysis contributed the understanding that organizational environments are more than technical and material factors and include subjective understandings and symbolic elements. Until recently, however, institutionalists have failed to examine how environment shapes understanding and social action, and how it is a product of and an influence on human agents. I am sympathetic to Roger Friedland and Robert Alford's attempt to conceptualize institutional environments in such a way as to "link individuals and organizations to society." "Bringing Society Back In: Symbols, Structures and Institutional Contradiction," paper delivered at the Conference on Institutional Change at the Center for Advanced Study in the Behavioral Sciences, Stanford, California, 15–16 May 1987, p. 16.

5. Harris sampled a cross section of 1015 households using a multistage random cluster sample ensuring every household an equal chance of being drawn. The sample was stratified by geographic region and by size of place to reflect the actual proportions of United States residents living in different regions. Sampling units were randomly selected within each stratum to reflect a probability proportional to census estimates of the given household populations.

6. United States Bureau of the Census, *Historical Statistics of the United States, Colonial Times to 1970* (Washington, D.C.: United States Government Printing Office, 1975), p. 126.

7. United States Bureau of the Census, *Statistical Abstracts of the United States, 1985,* (Washington, D.C.: United States Government Printing Office, 1984), p. 395.

8. United States Bureau of the Census, *Historical Statistics,* p. 132.

9. United States Bureau of the Census, *Statistical Abstracts,* p. 392.

10. Ibid., p. 398.

11. This redefinition did not come without opposition from husbands defending their role as provider (and by extension their

masculinity) and from women upholding the traditional role of home-maker. See, for example, Lillian Rubin, *Worlds of Pain: Life in the Working-Class Family* (New York: Basic Books, 1976), for an account of blue-collar men's resistance to working wives, and Marabel Morgan, *The Total Woman* (New York: Pocket Books, 1975), for a best-selling book advising women to retain their traditional place in the home, subordinate to their husbands' will.

12. Julie A. Matthaei, *An Economic History of Women in America* (New York: Schocken Books, 1982), p. 251.

13. On a list of nine possible reasons for entering direct sales, "supplementing my family income or making a little extra money for myself" emerged as the most frequently cited reason for inactive direct sellers and the second most important reason for active distributors. Active distributors cited "being independent and working when I want to" as the most important reason for their involvement.

14. Ibid., p. 254.

15. United States Department of Labor, *Dual Careers: A Longitudinal Study of Labor Market Experience of Women*, Manpower Research Monograph 21 (Washington, D.C.: United States Government Printing Office, 1970), 1: 21.

16. David M. Gordon, Richard Edwards, and Michael Reich, *Segmented Work, Divided Workers* (Cambridge: Cambridge University Press, 1982), p. 206.

17. Val Burris and Amy Wharton, "Sex Segregation in the U.S. Labor Force," *Review of Radical Political Economics*, fall 1982: 43–56.

18. James N. Baron and William T. Bielby, "The Organization of Work in a Segmented Economy," *American Sociological Review* 49, no. 4(1984): 454–73. See also Jeffrey Pfeffer and Yinon Cohen, "Determinants of Internal Labor Markets in Organizations," *Administrative Science Quarterly* 29, no 4.(1984): 550–72; and Rosabeth Moss Kanter, *Men and Women of the Corporation* (New York: Basic Books, 1977).

19. DSOs vary somewhat in this regard. For example, in Tupperware one can buy into an upper dealership level, although activity and success as a distributor are prerequisites. In Home Interiors and Gifts, a DSO that emphasizes Christian values, informants suggested that evidence of good moral character is critical to achieving top status.

20. Carol Hymowitz and Timothy D. Schellhardt, "The Glass Ceiling," *Wall Street Journal*, 25 March 1986, sec. 4, p. 1.

21. For a review of the dominant theories see Burris and Wharton, "Sex Segregation."

22. For an international comparison of child-care benefits in major industrialized nations, see Sheila Kamerman, "Childcare and Family Benefits," *Monthly Labor Review*, November 1980, p. 27.

23. "Services" is a miscellaneous category used by the United States census and other economic observers to include all productive activity that is not manufacturing or agriculture. Services include everything from banking and medicine to shoe repair and entertainment. Although services are associated with a "postindustrial society" no longer dominated by manufacturing, it is not true that services are synonymous with high technology. Certainly many high-technology occupations, such as communications specialists and engineering researchers, are part of the new shift to services, but so are bank tellers and letter carriers.

24. United States Bureau of the Census, *Statistical Abstracts*, p. 431.

25. Thomas M. Stanback, Jr., *Understanding the Service Economy: Employment, Productivity, Location* (Baltimore: Johns Hopkins University Press, 1979), p. 3.

26. Valerie A. Personik, "The Job Outlook through 1995," *Monthly Labor Review*, November 1983, p. 25.

27. Daniel Bell, *The Coming of Post-Industrial Society: A Venture in Social Forecasting* (New York: Basic Books, 1976).

28. Stanback, *Understanding the Service Economy*, p. 70.

29. Harry Braverman's important book *Labor and Monopoly Capital: The Degradation of Work in the Twentieth Century* (New York: Monthly Review Press, 1974) was among the first to describe the routinization of clerical labor. Although his prediction that white-collar workers would develop a class consciousness has failed to develop, his characterization of the transformation of modern white-collar work is significant. See also Rosemary Crompton and Gareth Jones, *White Collar Proletariat: Deskilling and Gender in Clerical Work* (Philadelphia: Temple University Press, 1984).

30. C. Wright Mills, *White Collar* (New York: Oxford University Press, 1953); William H. Whyte, *The Organization Man* (New York: Simon and Schuster, 1956).

31. Whyte, *Organization Man*, p. 3.

32. Edward Shepherd Mead, *How to Succeed in Business without Really Trying* (New York: Simon and Schuster, 1952).

33. Michael Maccoby, *The Gamesman* (New York: Simon and Schuster, 1976).

34. For discussion of professionals in bureaucracies see W. Richard Scott, "Reactions to Supervision in a Heteronomous Professional Organization," *Administrative Science Quarterly* 10, no. 2

(1965): 65–81, and Richard Hall, "Professionalization and Bureaucratization," *American Sociological Review* 33, no. 1(1968): 92–104.

35. Remarks at Direct Selling Education Foundation Academic Seminar, Boston, 1–2 November 1984, p. 23.

36. Paul M. Hirsch, "From Ambushes to Golden Parachutes: Corporate Takeovers as an Instance of Cultural Framing and Institutional Integration," *American Journal of Sociology* 91, no.4(1986): 801.

37. Michael Schrage and Warren Brown, "Middle Managers under Siege: No Longer Immune from Layoffs," *Washington Post*, 1 September 1985, pp. M1, M5.

38. There are no figures that authoritatively describe the number of corporate workers affected by mergers and takeovers, but Hirsch cites a *Fortune* estimate that the ten largest of 1983's 1,500 mergers influenced 220,000 employees. Hirsch, "From Ambushes to Golden Parachutes."

39. United States Bureau of National Affairs, *Bulletin to Management* (Washington, D.C.: Bureau of National Affairs, 1982).

40. Philip Selznick, *Law, Society, and Industrial Justice* (New York: Russell Sage Foundation, 1969).

41. Ibid., p. 135.

42. Proceedings of the Direct Selling Education Foundation Academic Seminar, Boston, 1–2 November 1984, p. 27.

43. Ibid., pp. 10–11.

44. Human resource management texts today invariably include a chapter on "Quality of Work Life" programs, or QWL, which aim to create an effective social environment for workers. Just as Taylor was concerned with the technology of work, today's workplace professionals are concerned with social technologies. See, for example, H. G. Heneman et al., *Personnel/Human Resource Management* (Homewood, Ill.: Richard D. Irwin, 1986), chaps. 18, 19.

45. See Reinhard Bendix, *Work and Authority in Industry* (Berkeley: University of California Press, 1963), p. 247.

46. Manuel Castells, *The Economic Crisis and American Society* (Princeton: Princeton University Press, 1980), p. 192.

47. The growth of subcontracting and the rise of the "informal sector" are important economic developments. The informal sector is often defined to include subsistence activities such as food growing, casually self-employed labor, petty production and trade, unprotected labor, and illegal trade such as drug trafficking. Because informal-sector work is unregulated and does not conform to government mandates for minimum wages, safety regulations, and other worker protections, it is a source of cheap labor. Data about the informal

sector are inherently unreliable but symptomatic of its growing size. See Alejandro Portes and John Walton, *Labor, Class, and the International System* (New York: Academic Press, 1981), for a discussion of the role of the informal sector in the changing world economy. See also Alejandro Portes and Saskia Sassen-Koob, "Making It Underground: Comparative Material on the Informal Sector in Western Market Economies," *American Journal of Sociology* 93, no.1(1987): 30–61.

48. Executives at Mary Kay Cosmetics have tried to confirm this claim by getting data on women's earnings in other industries such as real estate and insurance, where successful salespeople have substantial success. The claim has never been verified, but all of Mary Kay's fifty-nine national sales directors make over $100,000 a year.

49. Louis A. Zurcher and David A. Snow, "Collective Behavior: Social Movements," in *Social Psychology: Sociological Perspectives*, ed. Morris Rosenberg and Ralph H. Turner (New York: Basic Books), p. 452.

CHAPTER FOUR

1. The rhetoric and the reality are not always the same. For example, bureaucratic workers may be expected to bring work home at night and on weekends. The Lynds called this "the long arm of the job." Robert S. Lynd and Helen Merrell Lynd, *Middletown: A Study in Contemporary American Culture* (New York: Harcourt, Brace, 1959), chap. 7.

2. Weber saw patrimonialism as a direct inhibitor of the instrumentalism critical to development of rational administration and a capitalist economy. *Economy and Society*, ed. Guenther Roth and Claus Wittich (Berkeley: University of California Press, 1978), pp. 237–41. Although impersonality is a professed ideal in firms, it does not always exist in practice precisely because families are such useful political resources. For example, as Charles Perrow describes it, "Relatives who work for you can be expected to hide your mistakes and incompetence, warn you about threats to your position, and support you in conflicts with others." *Complex Organizations: A Critical Essay* (New York: Random House, 1986), p. 7. Moreover, even where work and family are kept formally separate they influence each other indirectly. For example, work usually determines a family's economic and social status, the amount and scheduling of their time together, and the presence or absence of stress in the household. See Jeylan T. Mortimer and Jayne London, "The Varying Linkages of Work and Family," in *Work and Family: Changing Roles of Men and Women*, ed. Patricia Voyandoff (Palo Alto, Calif.: Mayfield, 1984), pp. 20–42.

3. Rosabeth Moss Kanter, *Work and Family in the United States: A Critical Review and Agenda for Research and Policy* (New York: Russell Sage Foundation, 1977), p. 15.

4. An important history of the family is Carl N. Degler, *At Odds: Women and the Family in America from the Revolution to the Present* (Oxford: Oxford University Press, 1980). Although based on the European experience, Louise A. Tilly and Joan W. Scott's work clearly shows the relation between the shape of the family and the shape of the economy under capitalist development. *Women, Work and Family* (New York: Holt, Rinehart and Winston, 1978).

5. Ann Oakley, *Woman's Work* (New York: Random House Vintage Books, 1976), p. 10.

6. Rosalyn Baxandall, Linda Gordon, and Susan Reverby, *America's Working Women: A Documentary History 1600 to the Present* (New York: Random House Vintage Books, 1976), p. 15.

7. Alice Kessler-Harris, *Out to Work: A History of Wage-Earning Women in the United States* (Oxford: Oxford University Press, 1982), pp. 24–27.

8. Kanter, *Work and Family in the United States*, p. 10.

9. See also Daniel Nelson, *Managers and Workers: Origins of the New Factory System in the United States, 1880–1920* (Madison: University of Wisconsin Press, 1975), chap. 5. Nelson argues that factories relied on families and ethnic communities as a recruiting source for unskilled labor into the early twentieth century, until the rise of scientific management.

10. Janet Clark, "Women and Their Work: A Theory of Sexual Division of Labor and Growth of Women in the Labor Force," *Social Science Journal* 21, no. 4(1984): 112.

11. The isolation of women as homemakers in the late nineteenth century and early twentieth centuries was not uniform. In general it occurred among middle-class women. Immigrant women, black women, and working-class women often continued to work outside the home. See Kessler-Harris, *Out to Work*, chaps. 3, 4, and 5.

12. Jessie Bernard, "The Good-Provider Role: Its Rise and Fall," in *Work and Family: Changing Roles of Men and Women*, ed. Patricia Voyandoff (Palo Alto, Calif.: Mayfield, 1984), p. 48.

13. The United States census assumed that the man was the head of household until the 1980 census.

14. Bernard, "Good-Provider Role," pp. 54–57.

15. Elizabeth Maret and Barbara Finley, "The Distribution of Household Labor among Women in Dual-Earner Families," *Journal of Marriage and the Family* 46, no.2(1984): 357–64, and Robert Weiss, "Men and the Family," *Family Processes* 24(1985): 49–58.

16. Other types of work outside the home might be said to

make women more interesting to men. What is important, though, is that direct selling makes this argument and most other businesses do not.

17. Stephen Butterfield, *Amway: The Cult of Free Enterprise* (Boston: South End Press, 1985), p. 116.

18. Children are welcome at some A. L. Williams rallies but typically not at Amway functions. Nor does Amway provide day care at events. Butterfield claims that daycare is viewed as "creeping socialism," and "hiring babysitters is more consistent with the ideal of the nuclear family motivated by the pursuit of wealth: couples provide for their own, the lines are kept apart, and the distributor must strive harder to boost his [sales] in order to meet the cost." Ibid., p. 123.

19. This is an instance of what Bennett Berger calls "ideological work," that is, reconciling beliefs with the exigencies of living. *The Survival of a Counterculture: Ideological Work and Everyday Life among Rural Communards* (Berkeley: University of California Press, 1981).

20. The family ideology of DSOs and other organizations that promote home work has a material basis too. These businesses profit by imposing on family members who answer phones, pack orders, baby sit, and otherwise sustain home workers. DSOs try to make a virtue of what is in their economic interests.

21. Direct selling is not the only form of enterprise to use the family metaphor. Large Japanese firms are also metaphorical families. Not coincidentally, Japanese business practice, like DSOs, stresses cooperation and mutes individualism.

22. C. Wright Mills, *White Collar* (New York: Oxford University Press, 1953), p. 109.

23. Paul M. Hirsch, "From Ambushes to Golden Parachutes," *American Journal of Sociology* 91, no. 4(1986): 815.

24. Graduate business programs give middle-class women a chance to learn the instrumental-rational skills valued in corporations. Most women I interviewed did not have even this chance, of course.

25. Marilyn Loden, "A Machismo That Drives Women Out," *New York Times*, 9 February 1986, sec. 3, p. 2.

26. This separatist strategy was pursued with vigor by American women from 1870 to 1930. They developed an extensive institutional network known as the "women's club movement" that was both a response to rejection by men's public-sphere organizations and a desire for more feminine forms of organizing. See Estelle Freedman, "Separatism as Strategy: Female Institution Building and American Feminism, 1870–1930," *Feminist Studies* 5, no. 3(1979): 512–29,

and Patricia Robinson, "The Organizational Contrast of Past and Present Women's Groups: A Comparison of the Women's Committee of the Council of National Defense and the National Organization for Women," paper presented at the meetings of the Pacific Sociological Association, Albuquerque, April 1985.

27. The studies of sociologist Nancy Chodorow and psychologist Carol Gilligan suggest reasons for some women's rejection of bureaucracy: girls' developmental experiences lead them to nurturing interpersonal orientations, in contrast to boys' being directed toward concern with individual rights and abstract responsibilities. The organizational implications of these developmental outcomes are profoundly different. Nancy Chodorow, *The Reproduction of Mothering* (Berkeley: University of California Press, 1978), and Carol Gilligan, *In a Different Voice* (Cambridge: Harvard University Press, 1982). For a review of extant literature on gender and organization see Jeff Hearn and P. Wendy Parkin, "Gender and Organizations: A Selective Review and a Critique of a Neglected Area," *Organization Studies* 4, no. 3(1983): 219–42. Kathy E. Ferguson has written an analysis of bureaucracy as a patriarchal system. *The Feminist Case against Bureaucracy* (Philadelphia: Temple University Press, 1984).

28. Of course, network DSOs are capitalist enterprises, not social movement organizations dedicated to the emancipation of women. In fact, I argue below that their success stems in part from their not challenging prevailing arrangements in a substantial way.

29. The sexual division of labor is the reverse in women's DSOs. When men become involved they do the "inside" tasks of bookkeeping while women do the sales management.

30. Quoted by Dee Wedemeyer, "There's a Tupperware Party Starting Every Ten Seconds," *Ms.* 4, no.2(1975): 82. This interesting article explores the congruence of women's gender and working-class culture in Tupperware.

31. Mary C. Crowley, *Be Somebody . . . God Doesn't Take Time to Make a Nobody* (Dallas: Crescendo, 1974), pp. 46–47.

32. Mary Kay Ash, *Mary Kay* (New York: Harper and Row, 1981), p. 75.

33. See Degler, *At Odds*, pp. 14–19.

34. This exchange is not an equal one. According to Francesca M. Cancian, defining love only as romantic and expressive "exaggerates women's dependency on men," who are assumed to need romantic love less (men depend on women for sex, practical help, and other loving activities that are not generally labeled as love in our society). Defining love only in romantic terms further devalues women's domestic sphere by associating love with sentimentalism, unappreciated in a society that prizes instrumental activity. See "Gender

Politics: Love and Power in the Private and Public Spheres," in *Gender and the Life Course*, ed. Alice Rossi (New York: Aldine, 1985), pp. 253–64.

35. Steven Butterfield, *Amway*, p. 117.

36. Cf. Herman R. Lantz, Jane Keyes, and Martin Schultz, "The American Family in the Preindustrial Period: From Base Lines in History to Change," *American Sociological Review* 40, no. 1(1975): 21–36; and Degler, *At Odds*, chap. 7.

37. This is a term suggested by Estelle Freedman. A prefeminist organization may become feminist if "the group experience leads to insights about male domination" and if the group is relatively autonomous from control by men. Freedman, "Separatism as Strategy," p. 527. My study suggests that the former condition holds in some women's DSOs but the latter does not.

CHAPTER FIVE

1. As quoted by Anne Bagamery, "Please Make Me Feel Special," *Forbes* 131 (28 March 1983): 88.

2. Ibid. Home Interiors and Gifts, like many DSOs, is privately held, and data about such companies' finances are usually unaudited voluntary statements or estimates. But Mary Crowley came into public view in 1974 when the Internal Revenue Service challenged her $1.6 million annual salary. The United States Tax Court judge, however, found that the salary was fully justified because of her extraordinary ability to motivate women to sell. He found that her company's fast growth was largely attributable to her and that she probably could not have been replaced.

3. In structuring my analysis I am following Weber's attempt to "demonstrate the limitations of the materialist as well as the idealist interpretation of history, without denying the relative justification for both views." Wolfgang Schluchter, "The Paradox of Rationalization: On the Relation of Ethics and World," in *Max Weber's Vision of History, Ethics and Methods*, ed. Guenther Roth and Wolfgang Schluchter (Berkeley: University of California Press, 1979), p. 16.

4. The intraorganizational belief system of top government officials, including cabinet officers, and the consequences of that system for interaction constitute the topic of Gary G. Hamilton and Nicole Woolsey Biggart, *Governor Reagan, Governor Brown: A Sociology of Executive Power* (New York: Columbia University Press, 1984).

5. Weber identified two basic foundations for organized social relations. One is a *constellation of interests*, or a group formed on the basis of common material and ideal interests where people come

together voluntarily—for example, a financial market. The second is organization on the basis of *authority relations*, where members of a group accept that some have the right to exercise power over others— for example, a student government. While analytically distinct, these two bases of social organization are usually combined in practice. Bendix gives the example of a church congregation that gathers because the members' feelings of solidarity and common religious beliefs find expression when they worship together (constellation of interests). But the congregation may also accept the authority of the minister in directing its actions (authority relations). Bendix argues that it is more accurate to see these two bases of group relations as a continuum grading from one extreme to the other. Direct selling distributors, just like a church congregation, are oriented to common beliefs and to the implicit directives of DSO executives. See Reinhard Bendix, *From Max Weber: An Intellectual Portrait* (Garden City, N.Y.: Doubleday Anchor, 1962), pp. 288–89.

6. Social action can be said to be "rational" when it, for example, is purposive, employs calculation in achieving ends, and attempts control. See Arnold Eisen, "The Meanings and Confusions of Weberian 'Rationality,'" *British Journal of Sociology* 29, no. 1(1978): 57–70, and Stephen Kalberg, "Max Weber's Types of Rationality: Cornerstones for the Analysis of Rationalization Processes in History," *American Journal of Sociology* 85, no. 5(1980): 1147–79.

7. Weber described bureaucracy as an "iron cage" in which people feel trapped. *The Protestant Ethic and the Spirit of Capitalism*, trans. Talcott Parsons (New York: Charles Scribner's Sons, 1958), p. 181.

8. A series of essays on this topic is found in Sam Whimster and Scott Lash, eds., *Max Weber, Rationality and Modernity* (London: Allen and Unwin, 1987).

9. The historical development of economic rationality as managerial ideology and its institutional expression in four different countries is the topic of Reinhard Bendix's classic study, *Work and Authority in Industry: Ideologies of Management in the Course of Industrialization* (Berkeley: University of California Press, 1956). See also chapter 1 of Randall Collins's *Weberian Sociological Theory* (Cambridge: Cambridge University Press, 1986). Though not concerned with the ideological bases of the firm, Alfred D. Chandler, Jr.'s, history of firm development in the United States, *The Visible Hand: The Managerial Revolution in American Business* (Cambridge: Harvard University Press, 1977), is testimony to the economic superiority of the firm over traditional forms of enterprise.

10. Economists have only a single conceptualization of "rationality," and that is economic rationality. Weber described several

forms of rationality, including practical, substantive, and value rationality, each of which directed social action in distinctive ways. Amitai Etzioni criticizes economists' notion of rationality in "A Case for a Multiple-Utility Conception," *Economics and Philosophy* 2(1986): 159–83. For discussions of Weber's views on rationality see Eisen, "Meanings and Confusions of Weberian 'Rationality,'" and Kalberg, "Max Weber's Types of Rationality."

11. Max Weber, *Economy and Society*, ed. Guenther Roth and Claus Wittich (Berkeley: University of California Press, 1978), p. 25.

12. Roberta Lynn Satow, "Value-Rational Authority and Professional Organizations: Weber's Missing type," *Administrative Science Quarterly* 20, no. 4(1975): 526–31.

13. Bennett M. Berger, *The Survival of a Counterculture: Ideological Work and Everyday Life among Rural Communards* (Berkeley: University of California Press, 1981).

14. Philip Selznick, *The Organizational Weapon: A Study of Bolshevik Strategy and Tactics* (New York: McGraw-Hill, 1952).

15. Nicole Woolsey Biggart, "A Sociological Analysis of the Presidential Staff," *Sociological Quarterly* 25, no. 1(1984): 27–43.

16. Joyce Rothschild-Whitt, "The Collectivist Organization: An Alternative to Rational-Bureaucratic Models," *American Sociological Review* 44, no. 4(1979): 509–27.

17. Howard Aldrich and Robert N. Stern, "Resource Mobilization and the Creation of U.S. Producer's Cooperatives, 1835–1935," *Economic and Industrial Democracy* 4(1983): 371–406.

18. In a perverse way, piracy and other forms of economic raiding may express a traditional morality by upholding ethical behavior within the community but declaring all outsiders fair game for economic conquest. Weber, *Protestant Ethic*, p. 57.

19. For example, alternative organizations like cooperatives may place political values, such as members' participation in decision making, before efficiency considerations. See Rothschild-Whitt, "Collectivist Organization."

20. Weber, *Protestant Ethic*.

21. Weber does not argue that there have been no individuals interested in pursuing gain in traditional societies, because clearly avarice has existed throughout history. Rather, he is arguing that acquisitiveness was not a widespread orientation in traditional Europe until embraced by the Calvinists.

22. "Protoindustrialization" is the term given to the cottage industries that flourished in rural areas of Europe before the development of factory-based industries. This rural economic development is coming to be understood as critical to the later formation of a true

industrial economy. See L. A. Clarkson, *Proto-Industrialization: The First Phase of Industrialization?* (London: Macmillan, 1985).

23. Weber believed that the writings of Benjamin Franklin were an important popular expression of the Protestant ethic, though by the time Franklin wrote the ethos was highly secularized. Weber cited such proverbs as "After industry and frugality, nothing contributes more to the raising of a young man in the world than punctuality and justice in all his dealings," to convey the moral character of the Protestant ethic. Weber, *Protestant Ethic*, p. 49.

24. Much of the debate surrounding *The Protestant Ethic* focuses on its supposed idealism, that is, asserting that Weber argued for the primacy of ideas in the development of capitalism. In fact, most Weber scholars recognize that Weber was not arguing that a particular set of beliefs led to a particular type of economic order; rather, he meant that "the spirit of capitalism" favored a set of economic practices. See Gianfranco Poggi, *Calvinism and the Capitalist Spirit: Max Weber's "Protestant Ethic"* (Amherst: University of Massachusetts Press, 1983), and Gordon Marshall, *In Search of the Spirit of Capitalism* (New York: Columbia University Press, 1983), for discussions of the debate.

25. I discuss this in more detail in "Rationality, Meaning, and Self-Management: Success Manuals, 1950–1980," *Social Problems* 30, no. 3(1983): 298–311.

26. For an extended discussion of contemporary Americans' belief in individualism and their ideas of success see Robert N. Bellah, Richard Madsen, William M. Sullivan, Ann Swidler, and Steven M. Tipton, *Habits of the Heart: Individualism and Commitment in American Life* (Berkeley: University of California Press, 1985).

27. Luck plays a role in network direct selling too. A sponsor whose downline recruits very successful distributors will benefit financially from their success even while doing little to sustain that success.

28. They are not entrepreneurs in the way usually defined by economists; that is, they do not risk capital except for a typically modest "starter kit" and do not create new combinations or new products. In fact, they are encouraged to follow to the letter the business plan and sales strategy defined by the DSO headquarters. Although they are legally free to sell as they wish, I found that most accept the headquarters' sales and pricing strategies.

29. The 1975 Louis Harris survey found that the racial composition of distributors was similar to that of the population as a whole. My attendance at rallies and conventions confirms that, at least for the DSOs I studied, the industry continues to be integrated.

A belief in equal access to "success," of course, serves organizational ends by expanding the boundaries of potential recruits to everyone willing to work to be successful through direct selling.

30. This company uses an equally American expression of individualism to promote business activity, however. According to the president, "We use a great deal of EST philosophy in terms of taking responsibility for one's success or failures in life."

31. I discuss the management of competition further in the next chapter.

32. Curiously, the term "proselytizing" is widely used in the industry to mean trying to recruit a distributor from another DSO. The practice is frowned upon and seen as akin to trying to convert a believer in one faith to another.

33. Forrest C. Shaklee, *Reflections on a Philosophy* (New York: Benjamin, 1973).

34. *Product Catalog* (San Francisco: Shaklee Corporation, 1983), p. 4.

35. Mary Kay Ash, *Mary Kay* (New York: Harper and Row, 1981), p. 203.

36. Marabel Morgan, *The Total Woman* (Old Tappan, N.J.: F. H. Revell, 1973).

37. Proceedings of the Direct Selling Education Foundation Academic Seminar, Dallas, 11–12 April 1985, pp. 66–67.

38. As quoted in Holly G. Miller, "The First Lady of Home Interiors," *Saturday Evening Post*, April 1983, pp. 58–61, 87–88.

39. Mary C. Crowley, *You Can Too* (Old Tappan, N.J.: Fleming H. Revell, 1980); Ash, *Mary Kay*; Shaklee, *Reflections on a Philosophy*; Richard M. DeVos, *Believe!* (New York: Pocket Books, 1975).

40. Mary Douglas with Baron Isherwood, *The World of Goods* (New York: Basic Books, 1979).

41. *What Is Shaklee?* (San Francisco: Shaklee Corporation, 1983).

42. Thomas C. Hayes, "Crusading for Term Life Insurance," *New York Times*, 11 May 1986, p. 25.

43. Ruth Stroud and Steven W. Colford, "Herbalife Aims 'Preemptive' Suit at FDA," *Advertising Age*, 6 December 1984, p. 42.

44. Pauline Yoshihashi, "The Questions on Herbalife," *New York Times*, 5 April 1985, pp. D1, D4. and Ellen Paris, "Herbalife Anyone?" *Forbes*, 25 February 1985.

45. "Herbalife to Pay $850,000 and Limit Its Health Claims," *San Francisco Chronicle*, 16 October 1986.

46. Lois J. Lyons, "Prudential, A. L. Williams Settle Suit out of Court," *National Underwriter* (Life and Health Insurance Edition), 31 August 1985, p. 1.

47. Victor F. Zonana, "Shaklee Shootout: Health-Products Firm Used Toxic Substance, Ex-Distributor Claims," *Wall Street Journal*, 21 January 1982, p. 16.

48. Louis A. Zurcher and David A. Snow, "Collective Behavior: Social Movements," in *Social Psychology: Sociological Perspectives*, ed. Morris Rosenberg and Ralph H. Turner (New York: Basic Books, 1981), p. 456.

49. Many distributors have small successes, however, and these are welcomed and praised by the organization. People are said to "choose" their level of success, as though success and failure were simply a matter of will.

50. J. Wilson, *Introduction to Social Movements* (New York: Basic Books, 1973), p. 169.

51. There are other DSOs, including Consumer Express and United States Consumer Club, that similarly recruit distributors who will in fact be wholesale buyers of products for personal use.

52. Proceedings of the Direct Selling Education Foundation Academic Seminar, San Francisco, 17–18 May 1984, pp. 11–12.

53. Executives in the direct selling industry predicted that the social welfare ideology of the New Deal would threaten their survival. In 1935 an industry executive said, "I think that any system of contribution of public money to give people a chance to eat interferes with direct selling." *Proceedings of the Annual Convention, 1935*, (Winona, Minn.: National Association of Direct Selling Companies, 1935), p. 23.

54. Ann Swidler, "Culture in Action: Symbols and Strategies," *American Sociological Review* 51, no. 2(1986): 275.

55. "Ideology and circumstance" is a phrase used in Berger, *Survival of a Counterculture*, to refer to a similar situation among rural communards.

CHAPTER SIX

1. Although the sales forces of most DSOs have a large proportion of women, women are no better represented in the DSOs' corporate headquarters than they are in any typical American corporation.

2. Rosabeth Moss Kanter, "Commitment and Social Organization: A Study of Commitment Mechanisms in Utopian Communities," *American Sociological Review* 33, no.4(1968): 499.

3. Frederick Winslow Taylor, the father of modern management thought, believed that workers were motivated only by money,

and he created controls based on that belief. But later thinkers, such as Elton Mayo and Chester Barnard, argued that workers had social as well as economic needs; they were preoccupied by the design of work groups and the role of management in creating harmonious relations. Modern management scholars recognize that different types of workers—for example, professionals and administrators—have different desires, and that organizations play an important role in shaping individual aspirations. The best review of schools of management thought is Charles Perrow, *Complex Organizations: A Critical Essay* (New York: Random House, 1986). An important study of the evolution of control strategies in industrial settings is Richard Edwards, *Contested Terrain: The Transformation of the Workplace in the Twentieth Century* (New York: Basic Books, 1979).

4. Max Weber, "Politics as a Vocation," in *From Max Weber*, trans. and ed. H. H. Gerth and C. Wright Mills (New York: Oxford University Press, 1946), p. 78.

5. Weber was concerned with the structure of large-scale social systems, but his analytic framework is equally appropriate to individual organizations, or categories of organizations, and has been so used by sociologists. Gary Hamilton and I have extended Weber's ideas in this direction. See Gary G. Hamilton and Nicole Woolsey Biggart, "Why People Obey: Theoretical Observations on Power and Obedience in Complex Organizations," *Sociological Perspectives* 28, no. 1(1985): 3–28, and Nicole Woolsey Biggart and Gary G. Hamilton, "The Power of Obedience," *Administrative Science Quarterly* 29, no. 4(1984): 540–49.

6. Weber, "Politics as a Vocation," pp. 78–80.

7. In fact there are a number of organizational typologies, some of which include forms of social control as a dimension. Amitai Etzioni's typology of organizations posits compliance strategies, and William Ouchi suggests three forms of social order: markets, hierarchies (bureaucracies), and clans. Although network DSOs could be characterized either as a "normative" organization in Etzioni's typology or as a "clan" in Ouchi's, neither theorist has developed as systematically as Weber a model of the relationship between belief, administrative arrangements, and organizational practice. Most other typologies focus exclusively on bureaucracies and are not helpful in studying DSOs. For a review of these and other typologies see W. Richard Scott, *Organizations: Natural, Rational, and Open Systems* (Englewood Cliffs, N.J.: Prentice-Hall, 1981).

8. Weber, "Politics as a Vocation," pp. 78–79.

9. For example, family firms and paternalistic Japanese management combine traditional with bureaucratic elements, and Rosabeth Kanter convincingly argues the patrimonial character of relations be-

tween bosses and secretaries in modern corporations. Rosabeth Moss Kanter, *Men and Women of the Corporation* (New York: Basic Books, 1977).

10. John Meyer and W. Richard Scott argue that some organizations conform to the trappings of bureaucracy only on the surface while pursuing quite different organizational dynamics. See *Organizational Environments: Ritual and Rationality* (Beverly Hills, Calif.: Sage, 1983).

11. These characteristics are true of another quite different form of organization based on substantive rationality—collectivist-democratic (sometimes called alternative) organizations. Their differences are important, however: collectivist organizations empower the group to decide for the good of the whole, while in DSOs action is decidedly individual, not a group venture. Distributors are autonomous persons pursuing the same goals in similar circumstances. That through sponsorship activities they can help themselves by helping others does not make their action oriented primarily to the good of the group. Status differences, disparaged in collectivist organizations, are celebrated in DSOs, and in decided contrast to collectivist organizations, DSOs celebrate materialism. See Joyce Rothschild and J. Allen Whitt, *The Cooperative Workplace: Potentials and Dilemmas of Organizational Democracy and Participation* (Cambridge: Cambridge University Press, 1986).

12. Max Weber, *The Theory of Social and Economic Organization*, ed. Talcott Parsons (New York: Free Press, 1947), pp. 358–59.

13. Bryan Wilson states this point well: "If a man runs naked down the street proclaiming that he alone can save others from impending doom, and if he immediately wins a following, then he is a charismatic leader: a social relationship has come into being. If he does not win a following, he is simply a lunatic." *The Noble Savages: The Primitive Origins of Charisma and Its Contemporary Survival* (Berkeley: University of California Press, 1975), p. 7.

14. Ibid., pp. 360–61.

15. Benjamin Zablocki, *Alienation and Charisma* (New York: Free Press, 1980), p. 282.

16. The headquarters of direct selling organizations are bureaucratically organized; although management pursues a different logic in managing the field, they are run similarly to other corporations. All staff workers, for example, are employees, and work is functionally and hierarchically differentiated.

17. Religion provides us with many examples of charismatic leaders, including the Dalai Lama, the Old Testament prophets, and more recently, the Reverend Moon.

18. According to Shils, "[Charisma] might be thought to reside

in the ultimate principles of law which should govern man's conduct, arising from or derived from the nature of the universe and essential to human existence, discerned or elucidated by the exercise of man's most fundamental rational and expressive powers. Scientific discovery, ethical promulgation, artistic creativity, political and organizational authority (*auctoritatem*, *auctor*, authorship), and in fact all forms of genius, in the original sense of the word as permeation by the 'spirit,' are as much instances of the category of charismatic things as is religious prophecy." "Charisma, Order, and Status,' *American Sociological Review* 30, no.2 (1965): 201.

19. Ibid., p. 200, and Kanter, "Commitment and Social Organization," p. 514.

20. Wolfgang Schluchter, "The Transformation of Charisma," unpublished lecture given at the University of California, Davis, 5 November 1986.

21. Wilson, *Noble Savages*, p. 112. This is the staff's function in direct selling, but they are also concerned with procuring or manufacturing products and maintaining of data about distributors and their line relationships.

22. For example, see Philip Selznick's study of a Bolshevik political cell, *The Organizational Weapon: A Study of Bolshevik Strategy and Tactics* (New York: McGraw-Hill, 1952), and Joyce Rothschild-Whitt, "The Collectivist Organization: An Alternative to Rational-Bureaucratic Models," *American Sociological Review* 44, no. 4 (1979): 509–27. I have written about personal staff organizations that are devoted solely to the well-being of a leader in "A Sociological Analysis of the Presidential Staff," *Sociological Quarterly* 25, no. 1 (1984): 27–43. All of these use nonbureaucratic forms of control.

23. Weber noted that reason, the basis of legal-rational organization, relied more on external means, whereas charisma had a propensity to lead to inner controls: "Reason works from *without*: by altering the situations of life and hence its problems, finally in this way changing men's attitudes toward them; or it intellectualizes the individual. Charisma, on the other hand, *may* effect a subjective or *internal* reorientation." *Economy and Society*, ed. Guenther Roth and Claus Wittich (Berkeley: University of California Press, 1978), p. 245.

24. Rosabeth Moss Kanter's extensive study of utopian communities is the best resource for understanding control strategies in communitarian settings, and I have relied on it for analyzing control mechanisms in DSOs. *Commitment and Community: Communes and Utopias in Sociological Perspective* (Cambridge: Harvard University Press, 1972).

25. Not all of these strategies are important in all DSOs, and they vary in how they are expressed. For example, DSOs that have an entrepreneurial orientation utilize identity-creation controls extensively, while women's DSOs stress the importance of group celebration.

26. Erving Goffman, *Asylums* (Garden City, N.Y.: Anchor Doubleday, 1961).

27. Edgar Schein, "Organizational Socialization and the Profession of Management," Industrial Management Review 9 (1968): 1–15.

28. Weber, *Theory of Social and Economic Organization*, p. 363.

29. This is not as unusual a strategy as it might first appear. The hiring of professionals, workers who have internalized occupational standards and work methods, is a strategy of hiring for self-control.

30. Norman Vincent Peale's *The Power of Positive Thinking* (New York: Prentice-Hall, 1952) is the source of the term. The book outsold every nonfiction work in the mid-1950s except the Bible and is still in print. It espouses proper outlook, rather than hard work, as the key to success. For a review of how-to-succeed themes in popular nonfiction and their relationship to economic change, see Nicole Woolsey Biggart, "Rationality, Meaning, and Self-Management: Success Manuals, 1950–1980," *Social Problems* 30, no. 3 (1983): 298–311.

31. Electronic technologies have become important parts of DSO control strategies. Amway has purchased radio stations to broadcast its message, and Herbalife uses lengthy late-night broadcasts on Cable News Network. Avon, Shaklee, and United Sciences of America make extensive use of video cassettes both to market products and to recruit. These technologies both assist the sales force and ensure that the headquarters has some limited control of the message being presented.

32. Stephen Butterfield, *Amway: The Cult of Free Enterprise* (Boston: South End Press, 1985), p. 100.

33. Proceedings of the Direct Selling Education Foundation Academic Seminar, Dallas, 11–12 April 1985, p. 70.

34. Kanter, *Commitment and Community*, pp. 108–10.

35. In truth, Mary Kay Cosmetics gives awards for even the smallest success, so that everyone is "a winner." One former Tupperware dealer said this was not true in that organization and was a reason for her switch to Mary Kay.

36. Kanter, *Commitment and Community*, p. 115.

37. While these reverent and emotional expressions may be

unusual in the business sphere, they recall the description of political leaders by personal staff members, who also serve in value-rational settings. See Gary G. Hamilton and Nicole Woolsey Biggart, *Governor Reagan, Governor Brown: A Sociology of Executive Power* (New York: Columbia University Press, 1984), chap. 2.

38. This generalization may be less true today as even direct selling becomes subject to economically rational calculus. For example, United Sciences of America was founded by a group of investors who made an apparent determination of the elements of success in network DSOs (e.g., entrepreneurial ideology, product ideology, charismatic leader). The president, an important investor, was a successful entrepreneur who apparently understood the importance of establishing himself as a "leader."

39. "Virtuoso" has a double meaning, referring both to skill and to being filled with the spirit or "virtue." Both meanings are reflected in the status elites of DSOs.

40. In addition to designation of a successor and hereditary succession, Weber identified the search for a new leader based on established criteria, revelation, and the ritual transfer of charisma as succession strategies. *Economy and Society*, pp. 246–49.

41. There are limits to this in direct selling, however. The children of successful founders have grown up leading privileged lives and cannot serve as exemplars.

42. In fact, this appears to be a common fear in direct selling, especially in new organizations. I heard several tales of secession of lines that formed their own companies.

43. For example, dealers, the lowest level, do not receive overrides on their recruits, just a one-time "finder's fee." Only the manager of the unit benefits from recruits' sales, limiting connectedness in the network. Distributors, the level above manager, are selected for managerial qualities as well as proven success as a dealer. These women give up selling too, contributing to differentiation of labor in the field and reducing the mechanical solidarity typical of DSOs. These bureaucratic elements may also be explained by the fact that Tupperware has been a subsidiary of a large conglomerate for some years.

44. Kanter, *Commitment and Community*, p. 120.

45. Butterfield, *Amway*, p. 74.

46. There are limits to guidance, though. Sponsors are expected to encourage and provide assistance as long as the recruit is willing to accept aid. The obligation is circumscribed, however, and does not approach that of a patron/client relationship in traditional social orders. For example, one sponsor said, "In our particular line of business we don't force anybody to do anything they don't want to

do. We ask them what they want to do, and we ask permission to help them. If they're willing to let us, fine." These limits help to relieve the sponsor of blame for the downline's failures.

47. Stephen Hill, *Competition and Control at Work* (Cambridge: MIT Press, 1981), p. 18.

48. Lewis Coser describes the "symbolic walls" that some organizations have used to limit social contact. See *Greedy Institutions* (New York: Free Press, 1974).

49. "Social Structure and Organization," in *Handbook of Organizations*, ed. James G. March (Chicago: Rand McNally, 1965), pp. 142–91.

50. Ibid., p. 82.

51. This is a common strategy in value-rational organizations that helps focus attention on the mission and reduce distractions. Gary Hamilton and I describe a similar strategy in the organization of political staffs in *Governor Reagan, Governor Brown*, pp. 26–29.

52. The lack of control over the distribution network is a fascinating marketing problem: DSOs find it difficult to target appeals to a shifting distributor base. Moreover, most do not even know the identity of their ultimate customers, although Mary Kay Cosmetics has made a successful effort to learn the names of beauty consultants' clients. Until now, when a beauty consultant dropped out, her customers were "lost" to the company. When other DSOs have made similar efforts to learn customers' names they have been met with obstinacy from distributors who fear losing business to direct solicitation by the headquarters. It is a mark of the beauty consultants' trust in Mary Kay that they have relinquished the data. The company is using the names to do supportive direct-mail advertising.

53. Kanter, *Commitment and Community*, p. 99.

54. Companies differ on their attendance policy for annual meetings. While everyone in Mary Kay may attend Seminar at her own expense, in Amway and Shaklee attendance is a privilege of rank, and the companies may pay all expenses, depending on productivity levels. For example, "coordinators" may attend the Shaklee meeting free, but they must achieve given productivity goals if they want to bring spouses or children. In these companies meeting attendance is a mark of honor.

55. Kanter, *Commitment and Community*, pp. 76–80.

56. Many kinds of jobs create emotional sets, as Arlie Hochschild has discussed, but direct selling, with its totalistic and ideological character, is an extreme example. See *The Managed Heart: Commercialization of Human Feeling* (Berkeley: University of California Press, 1983).

57. I am generalizing from my interviews, but Butterfield's

book, *Amway*, is evidence that disaffected distributors can be insightful critics of a controlling organization.

58. Turnover figures, when they were given to me by DSOs, varied from a "good" figure of 20% to 40% annually to over 100%. The largest DSOs would not reveal their turnover rates but admitted that turnover was a continuing management concern. Trade association executives estimate that turnover is probably 100% annually for the industry as a whole. Turnover figures cannot really be compared with those for firms, however, and are not even comparable across DSOs. For example, a distributor who sold products every fall for years for "Christmas money" but "quit" every winter would represent a 100% turnover figure. Turnover is also measured differently at various DSOs. A woman distributor for Avon must place an order every month or so to be considered active, whereas some clothing concerns consider an order every year evidence of active status.

59. To reduce turnover, in 1985 the giant Avon Corporation tried a pilot program to make some Avon distributors employees but abandoned it in less than a year.

60. Proceedings of the Direct Selling Education Foundation Academic Seminar, Dallas, Texas, 11–12 April 1985, p. 69.

61. Reinhard Bendix, *Max Weber: An Intellectual Portrait* (Garden City, N.Y.: Doubleday Anchor, 1962), p. 306.

62. Gary G. Hamilton, "The Structural Sources of Adventurism: The Case of the California Gold Rush," *American Journal of Sociology* 83, no. 6 (1978): 1487. In this article Hamilton shows the social structural sources of differing orientations to economically risky activity.

63. It is a curious feature of the industry, however, that it has rationalized through collective organizing strategies the very conditions under which emotional, individualized ambition may be pursued.

CHAPTER SEVEN

1. I do not want to argue that executives in DSOs were omnipotent and omniscient in structuring a successful business strategy. I believe it is more likely that there were a number of different attempts to deal with the control challenge and that those suited to changing conditions helped their companies succeed ("survive" in population ecology terms). Certainly, for example, there is no evidence that Mary Kay Ash calculated a strategic plan for her fledgling company in the 1960s. She makes quite clear in her autobiography that she tried to design a direct selling company she herself would like to work in. Her preferences in this instance were widely shared by women in a

particular set of circumstances, but no doubt there were other attempts, lost to history, that failed. Indeed, the number of start-up DSOs is reputed to be very high because the entry costs are very, very low. A company needs only a few weeks of the product on credit from a manufacturer to begin recruiting and selling.

2. Frederick Winslow Taylor, *The Principles of Scientific Management* (New York: Harper, 1911).

3. Industrial psychology of this type is often referred to as the "human relations school" of organizational analysis. The major works of the school are summarized by Charles Perrow, *Complex Organizations: A Critical Essay* (New York: Random House, 1986), chap. 3.

4. These questions are central topics of organizational behavior courses in business schools, which are dominated by a psychological paradigm. They represent major topics in texts that examine motivation, leadership, and job design in organizations. See, for example, Stephen P. Robbins, *Organizational Behavior: Concepts, Controversies, and Applications* (Englewood Cliffs, N.J.: Prentice-Hall, 1983).

5. The "economic man" assumed by economists is a rational, atomized person who maximizes individual interests. Psychologists emphasize people's innate needs and inclinations, whereas sociologists are concerned with how social experiences and relations shape people's self-concepts and actions. Howard Aldrich and Catherine Zimmer review the economic and psychological approaches to entrepreneurship and suggest the utility of a more socially embedded approach in "Entrepreneurship through Social Networks," in Howard Aldrich, *Population Perspectives on Organizations*, Studia Oeconomiae Negotiorum (Acta Universitatis Upsaliensis) (Uppsala: University of Uppsala, 1986), chap. 1. An excellent description of a sociologically informed approach to economic analysis is Amitai Etzioni, "Socio-economics: Humanizing the Dismal Science," *Washington Post*, 11 January 1987, p. C-3.

6. James W. Carland, Frank Hoy, William R. Boulton, and Jo Ann C. Carland review definitions in "Differentiating Entrepreneurs from Small Business Owners: A Conceptualization," *Academy of Management Review* 9, no.2 (1984): 354–59.

7. J. A. Schumpter, *The Theory of Economic Development* (Cambridge: Harvard University Press, 1934).

8. Schumpeter, *Theory of Economic Development*, and some other economists do not believe risk bearing is a necessary factor. They argue that investors and owners bear risk but are not necessarily entrepreneurs.

9. John W. Meyer and Brian Rowan demonstrated how organizational practices may have little relation to the technical activi-

ties of the organization; practices become ritual signals that solicit legitimacy. "Institutional organizations: Formal Structure as Myth and Ceremony," *American Journal of Sociology* 83, no. 2 (1984): 440–63. Similarly, the use of the term "entrepreneur" serves a legitimating function for the nonentrepreneurial selling activities of distributors.

10. See, for example, John G. Cawelti, *Apostles of the Self-Made Man* (Chicago: University of Chicago Press, 1964); Lawrence Chenoweth, *The American Dream of Success* (North Scituate, Mass.: Duxbury Press, 1974); and Richard M. Huber, *The American Idea of Success* (New York: Free Press, 1954).

11. This observation is the topic of Orrin E. Klapp, *Heroes, Villains and Fools: The Changing American Character* (Englewood Cliffs, N.J.: Prentice-Hall, 1962).

12. I studied the changing ideals of success in "Rationality, Meaning, and Self-Management: Success Manuals, 1950–1980," *Social Problems* 30, no. 3 (1983): 298–311.

13. Mary C. Crowley, *Be Somebody . . . God Doesn't Take Time to Make a Nobody* (Dallas: Crescendo, 1974), p. 59.

14. Bureaucratic work also draws on cultural ideals—for example, integrity, efficiency, and orderliness.

15. Karl Polanyi, *The Great Transformation* (Boston: Beacon Press, 1957), p. 163.

16. Perrow, *Complex Organizations*, p. 49.

17. Richard Edwards, *Contested Terrain: The Transformation of the Workplace in the Twentieth Century* (New York: Basic Books, 1979).

18. Max Weber, *The Protestant Ethic and the Spirit of Capitalism*, trans. Talcott Parsons (New York: Charles Scribner's Sons, 1958). p. 181.

19. For example, marriage is increasingly subject to contractual arrangements such as prenuptial agreements.

20. Sociologists recognize that the presence and character of social networks are crucial to whether someone joins and remains in an ideological crusade. See David A. Snow, Louis A. Zurcher, Jr., and Sheldon Ekland-Olson, "Social Networks and Social Movements: A Microstructural Approach to Differential Recruitment," *American Sociological Review* 45, no.5 (1980): 787–801.

21. Gifford Pinchot, *Intrapreneuring: Why You Don't Have to Leave the Corporation to Become an Entrepreneur* (New York: Harper and Row, 1985).

22. Jacob M. Schlesinger, "Auto Firms and UAW Find That Cooperation Can Get Complicated," *Wall Street Journal*, 25 August 1987, pp. 1, 14.

23. For example, Harvard Business School professor Richard E. Walton has argued for the movement from control to commitment strategies. By commitment he means control of the worker through social relations and identification with the organization. "From Control to Commitment in the Workplace," *Harvard Business Review*, March-April 1985, 77–84.

24. Much of Weber's writings concerns the spread of rationality in the West as evidenced by the increasing depersonalization of social relations, the use of rational calculus in many life spheres, and increasing technical control over the social and natural worlds. He recognized, however, that the rationalization process had limits. For a discussion of Weber's sociological and philosophical views on rationality see Rogers Brubaker, *The Limits of Rationality: An Essay on the Social and Moral Thought of Max Weber* (London: George Allen and Unwin, 1984).

25. Walter W. Powell examines the recent proliferation of organizational forms that are neither bureaucracies nor markets of individuals but that in different ways rely on social networks of relationships. My study of DSOs emphasizes the experiential limits of bureaucracy and the costs of the employment relationship to owners, but some of the environmental and reciprocity factors described by Powell apply to DSOs. "Hybrid Organizational Arrangements," *California Management Review* 30, no. 1 (1987): 67–87. Howard Aldrich and Ellen Auster discuss this same effect at the population level. They argue that networklike strategies such as subcontracting and franchising, typical of smaller and newer companies, may be emulated by large firms to mitigate problems of age and size. "Even Dwarfs Started Small: Liabilities of Age and Size and Their Strategic Implications," in Howard Aldrich et al., *Population Perspectives on Organizations*, Studia Oeconomiae Negotorium (Acta Universitas Upsaliensis) (Uppsala: University of Uppsala, 1986), chap. 2.

26. The relatively greater importance of social bonds in dangerous coal mines, rather than more "efficient" bureaucratic relations, was the topic of two classic works: Alvin W. Gouldner, *Patterns of Industrial Bureaucracy* (Glencoe, Ill.: Free Press, 1954), and E. L. Trist and K. W. Bamforth, "Social and Psychological Consequences of the Longwall Method of Coal-Getting," *Human Relations* 4, no. 1 (1951): 3–28.

27. Arlie Hochschild, *The Managed Heart: Commercialization of Human Feeling* (Berkeley: University of California Press, 1983).

28. See Howard E. Aldrich, *Organizations and Environments* (Englewood Cliffs, N.J.: Prentice-Hall, 1979), chap. 7, for a discussion of the conditions necessary to sustain new organizational forms.

29. "Direct Selling: A World of Business," brochure published

by the World Federation of Direct Selling Associations, Washington, D.C., 1985.

30. Kenneth F. Englade, "Door to Door Car Salesmen in Japan Reap Billions," *Toronto Globe and Mail*, 23 July 1985.

31. The World Federation of Direct Selling Associations reported that in 1985 Hong Kong had 20,000 distributors and $15 million in retail sales; Malaysia had 95,000 distributors and $135 million in sales; and Singapore had 15,000 distributors and $23 million in sales. Officials say that at best the figures are rough estimates. "Direct Selling: A World of Business."

32. Other industry officials have noted that direct selling succeeds in some countries, including Asian nations, where women have few or poor ways of entering the labor force. This is an important reason for the success of direct selling in Mexico, for example.

33. Gary Hamilton and I make this same argument in "Market, Culture, and Society: A Comparative Analysis of Management and Organization in the Far East," *American Journal of Sociology*, in press.

34. Mark Granovetter, "Economic Action and Social Structure: The Problem of Embeddedness" *American Journal of Sociology* 91, no. 3 (1985): 481–510.

APPENDIX

1. In fact, Weber explictly argued for the superiority of ideal types over the "synthetic constructs" favored by economists. He believed that economic models work only under utopian conditions such as free competition and rigorously rational behavior. Instead, he believed it far more useful to build models based on an empirical reality, not a utopian one. Max Weber, *The Methodology of the Social Sciences*, ed. and trans. Edward A. Shils and Henry A. Finch (New York: Free Press, 1949), pp. 86–92.

2. Guenther Roth, "Epilogue: Weber's Vision of History," in *Max Weber's Vision of History: Ethics and Methods*, ed. Guenther Roth and Wolfgang Schluchter (Berkeley: University of California Press, 1984), p. 198.

3. For additional insight into the utility of typological analysis see John C. McKinney, "Methodology, Procedures, and Techniques in Sociology," in *Modern Sociological Theory*, ed. Howard Becker and Alvin Boskoff (New York: Dryden Press, 1957), pp. 186–235, and Don Martindale, "Sociological Theory and the Ideal Type," in *Symposium on Sociological Theory*, ed. Llewellyn Gross (Evanston, Ill.: Row, Peterson, 1959), pp. 57–91.

4. Roth, "Epilogue," pp. 195–201.

5. The ten largest DSOs are Amway Corporation, Avon Products, Electrolux Corporation, Encyclopaedia Britannica, Home Interiors and Gifts, Mary Kay Cosmetics, Princess House, Scott Fetzer (Kirby Company and World Book, Inc.), Shaklee Corporation, and Tupperware Home Parties. This list compiled by the Direct Selling Association does not include insurance companies such as A. L. Williams that use the same form of organization.

6. Max Weber, *Economy and Society*, ed. Guenther Roth and Claus Wittich (Berkeley: University of California, 1978), p. 4.

Index